Sai Keung Wong

High Performance Virtual Clothing Dynamics

Sai Keung Wong

High Performance Virtual Clothing Dynamics

High Performance Collision Detection, Response and Dynamics for Virtual Clothing Simulation

VDM Verlag Dr. Müller

Impressum/Imprint (nur für Deutschland/ only for Germany)
Bibliografische Information der Deutschen Nationalbibliothek: Die Deutsche Nationalbibliothek
verzeichnet diese Publikation in der Deutschen Nationalbibliografie; detaillierte bibliografische
Daten sind im Internet über http://dnb.d-nb.de abrufbar.
Alle in diesem Buch genannten Marken und Produktnamen unterliegen warenzeichen-, marken-
oder patentrechtlichem Schutz bzw. sind Warenzeichen oder eingetragene Warenzeichen der
jeweiligen Inhaber. Die Wiedergabe von Marken, Produktnamen, Gebrauchsnamen,
Handelsnamen, Warenbezeichnungen u.s.w. in diesem Werk berechtigt auch ohne besondere
Kennzeichnung nicht zu der Annahme, dass solche Namen im Sinne der Warenzeichen- und
Markenschutzgesetzgebung als frei zu betrachten wären und daher von jedermann benutzt
werden dürften.

Coverbild: www.purestockx.com

Verlag: VDM Verlag Dr. Müller Aktiengesellschaft & Co. KG
Dudweiler Landstr. 125 a, 66123 Saarbrücken, Deutschland
Telefon +49 681 9100-698, Telefax +49 681 9100-988, Email: info@vdm-verlag.de
Zugl.: Hong Kong, The Hong Kong University of Science and Technology, 2004

Herstellung in Deutschland:
Schaltungsdienst Lange o.H.G., Zehrensdorfer Str. 11, D-12277 Berlin
Books on Demand GmbH, Gutenbergring 53, D-22848 Norderstedt
Reha GmbH, Dudweiler Landstr. 99, D- 66123 Saarbrücken
ISBN: 978-3-639-08967-7

Imprint (only for USA, GB)
Bibliographic information published by the Deutsche Nationalbibliothek: The Deutsche
Nationalbibliothek lists this publication in the Deutsche Nationalbibliografie; detailed
bibliographic data are available in the Internet at http://dnb.d-nb.de.
Any brand names and product names mentioned in this book are subject to trademark, brand or
patent protection and are trademarks or registered trademarks of their respective holders. The use
of brand names, product names, common names, trade names, product descriptions etc. even
without
a particular marking in this works is in no way to be construed to mean that such names may be
regarded as unrestricted in respect of trademark and brand protection legislation and could thus
be used by anyone.

Cover image: www.purestockx.com

Publisher:
VDM Verlag Dr. Müller Aktiengesellschaft & Co. KG
Dudweiler Landstr. 125 a, 66123 Saarbrücken, Germany
Phone +49 681 9100-698, Fax +49 681 9100-988, Email: info@vdm-verlag.de

Copyright © 2008 VDM Verlag Dr. Müller Aktiengesellschaft & Co. KG and licensors
All rights reserved. Saarbrücken 2008

Produced in USA and UK by:
Lightning Source Inc., 1246 Heil Quaker Blvd., La Vergne, TN 37086, USA
Lightning Source UK Ltd., Chapter House, Pitfield, Kiln Farm, Milton Keynes, MK11 3LW, GB
BookSurge, 7290 B. Investment Drive, North Charleston, SC 29418, USA
ISBN: 978-3-639-08967-7

Acknowledgments

I would like to thank my supervisors Prof. George Baciu and Prof. Andrew Horner. In particular, I thank Prof. George Baciu for his guidance and assigning me in a nice lab for studying. He taught me how to package and deliver ideas to people. I also thank my Ph.D. thesis examination committee members, Prof. Cheng Siu-Wing, Prof. Tang Chi-Keung, Prof. Metthew Yuen, and Prof. Wu Enhua, for their comments about my thesis. Their comments definitely helped me refine the thesis in every aspect.

Thanks go to Mr. Martin Kyle for helping me proofread the draft of this monograph. Thanks my friends for their kindly concerns about the development of my project.

Last but not least, I thank my wife and family for their patience and love. Without their support, I would not be able to finish this monograph.

SAI-KEUNG WONG

Contents

Abstract

There are three major problems in modeling the natural motion of virtual clothing in a 3D environment: (1) a large number of contact points, (2) the computations of collision information in the presence of numerical errors, and (3) interactions with objects having sharp features. This thesis proposes new techniques that successfully address these three problems. The results show that these new techniques can be applied on virtual garments with complex geometry and on unique interactions between continuous and non-smooth surfaces. Our techniques are classified into four categories: (1) culling non-colliding subsurfaces in collision detection, (2) intrinsic collision detection, (3) collision response, and (4) the editing and simulation of special virtual garments.

For culling non-colliding subsurfaces in collision detection, we propose an image-based method for interference test, a method of decomposition of a surface into a new type of $(\pi, \beta, \mathbf{I})$-surfaces for exact collision detection in the time domain and an adaptive backward voxel-based hierarchical structure for dealing with highly compressed deformable surfaces. For intrinsic collision detection, we propose a new system architecture. Robust treatments of numerical errors are devised. For collision response, a penetration-free motion space is proposed for handling features involved in multiple collision events, and a static analysis method is suggested for handling friction and stiction. Thus, interactions with objects having sharp features are handled efficiently. For the editing and simulation of special virtual garments, we propose techniques to handle multi-layered surfaces, surfaces with sharp features and sewn surfaces. A multi-layered surface is constructed by gluing several surfaces together either along lines or over regions. A surface with sharp features is represented by two meshes. A sewn surface is obtained by systematically performing a stable sewing process.

These techniques have been integrated into a high performance system for virtual clothing dynamics.

Nomenclature

Admissible space of canonical cones: We define an admissible space of a set of canonical cones $\mathcal{C} = \{C_1, C_2, \cdots, C_m\}$ as $L(\mathcal{C}) \equiv \{n : n \cdot C = n \ \forall C \in \mathcal{C}, n \in R^3\}$. The normalized admissible space is defined as $\hat{L}(\mathcal{C}) = \{n : \forall n \in L(\mathcal{C}), |n| = 1\}$. Therefore, for any vector $v \in L(\mathcal{C})$, there exists $n \in \hat{L}(\mathcal{C})$ s.t. $v = \alpha n$, and $\alpha > 0$.

A direct result from the above definition is that the intersection of the canonical cones is a subset of their admissible space, i.e. $\bigcap_{i \in \{1,2,\cdots,m\}} C_i \subseteq L(\{C_1, C_2, \cdots, C_m\})$.

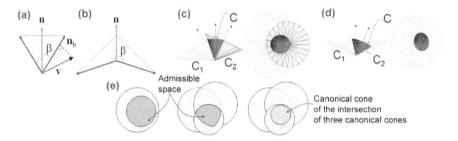

Figure 1: Canonical cone, admissible space and intersection of cones. (a, b): canonical cone; (a): convex for $\beta \leq 90deg$ and (b): concave for $\beta > 90deg$; (c, d): intersection of two cones: $C = C_1 \cap C_2$. (e): admissible space and intersection of cones.

Canonical cone: A canonical cone $C(n, \beta, I)$ has three components: n the cone axis vector, β the cone angle, and I the time interval (Figure 1(a)(b)). We denote the normalized canonical cone as $\hat{C}(n, \beta, I)$ if $|n| = 1$. We suppress the term I if $I = [0, 1]$.

Cone of collision constraint: We denote a cone of collision constraint as $\mathcal{Z}(C, N)$, where C is a canonical cone and N is a set of unit vectors. We define the intersection of two collision constraints $\mathcal{Z}_1$ and $\mathcal{Z}_2$ as follows:

$$\mathcal{Z}(C, N) \equiv \mathcal{Z}_1 \cap \mathcal{Z}_2 = \mathcal{Z}(C_1 \cap C_2, N_1 \cup N_2) \tag{1}$$

In short, we say that $\mathcal{Z}$ is a collision constraint.

Dot product between a canonical cone and a vector: The dot product between a canonical cone $C(\mathbf{n}, \beta, \mathbf{I})$ and a vector $\mathbf{v}$ (Figure 1) is given by:

$$
\mathbf{v} \cdot C(\mathbf{n}, \beta, \mathbf{I}) =
\begin{cases}
\mathbf{v} & \mathbf{n} \neq \mathbf{0},\ \mathbf{v} \cdot \mathbf{n} \geq \cos\beta \\[6pt]
(\mathbf{v} \cdot \mathbf{n}_b)\mathbf{n}_b & \mathbf{n} \neq \mathbf{0},\ \mathbf{v} \cdot \mathbf{n} < \cos\beta, \\[6pt]
& \mathbf{n} \neq \mathbf{0}, \\[6pt]
& \exists \alpha_1, \alpha_2 \in R,\ \mathbf{n}_b = \frac{\alpha_1 \mathbf{v} + \alpha_2 \mathbf{n}}{|\alpha_1 \mathbf{v} + \alpha_2 \mathbf{n}|}, \\[6pt]
& \mathbf{v} \cdot \mathbf{n}_b > 0,\ \mathbf{n}_b \cdot \mathbf{n} = \cos\beta, \\[6pt]
\mathbf{0} & \text{otherwise}
\end{cases}
$$

If $\mathbf{v} = \mathbf{v} \cdot C(\mathbf{n}, \beta, \mathbf{I})$, then $\mathbf{v}$ is inside the canonical cone. The unit vector $\mathbf{n}_b$ is in the space spanned by $\mathbf{n}$ and $\mathbf{v}$, and it is on the boundary of the canonical cone, i.e. $\mathbf{n}_b \cdot \mathbf{n} = \cos\beta$.

Edge-connected triangles of depth d: We denote $E(T, d)$ as a set of triangles which can be reached by triangle T by traveling d triangles (excluding itself) through the edge-connected triangles.

Intersection of canonical cones: We define the intersection of a set of canonical cones $\{C_1, C_2, \cdots, C_m\}$ to be the largest convex canonical cone C lying inside the common region of the given cones. We denote the relationship as $C \equiv \bigcap_{i \in \{1,2,\cdots,m\}} C_i$. Figure 1(c)(d) shows the intersection of two canonical cones.

Isolated triangles: The triangles that do not belong to any (π, β)-surfaces or $(\pi, \beta, \mathbf{I})$-surfaces.

Normal of triangle in time domain: We denote $\mathbf{x}_i(t)$ as $\mathbf{x}_i + \mathbf{w}_i(t)$, where $\mathbf{w}_i$ is a second order differentiable function of t and $\mathbf{w}_i(0) = \mathbf{0}$. We define $\vec{x}_{ij}(t)$ as $(\mathbf{x}_j + \mathbf{w}_j(t)) - (\mathbf{x}_i + \mathbf{w}_i(t))$. Given a deformable triangle $T(\mathbf{x}_1(t), \mathbf{x}_2(t), \mathbf{x}_3(t))$, the time domain normal $\mathbf{n}_T(t)$ of T is defined as: $\mathbf{n}_T(t) \equiv \vec{x}_{12}(t) \times \vec{x}_{13}(t)$ where $\mathbf{x}_1(t)$, $\mathbf{x}_2(t)$, and $\mathbf{x}_3(t)$ are the vertices of T. We assume that the triangle does not degenerate into a line segment or a point. Therefore, $\mathbf{n}_T(t)$ is a non-zero vector.

Dot product between a cone of collision constraint and a vector: The dot product between a cone of collision constraint $\mathcal{Z}(C, N)$ and a vector $\mathbf{v}$ is given by:

$$\mathbf{v} \cdot \mathcal{Z}(C(\mathbf{n}, \beta), N) = \begin{cases} \mathbf{v} & \forall \mathbf{n} \in N \ \ \mathbf{v} \cdot \mathbf{n} \geq \cos \beta \\ \mathbf{v} \cdot C & \text{otherwise} \end{cases}$$

If $\mathbf{v} = \mathbf{v} \cdot \mathcal{Z}(C(\mathbf{n}, \beta), N)$, then $\mathbf{v}$ is satisfied the collision constraint $\mathcal{Z}$ or equivalently $\mathbf{v}$ is inside the admissible space of the collision constraint.

A (π, β)-surface: We define a polygonal surface $\mathcal{S} \equiv \{T_1, T_2, \cdots, T_n\}$ to be (π, β) if there exist a unit vector π_s and an angle β_s, such that for all $i \in \{1, 2, \cdots, n\}$, we have $\pi_s \cdot \mathbf{n}_i \geq \cos\beta_s$, where $0 \leq \beta_s < \pi/2$ and $\mathbf{n}_i$ is the unit normal of triangle T_i. Alternatively, we call this surface a (π_s, β_s)-surface, where π_s is the surface direction and β_s is the surface angle.

A $(\pi, \beta, \mathbf{I})$-surface: Let $\mathcal{S}$ be a 2-manifold surface. It is associated with a set of triangles $\{T_1, T_2, \cdots, T_n\}$ after it is discretized. If there exists a non-zero vector $\mathbf{n}(t)$ and a scalar β_s, s.t. $0 \leq \beta_s < \frac{\pi}{2}$, for all $T_i \in \mathcal{S}$ and for all $t \in \mathbf{I} = [0, I_{max}]$, we have $\frac{\mathbf{n}(t)}{|\mathbf{n}(t)|} \cdot \frac{\mathbf{n}_{T_i}(t)}{|\mathbf{n}_{T_i}(t)|} \geq \cos \beta_s$. Then $\mathcal{S}$ is a $(\pi, \beta, \mathbf{I})$-surface. Specifically, we call this surface a $(\mathbf{n}(t), \beta_s, \mathbf{I})$-surface. It is associated with a canonical cone $C(\mathbf{n}(t), \beta_s, \mathbf{I})$, where $\mathbf{n}(t)$ is the surface axis and β_s is the surface angle. If β_s is the smallest among all the canonical cones, we call the corresponding cone the optimal canonical cone associated with the surface. If $\mathbf{I} = [0, 1]$, we suppress this term.

Potential colliding pair: Two triangles form a potential colliding pair if their bounding volumes overlap. Collision information of a potential colliding pair is computed in the intrinsic collision detection unit.

Tangential and normal components of a vector: Assume that a vector $\mathbf{v}$ is not inside the admissible space of the collision constraint $\mathcal{Z}(C, N)$. We define the tangential component $\mathbf{v}_T$ and normal component $\mathbf{v}_N$ of $\mathbf{v}$ with respect to $\mathcal{Z}(C, N)$ as follows:

$$\mathbf{v}_T \equiv \mathbf{v} \cdot \mathcal{Z}(C, N), \quad \mathbf{v}_N \equiv \begin{cases} \mathbf{v} - \mathbf{v}_T & \text{if } \mathbf{v}_T \neq \mathbf{0} \\ \mathbf{0} & \text{otherwise} \end{cases}$$

Chapter 1

Introduction

Modeling the natural motion of virtual clothing in a 3D environment is currently one of the most computationally demanding tasks. The interactive manipulation of virtual clothing has become possible with advances in computational power and more efficient algorithms. Building a high performance system for computing virtual clothing dynamics efficiently, robustly and realistically is no longer a tale. We have developed a set of robust techniques for scalable dynamics and interactions of virtual clothing. We achieve interactive rates if the complexity of virtual clothing is about thousands of triangles.

A high performance system should be robust and efficient in handling dynamics computation, collision detection and collision response. The system should be able to handle different kinds of clothes in different environments dynamically. The animation produced by the system should be physically realistic. Although we need not model the motion of clothes as accurate as the one developed in continuum mechanics but the derivation of the motion of clothes should be built based on the model of Newtonian mechanics. By employing Newtonian mechanics alone for modeling clothes with a large number of particles, realistic simulation of clothing can be produced.

There are three major problems in simulating virtual clothing: (1) a large number of potential colliding pairs in collisions, (2) the computations of the relative orientation between colliding pairs in the presence of numerical errors, and (3) friction, stiction and dynamic response in the presence of objects with sharp features. These three problems affect the performance of virtual clothing simulation. Due to these problems in the past, we used small mesh sizes, used objects with smooth surfaces, avoided performing interactions, and used a single piece of cloth without sharp features. Based on the previous work, we have developed a set of new techniques for handling these three problems efficiently and robustly. The results show that these new techniques can be applied on virtual clothing with complex geometry and on unique interactions between continuous and non-smooth surfaces. By using our techniques, the realism of complex simulations for virtual clothing has been improved. Moreover, we can perform editing and simulation of three kinds of special virtual clothing: deformable surfaces with sharp features, multi-layered surfaces constructed by gluing several surfaces along lines or over regions, and sewn surfaces composed of several panels.

Although we focus on virtual clothes, our techniques can be applied to other kinds of deformable surfaces, for example, rubber and skin. Throughout this thesis, we will use the term "deformable surface" as a synonym for "virtual clothing" and other cloth-like objects.

1.1   Motivation

There is a wide range of applications of deformable surfaces across different areas, for example, computer graphics and animation, virtual reality, computer-aided design and computer-aided apparel design, image analysis, engineering simulation, and surgical simulation and training. Different aspects of the deformable surfaces are emphasized, in particular, visual realism and computation complexity. Visual realism and computation complexity are two essential factors which are required to be compromised in order to achieve the desired effect.

In computer graphics and animation, deformable models have been used for clothing [139, 114, 20, 33, 39], face modeling [154], and animal or human characters [135, 104]. In virtual reality, deformable objects are used for modeling different kinds of objects which can be manipulated at real-time or interactive rates. In computer-aided design, deformable models are used for editing curves, surfaces, and solids. In computer-aided apparel design, deformable models are used for simulating fabric draping and folding [129, 38]. In image analysis, deformation surfaces are used for segmentation of images and curved surfaces fitting. In engineering simulation, an accurate and precise deformable modeling helps the analysis of a certain material. Surgical simulation and training systems have a strict requirement on both the performance and the accuracy of the modeling techniques. Real-time response and physically realistic modeling of human-body tissues are demanded [46, 104, 26, 35, 34]. Readers are referred to cloth modeling techniques in [105]. Deformable image analysis can be found in [95], and deformable modeling techniques in computer graphics can be found in [56].

1.2 Challenges

In the wide spreading virtual reality, the visual effect is much more important than the accuracy of the underlying model. It is more important to have interactive performance instead of waiting in a virtual reality application. The computation should be fast so that real-time or interactive refresh rates can be achieved. Although the computation power of the conventional computers has been improved in the past twenty years, it is still not easy to achieve real-time or interactive performance for simulations which involve complex deformable objects due to a large number of potential colliding pairs in collisions, the computations of the relative orientation between colliding pairs in the presence of numerical errors, and interactions with objects having sharp features. Moreover, the editing and simulation of three kinds of special deformable surfaces, surfaces with sharp features, multi-layered surfaces, and sewn surfaces, are difficult. In order to simulate these three types of surfaces efficiently and robustly, we not only need to handle the three problems but also to employ other mechanisms.

Deformable materials, such as cloth, are subject to a large number of contact points in the proximity of other moving objects. There is a lot of potential colliding pairs that

3

is required for further processing in order to determine these contact points. Furthermore, deformable objects often fold, roll, and drape within themselves generating a large number of self-collisions areas. The interactive requirements of 3D games and physically driven virtual environments make inter-collision and self-collision computations more challenging. We call a designated unit for handling collisions a *collision detector*.

The role of a collision detector is to report not only the colliding pairs but also collision information about the pairs. There is one piece of information that is difficult to compute: the collision orientation of the colliding pairs. Surfaces can interact with other objects on both sides. The colliding regions of the surfaces may be determined lying on the wrong sides owing to numerical errors. In this case, either a fault collision event may be reported or a true collision event may be missed. Consequently, the motion of the colliding regions will be computed incorrectly. This will result in penetration and affect the realism of the motion of the deformable surfaces.

The deformable surfaces not only interact with themselves but also with other rigid bodies. These rigid bodies may have sharp features (discontinuity across some regions). The interaction of deformable surfaces with such objects poses a significant challenge to the current collision detection methods. The dynamic response has been an open problem for the interaction of a large number of sharp features with folding materials for real applications such as cloth modeling, draping and design.

There are some composite deformable surfaces which require other treatments: surfaces with sharp features, multi-layered surfaces and sewn surfaces. Not only that we need to handle the dynamics, collision detection and collision response for them but also we need other mechanisms in order to animate them efficiently.

When there are sharp features in a deformable surface, the issues of the stability and computation power arise. An intuitive way for handling this kind of surface is to increase the mesh resolution by performing triangulation. By performing triangulation up to a certain degree, the sharp features still remain. At this moment, adaptive meshing could be applied for the sharp feature regions. The major problem is that we cannot change the smoothness condition of the features. Moreover, by increasing the mesh resolution, it will take a longer time to evaluate the motion equation. The added cost to the collision detection process is also tremendous during the mechanical simulation. When the mesh resolution gets higher, the area of triangles becomes smaller. As a result, we need relatively small time step in order to carry out the integration process. The total cost dramatically increases.

In garment design, it is common practice to attach different pieces of cloth onto one another in order to make pockets or to embellish garments. They can be attached along lines or over regions. The resulting surface is a composite surface which is called a *multi-layered surface*. We need to preserve the anisotropic properties of each piece of cloth compositing the multi-layered surface. This multi-layered surface may be a non-manifold surface. The other kind of collision detection method is required for dealing with it.

In computer-aided apparel design, it is common process to sew (or merge) several panels together or a panel itself according to the seaming information. The resulting surface is called a *sewn surface*. A control system should be developed so as to compute the final shape of the sewn surface quickly. This shortens the time in designing virtual clothing.

1.3   Goals

We develop techniques for building a high performance system for virtual clothing dynamics. The goals that we have fulfilled include the following items:

- *Our collision detection techniques are accurate, efficient and robust. By accuracy, we mean that the distance between two contact points is in the same order of magnitude as $\tilde{d}_{max}$, where $\tilde{d}_{max}$ is the possible maximum computed shortest* *distance* [1] *of two features in a 0-collision event.*

Justification: Our collision detector can report reliable and meaningful collision information. The exact meshes of the objects are used in collision detection. We adopt floating point computation in our velocity-based collision detection method in order to compute collision information. Moreover, we optimize the performance at each stage of the collision detection pipeline so that the overall performance of collision detection is improved. From experiment results, they show that our techniques perform the best. The problems induced by numerical errors are tackled with careful treatments so that complex collision situation can be handled.

- *Our system is reasonable, robust and efficient in handling collision response and dynamics computation.*

Justification: We develop techniques based on the laws of motion in order to handle collision response and dynamics computation. The techniques capture the major elements from the laws of motion. For example, in handling friction and stiction, we develop techniques according to the Coulomb model of friction.

The techniques are robust since they are simple and they can manage complex interaction between deformable surfaces and rigid bodies with sharp features. In order to perform collision response and dynamics computation efficiently, we reduce the computation so that we need to handle only the involved particles and features.

- *Our system is able to handle different kinds of clothes in different environments stably.*

Justification: We develop techniques for handling interaction between cloth pieces and rigid bodies of different shapes. The rigid bodies and the cloth pieces may have sharp features. Moreover, the cloth pieces may be glued or sewn

---

[1] The computed distance of two colliding features is the distance obtained from a velocity-based collision detection method.

together. Our system can handle this kind of complex interaction without becoming numerically unstable. The cloth pieces do not behave weirdly.

- *Our system can produce physically realistic simulation.*

  Justification: We employ an existing physical technique for modeling the physical structure of virtual clothing. The physical model is based on the model of Newtonian mechanics. By employing Newtonian mechanics alone for modeling virtual clothing with a large number of particles, we can produce realistic simulation of virtual clothing.

1.4   Contributions

We have devised techniques for simulating deformable surfaces efficiently, robustly and physical realistically. These techniques can be applied in four areas: (1) culling non-colliding subsurfaces for collision detection, (2) intrinsic collision detection, (3) collision response, and (4) the editing and simulation of three kinds of special deformable surfaces. The techniques developed in these four areas range from the basic operations in the pipeline of collision detection for deformable surfaces and the mechanism of handling their interactions to the methods of handling composite surfaces and editing tools. The techniques have been integrated and successfully applied to perform simulation of virtual clothing. We summarize them as follows:

1. **Culling non-colliding subsurfaces for collision detection**

   - **An image-based method for interference test:** This method is used as a front-end for decomposing surfaces into low curvature surfaces. After that *potential colliding pairs* (PCPs) are collected in the process of frame buffer scanning. If the relative deformation of elements of a subsurface is less than half of a pixel, the method is also capable of collecting PCPs for this subsurface. The related materials have been published/accepted in [10, 12, 151].

7

- $(\pi, \beta, \mathbf{I})$-**surface decomposition:** This method is used as a front-end for decomposing surfaces into $(\pi, \beta, \mathbf{I})$-surfaces in the time domain. During the collision detection process, we perform only inter-collision detection among these $(\pi, \beta, \mathbf{I})$-surfaces. This method can detect the first contact point for a closed orientable two-manifold. For a surface with convex shape initially in 2D space[2], large out of plane deformation and small inplane deformation are allowed. The related materials will be published in [150].

- **An adaptive backward voxel-based (BVOX) hierarchical structure:** An adaptive BVOX-AABB hierarchical structure is proposed for collection of PCPs. This kind of hierarchical structure suits to highly compressed deformable surfaces. This hierarchical structure adapts to the shape of the deformable surfaces. The sub-objects which are in the same spatial neighborhood are likely to be assigned to the same branch of the hierarchical structure. Thus, the hierarchical structure shortens the time in traversal. The related materials have been published in [12].

2. **Intrinsic collision detection**

An architecture is proposed for implementing the unit of the intrinsic collision detection in the bottom-most layer of a collision detector. We have implemented this architecture for performing the intrinsic collision detection in the time domain successfully. By exploiting the coherent and temporal properties of the motion of the PCPs, we have improved the overall performance of the collision detection process. Frequently used values are maintained in the database of the unit of intrinsic collision detection. The velocity-based approach is employed for computing exact collisions of feature pairs with certain thicknesses. Numerical error which has been a major problem in collision detection is managed robustly in the intrinsic collision detection unit.

---

[2]After a developable surface is flattened in plane, its shape is convex.

3. **Collision response**

- **Penetration-free motion space:** A penetration-free motion space is proposed to prevent penetration for features involved in multiple collision events. The penetration-free motion space is computed for each particle of the colliding features. The velocities of the particles and the forces exerting on the particles are adjusted so that the colliding feature pairs will not intersect each other in the current frame. We have shown that the motion of the deformable surfaces is computed realistically by using this method. The related materials will be published in [150].

- **Handling friction and stiction:** In order to handle friction and stiction, we propose to adopt a static analysis before evaluating the motion equation. The forces exerting on the particles are modified according to the Coulomb's model of friction. The related materials will be published in [150].

4. **The editing and simulation of three kinds of special deformable surfaces**

We propose three methods to perform simulation of three kinds of special deformable surfaces. These methods can be treated as editing tools for compositing and manipulating these deformable surfaces. The three methods are a two-layer scheme, a master-slave scheme, and a scheme of controlled sewing process.

- **A two-layer scheme:** A two-layer scheme is designed for stably animating a deformable surface with sharp features (and probably with holes). In the scheme, we use two meshes, an appearance mesh and a ghost mesh, to represent the deformable surface. By employing this scheme, we avoid using high resolution mesh. We have shown that this method performs stably even though there are collisions.

- **A master-slave scheme:** A master-slave scheme is devised for gluing several surfaces together either along lines or over regions. The resulting surface is a composite surface, namely, *multi-layered surface*. The scheme

9

preserves the anisotropic properties of the composite surface. The composite surface may be a non-manifold surface. A scheme of collision detection is proposed for this kind of surface. The related materials will be published in [152].

- **A scheme of controlled sewing process:** A method has been proposed for systematically controlling the sewing (or merging) process for deformable surfaces. The product of the sewing process is a composite surface, namely *sewn surface*, which is composed of several surfaces. By controlling the internal physical parameters and internal structure of the deformable surfaces, quickly we bring the surfaces into or near the equilibrium state without producing unnecessary self-collisions. We have successfully employed the sewing process for creating realistic Chinese dresses.

1.5   System overview

There are three major components in a simulation system: a modeling unit, a collision detection unit and a collision response unit. The modeling unit is responsible for modeling the physical structure of deformable objects. The dynamics computation is strongly related to the underlying models of the deformable objects. The collision detection unit is responsible for detecting collision events. It reports collision information and passes collision information to the collision response unit. The collision response unit handles the collision events so that the involved colliding objects (or colliding features) will not penetrate each other. Our simulation system consists of the following eleven stages:

1. **Selection of modeling techniques:**   Appropriate modeling techniques are selected for modeling the physical structure of the deformable surfaces. The selection of a modeling technique for a deformable surface is provided by a user.

10

2. **Initialization and Preprocessing:** Initialize the data structure, and compute the quantities and data structure which will not change over time.

3. **Selection of a time step** Δt**:** The time step indicates the time difference between two frames. It affects the stability of the integration of the motion equation.

4. **Computation of the current collision constraints:** The current collisions affect the force distribution among involved objects. Appropriate collision constraints should be applied in order to prevent penetration.

5. **Computation of forces acting on the objects:** The forces should be computed so that they do not violate the collision constraints.

6. **Motion equation construction:** The motion equation of the objects is constructed at run-time depending on the status of the objects.

7. **Integration of the motion equation:** The positions and velocities of the objects are computed for the next frame. This requires to perform numerical integration for the motion equation.

8. **Computation of collisions:** The collision events are computed so that the objects will not intersect or pass through each other. The related collision information is reported for further processing.

9. **Update object positions:** Objects move to their new positions. If the objects are unbreakable, they should not intersect with each other.

10. **Geometry post-refinement:** Detailed geometric information is added to the objects before/when they are rendered.

11. **Rendering objects:** Finally, the objects are rendered. One time step is completed for the simulation.

The stages (3)-(9) may be executed several times before the objects are rendered. Without other specifications, we invoke only the collision detection unit one time per frame for each object pair.

The deformable surfaces are orientable two-manifold. We assume that the data representation of a deformable surface is a triangular mesh $\mathcal{T} = \{T_i, i = 1...n\}$. The normal of a triangle T_i is denoted by $\mathbf{n}_i$. These triangles are inter-connected with known topology information. For example, the adjacent triangles are known for each triangle and the edges attached at a vertex are given.

The physical models of deformable surfaces are modeled using spring-mass systems similar to the model described in [114]. The semi-implicit Crank-Nicolson method is adopted for integrating the motion equation. The underlying physical model of deformable surfaces can be replaced by other models such as [82, 67]. The numerical integration method can also be replaced with other methods [112].

Numerical integration

We have worked with a number of numerical integration methods such as Forward Euler, Runge-Kutta, and, most importantly the first-order semi-implicit method discussed by Baraff and Witkin [20]. The Crank-Nicolson semi-implicit method (or semi-midpoint scheme) provides the most accurate solution for sliding, stiction and friction. (A discussion on the issue of the stability of the implicit integration methods can be found in [75].) The Crank-Nicolson semi-implicit method is a second order method. Denote $\mathbf{x}_i$ and $\mathbf{v}_i$ as the position and velocity of a particle i, respectively. The formula for computing the change of positions of particles $\Delta \mathbf{x}$ and the change of velocities of particles $\Delta \mathbf{v}$ between two consecutive frames is based on Newton's second law of motion. By expanding $\mathbf{f}$ in the Taylor series and using the first order approximation $\mathbf{f}(\mathbf{x}_0 + \Delta \mathbf{x}, \mathbf{v}_0 + \Delta \mathbf{v}) = \mathbf{f}_0 + \frac{\partial \mathbf{f}}{\partial \mathbf{x}} \Delta \mathbf{x} + \frac{\partial \mathbf{f}}{\partial \mathbf{v}} \Delta \mathbf{v}$, we obtain

$$\begin{pmatrix} \Delta \mathbf{x} \\ \Delta \mathbf{v} \end{pmatrix} = \frac{h}{2} \begin{pmatrix} (\mathbf{v}_0 + \Delta \mathbf{v}) + \mathbf{v}_0 \\ \mathbf{M}^{-1}[(\mathbf{f}_0 + \frac{\partial \mathbf{f}}{\partial \mathbf{x}} \Delta \mathbf{x} + \frac{\partial \mathbf{f}}{\partial \mathbf{v}} \Delta \mathbf{v}) + \mathbf{f}_0] \end{pmatrix} \qquad (1.1)$$

By arranging the terms for the second row of the equation, we obtain:

$$\left(\mathbf{I} - \frac{h}{2} \mathbf{M}^{-1} \frac{\partial \mathbf{f}}{\partial \mathbf{v}} - \frac{h^2}{4} \mathbf{M}^{-1} \frac{\partial \mathbf{f}}{\partial \mathbf{x}} \right) \Delta \mathbf{v} = h \mathbf{M}^{-1} \left[\mathbf{f}_0 + \frac{h}{2} \frac{\partial \mathbf{f}}{\partial \mathbf{x}} \mathbf{v}_0 \right] \qquad (1.2)$$

where the subscript 0 indicates the value obtained from the previous frame, $\mathbf{f}$ is the force vector, $\mathbf{M}$ is the mass matrix, and h is the time step size. The changes $\Delta\mathbf{x}$ and $\Delta\mathbf{v}$ are the two vectors formed by compositing $\Delta\mathbf{x}_i$ and $\Delta\mathbf{v}_i$, for all particles i, respectively. The same operation is done on $\mathbf{x}_i$ and $\mathbf{v}_i$ to obtain $\mathbf{x}$ and $\mathbf{v}$.

In a spring-mass system, the matrix on the left hand side of Equation 1.2 is symmetric and positive definite. The Conjugate Gradient method [120] is applied to solve Equation 1.2. Usually, for a small h, the matrix on the left hand side is diagonally dominant. Alternatively, the Jacobi iterative method [112] can be applied to solve Equation 1.2.

From the first row of Equation 1.1, we have $\Delta\mathbf{x} = \frac{h}{2}(2\mathbf{v}_0 + \Delta\mathbf{v})$. Therefore, the particles will move from the positions $\mathbf{x}$ in the previous frame to the new positions $\mathbf{x} + \Delta\mathbf{x}$ in the current frame if there is no collision. The final velocities of the particles are adjusted to $\mathbf{v} + \Delta\mathbf{v}$. If there are collisions, the particles move to the new positions $\mathbf{x}_0 + \mathbf{C}_t\Delta\mathbf{x}$, where $\mathbf{C}_t$ is a diagonal matrix of the collision time c_t of the particles.

The dynamic model in our system includes gravity, spring forces, viscous damping forces, and external force drivers such as wind loading. Wind loading is modeled as: $-k_f|\mathbf{v} - \mathbf{v}^{wind}|(\mathbf{n}\cdot(\mathbf{v}-\mathbf{v}^{wind}))\mathbf{n}$, where $\mathbf{n}$ is the particle (or surface) unit normal, k_f is a constant coefficient, and $\mathbf{v}^{wind}$ is the velocity of wind. The stochastic wind modeling is described in [91]. Readers are referred to [114, 48] for the formulation of the forces and the computation of $\frac{\partial\mathbf{f}}{\partial\mathbf{x}}$ and $\frac{\partial\mathbf{f}}{\partial\mathbf{v}}$.

1.6 Outline

Each proposed technique will be analyzed empirically. The experimental results, summaries and discussions are given in the end of each chapter. The organization of this thesis is as follows. We review the related work on modeling, collision detection and collision response in Chapter 2, Chapter 3, and Chapter 4, respectively. The modeling techniques include the geometrical techniques, physical techniques and hybrid techniques. The collision detection techniques include object-based techniques and image-based techniques. The collision response techniques include the analytical approach, penalty approach, constraint approach and methods of modifying particle state.

Chapter 5 proposes an image-based collision detection method. This method performs the subsurface culling and collects potential colliding pairs for further processing. A multi-viewport assignment scheme is proposed for assigning a set of viewports into a rendering window efficiently. The adaptive BVOX-AABB hierarchical structure is proposed for handling highly compressed deformable surfaces.

Chapter 6 develops an architecture for the intrinsic collision detection unit. A velocity-based collision detection method is employed. This method suits to handling collision detection in the time domain for triangular meshes. Optimization methods are proposed for improving the collision detection process. Robust treatments for numerical errors in computing collision orientation are proposed. A phenomenon called ghost particle pulling is discussed.

Chapter 7 describes a new class of surface: $(\pi, \beta, \mathbf{I})$-surface. We propose a method for improving the performance of self-collision detection by decomposing a surface into a set of $(\pi, \beta, \mathbf{I})$-surfaces. We show that the method can compute the first contact point for a closed orientable two-manifold. It can also detect the first contact point for a two-manifold with boundary under certain condition. A penetration-free motion space is proposed for preventing colliding features penetrating each other. A static analysis approach is proposed to handle friction and stiction in the dynamic response.

Chapter 8 presents a two-layer method for handling deformable surfaces with sharp features. A deformable surface with sharp features is represented by two meshes: an appearance mesh and a ghost mesh. By manipulating these two meshes appropriately, we can animate the deformable surface without using high resolution mesh and small time step.

Chapter 9 discusses a master-slave scheme for animating multi-layered surfaces.

The multi-layered surfaces may have non-manifold features. We need to employ other treatments for the non-manifold features when performing collision detection for these multi-layered surfaces.

Chapter 10 and Chapter 11 develop a control system for performing a sewing process and a piecewise stable sewing process, respectively. We can produce realistic Chinese dresses by using the proposed techniques.

Finally, we conclude this thesis in Chapter 12. We summarize our proposed techniques and propose potential extensions for them. We also present some other problems related to simulation of virtual clothing.

16

Chapter 2

Related Work on Modeling

2.1 Introduction

There are three classes of modeling techniques for deformable surfaces: geometrical, physical, and hybrid. In geometrical techniques, individual or a set of points or shape parameters are manually adjusted or computed based on some predefined rules for shape editing. The geometrical techniques are adequate for modeling the static appearance of the objects. Physical techniques are designed for modeling the deformation effect of the objects according to the laws of motion. They account for the physical properties, forces and the constraints of the environment. A large set of differential equations which governs the motion of the objects is produced. Hybrid techniques integrate both of the geometric features and physical behavior of the objects together. The hybrid techniques provide a way to refine the details of the objects.

2.2 Geometrical techniques

The geometrical techniques are adopted when we want to model the static appearance of deformable objects without considering their dynamic behavior. The geometrical techniques are relatively simple and computationally efficient. There are three categories: (1) constrained-based techniques, (2) control point-based techniques, and (3) techniques of free-form deformation.

2.2.1 Constrained-based techniques

In constrained-based techniques, a set of constraints and the shape functions connecting two points are given. The shape of the deformable objects is computed accordingly. An iterative relaxation process is applied to adjust the final shape of the objects. We discuss four constrained-based techniques as follows.

Using catenary and relaxation process: Weil [148] presented a two-stage method for modeling a piece of cloth hanging from some constrained points in three-dimension space. The piece of cloth is represented as a set of grid points organized uniformly in a rectangle initially. The shape of the cloth piece within the convex hull is approximated using catenaries [1] and then an iterative relaxation process is employed for enforcing displacement constraint between the grid points. Consequently, folds are created. Finally, the spline surface is used to interpolate the grid points and this surface is treated as a collection of small cylindrical segments so as to capture the translucent effect of cloth. A ray-tracer is used to render the surface.

Using hollow cylinder: Agui et al. [5] represented the cloth object as a hollow cylinder for modeling a sleeve on a blending arm. The hollow cylinder consists of a series of circular rings. The circular rings are transformed into polygons for producing folds.

Using superimposing harmonic functions: Hinds et al. [65] presented a system for garment design. A garment is modeled by using a number of 3D surfaces (panels). C^0 continuity is maintained at the connection between panels. They developed a method for creating simple fold embellishments to the cloth surface by using superimposing harmonic functions, e.g. sinusoidal functions. Figure 2.1 shows how folds are created. A quadrilateral region (a, b, c, d) is selected. This region is deformed by applying a decaying sinusoidal function which reaches maximum amplitude at the lowest middle point of the region and decays to zero at the region boundary.

---

[1]A catenary [60] is a uniform density curve, which is perfectly flexible inextensible, hanging from two fixed points under gravity.

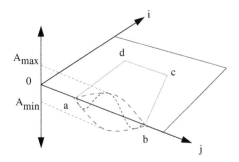

Figure 2.1: Fold superimposing.

Using layers: Ng et al. [106, 105] proposed a modeling technique that generated the folds in the gaps between cloth layer and the skin layer. Fold lines are specified and then the sinusoidal functions are used to create folds along the lines. A set of rules is developed to simplify the process.

2.2.2 Control point-based techniques

Control point-based techniques require designers to manipulate a set of control points of the deformable objects as well as the shape parameters. There is a variety of techniques, such as Bezier curves, B-Splines, rational B-Spline, non-uniform rational B-Splines(NURBS) and β-Spline. There are some curve types and patches which require specific set of control points and parameter values. A comprehensive coverage on NURBS can be found in [108] for modeling curves and surfaces.

2.2.3 Free-form deformation

Free-form deformation (FFD) provides a more powerful editing capability than the approaches based on the manipulation of control points. FFD changes the shape of the objects by deforming the space in which the objects lie. FFD can be applied to points, splines, polygons, implicit surfaces, and parametric patches. Three free-form deformation techniques are discussed as follows.

Jacobians: Barr [23] employed Jacobians to deform solid objects with the operators, namely, twist, taper and bend. The volume of the objects is conserved.

Trivariate polynomials: Sederberg and Parry [117] proposed a method to deform space in which the objects are embedded based on trivariate Bernstein polynomials. The volume change of the object can be computed after the object is deformed.

Lattices: Coquillart [43] extended the work of Sederberg and Parry to deform the shape of an existing surface either by bending it along an arbitrarily shaped curve or by adding arbitrarily shaped bumps to it. The objects are embedded inside lattices. If the shape of the lattices is modified, the corresponding parts of the objects are changed accordingly.

2.2.4   Advantages and limitations

Geometric techniques are simple and fast. However, the deformable objects are either static or are subject to some prescribed trajectories. They do not interact with each other or with the external environment. These models are usually referred as passive models. There are three main drawbacks as stated in [6]:

1. These techniques are limited to some specific situations. Complex situations such as interaction between the objects and the environment cannot be applied, in general. It requires a significant involvement of the designers to change the shape of the deformable objects.

2. As there are no quantities varying with time, it is not easy to produce animation. This makes the motion simulation of deformable objects a tedious and very time consuming task for animators. Although there are some interpolation techniques for morphing objects from one shape to another shape [29], the process requires the manipulation from animators.

3. It is difficult to model the dynamic behavior of deformable objects as the geometrical techniques are weak in representing physical properties of the deformable objects such as elasticity, anisotropy, and viscoelasticity.

2.3 Physical techniques

Physical techniques employ physical principles for realistic simulation of complex physical processes that would be difficult or impossible to model with purely geometric techniques. The physical properties, such as mass, stiffness, damping factors, anisotropy, inhomogeneity, and viscoelasticity can be captured in a physical model. There are two popular physical systems for modeling deformable surfaces: particle system and continuum system. In particle systems, a deformable surface is modeled as a set of punctual masses (or particles). Each particle influences its neighboring particles through some kinds of forces. The motion equation of a particle system is derived from the Newtonian mechanics. In continuum systems, a deformable surface is modeled as a continuous object. The motion equation of a continuum model is derived from the continuum mechanics.

2.3.1 Particle systems

Particle systems have been used in computer graphics to model natural phenomena, for example, fire and waterfalls [116, 122]. In a particle system, an object is represented by a set of particles. The particles influence each other through some kinds of forces. We discuss two kinds of particle systems: spring-mass system and oriented particle system. In a spring-mass system, particles are connected by massless springs of non-zero natural length. Some springs may be composed of more than two particles. In an oriented particle system, particles interact with each other through certain forces among the particles. The forces are depended on the distance and orientation of particles. We summarize five particle systems as follows.

The Work of T.L. Kunii et al.: T.L. Kunii et al. [82] represented a cloth model

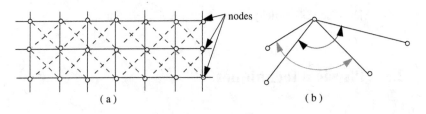

Figure 2.2: A particle system proposed by Kunii et al.

as a collection of a finite number of lines and a finite number of nodes. Figure 2.2 shows the structure of the model. The lines correspond to the threads and the nodes correspond to the crossings of these threads. Each line works as a spring that reacts to the change of the length of the line, and each arc also works as a spring that reacts to the change of the angle of the arc. The dotted lines also work as springs.

The Work of D. Breen et al.: D. Breen et al. [31] modeled a piece of cloth as a set of 3-D points lying on a 2-D rectangular grid. Each point represents a thread crossing in a plain-weave fabric. Each point i has a certain amount of energy which is given by:

$$U_{total_i} = U_{repel_i} + U_{stretch_i} + U_{bend_i} + U_{trellis_i}$$

U_{total_i} total energy of a particle i

U_{repel_i} energy due to repulsion, preventing interpenetration

$U_{stretch_i}$ energy function that connects each particle to four of its neighboring particle

U_{bend_i} energy due to threads bending over one another out of the plane

$U_{trellis_i}$ energy due to bending around a thread crossing in the plane of the cloth

The Work of Eberhardt et al.: Eberhardt et al. [50] described a model which is an extension of the work of Breen et al. [32]. They applied D'Alembert and Lagrange equation to setup the relationship between the trajectory and potential energy of particles. Let V be a cloth-specific potential, $L = E_{kin} - V$ be the sum of all energies of all particles and E_{kin} be kinetic energy of the system. Then L is given by:

$$L = \sum_i U_{kin_i} - \left(\sum_i U_{pot_i} + \sum_i U_{tension_i} + \sum_i U_{shear_i} + \sum_i U_{bend_i} \right)$$

where

U_{kin_i} kinetic energy for particle i

U_{pot_i} potential energy for particle i under effect of gravitational field

U_{bend_i} energy for particle i due to bending force

U_{shear_i} energy for particle i due to shearing force

$U_{tension_i}$ energy for particle i due to tension force

The partial differential equation is reduced to a system of ordinary differential equations, one for each particle.

The Work of Provot: Provot [113] employed a spring-mass net to model cloth. The cloth model is a mesh of $m \times n$ particles. Each mass is linked to its neighbors by springs. There are three kinds of springs to link neighbors of point masses together: structural springs, shear springs, and flexion springs. Figure 2.3 shows the structure of the springs in the mesh. If the properties of the springs are specified and suitable physical methods are employed, the motion equation of the particles can be derived. This structure is similar to the model proposed by Kunii et al. [82]. A similar structure was adopted by Fan et al. [51].

The Work of Szeliski and Tonnesen: Szeliski and Tonnesen [127] presented a deformable surface which is formed by oriented particles. Long-range attractive forces and short-range repulsion forces are used to model the interaction between particles. They demonstrated welding two surfaces together, cutting a surface into two, putting a crease into a surface, and stretching between particles.

23

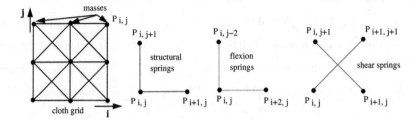

Figure 2.3: A spring-mass system proposed by Provot.

2.3.2 Advantages and limitations of particle systems

A particle system is a simple physical model with well-known understood dynamics. The formulation of the motion equation is easily constructed. A particle system demonstrates the utility in animating deformable objects that would be difficult if they are manually manipulated. It is possible to animate the deformation objects at interactive rates that the continuum models with the same scale cannot be achieved. It suits to parallel computation due to the local nature of the interactions between particles. However, there are three drawbacks [56]:

- A particle system is an approximation of the true physics that occurs in a continuous body. It is not easy to obtain the correct springs or parameters.

- In order to model incompressible volumetric objects or thin surfaces which are resistant to bending is not easy. Although extra springs can be added, this will increase the cost of computation.

- Another problem is called stiffness. When the spring constants are too large, the stiffness problem leads to instability if explicit integration methods are adopted. Although an implicit integration method can be employed for large time step, the accuracy is paid off. A description about this problem can be found in [19].

2.3.3 Continuum systems

In continuum systems, mass and energies are distributed throughout the objects. The motion equations of the continuum objects are derived based on continuum mechanics. The continuum modeling techniques model the physical properties of an object accurately. A set of representative points within the material is selected. Their positions and velocities form the elements of a finite state vector. Each continuum model is associated with the finite state vector which describes the current state of the model. We summarize four continuum systems as follows.

The Work of Terzopoulos et al.: Terzopoulos et al. [131, 132, 130] proposed a method based on the variational principle of mechanics in Lagrange's form [98]. The proposed method suits to modeling generalized flexible objects. The formulation includes the inertia force, damping force, elastic force and net external force. The elastic force is expressed as a variational derivative of potential energy of deformation and potential energy is defined by using the metric tensor and curvature tensor.

The material coordinates of a point $\mathbf{a}$ in a body Ω is defined in the Cartesian coordinate system $[a_1, a_2, a_3]$ as

$$\mathbf{r}(\mathbf{a}, t) = [r_1(\mathbf{a}, t), r_2(\mathbf{a}, t), r_3(\mathbf{a}, t)] \tag{2.1}$$

where t is time.

The Lagrange's form governing a deformable model's motion under the action of externally applied forces is given by:

$$\underbrace{\frac{\partial}{\partial t}\left(\mu\frac{\partial \mathbf{r}}{\partial t}\right)}_{\text{inertial force}} + \underbrace{\gamma\frac{\partial \mathbf{r}}{\partial t}}_{\text{damping force}} + \underbrace{\frac{\delta \mathcal{E}(\mathbf{r})}{\delta \mathbf{r}}}_{\text{elastic force}} = \underbrace{f(\mathbf{r}, t)}_{\text{net external forces}} \tag{2.2}$$

$\mu(\mathbf{a})$ mass density of the body at $\mathbf{a}$

$\mathbf{r}(\mathbf{a}, t)$ position of the particle $\mathbf{a}$ at time t

where $\gamma(\mathbf{a})$ damping density

$f(\mathbf{r}, t)$ net externally applied forces

$\mathcal{E}(\mathbf{r})$ net instantaneous potential energy of elastic deformation of the body

$\frac{\mathcal{E}(\mathbf{r})}{\delta \mathbf{r}}$ elastic force

The metric tensor and curvature tensor are used to define potential energy $\mathcal{E}(\mathbf{r})$.

The metric tensor is given by

$$G_{ij}(\mathbf{r}(\mathbf{a})) = \frac{\partial \mathbf{r}}{\partial a_i} \cdot \frac{\partial \mathbf{r}}{\partial a_j} \tag{2.3}$$

and the curvature tensor is given by

$$B_{ij}(\mathbf{r}(\mathbf{a})) = \mathbf{n} \cdot \frac{\partial^2 \mathbf{r}}{\partial a_i \partial a_j} \tag{2.4}$$

where the vector $\mathbf{n}$ is the unit surface normal. Now, $\mathcal{E}(\mathbf{r})$ is defined as

$$\mathcal{E}(\mathbf{r}) = \int_{\Omega} \|\mathbf{G} - \mathbf{G}^0\|_{\alpha}^2 + \|\mathbf{B} - \mathbf{B}^0\|_{\beta}^2 da_1 da_2 \tag{2.5}$$

where $\| \cdot \|_{\alpha}$ and $\| \cdot \|_{\beta}$ are weighted matrix norms. The superscript 0 indicates that the value is taken when the corresponding points are in rest state.

The Work of Carignan et al.: Carignan et al. [37] suggested in their cloth modeling technique that a more accurate damping term ([119]) could be used to replace the original damping term by introducing a dissipation function $\dot{\mathbf{G}}$ in the model of Terzopoulos et al. The dissipation function $\dot{\mathbf{G}}$ measures the rate of change of the deformation. The surface integral may be interpreted as a rate of energy dissipation due to the internal friction. The dissipation function $\dot{\mathbf{G}}$ minimizes the deformation speed. An advantage of this formulation is that there will be no energy dissipation when the surface undergoes a rigid body displacement.

The Work of Aono: Aono [6] proposed a model based on the equilibrium of equation in the field of elasticity and D'Alembert's principle. The fundamental model of cloth is developed based on three assumptions: (1) cloth is homogeneous, isotropic,

26

and linearly elastic in its initial state, (2) cloth is in equilibrium at any time under given applied forces, according to D'Alembert's principle, and (3) cloth is a perfectly thin surface, and never expands or contracts along the surface normal. After obtaining the fundamental model of cloth, the damping factor, inhomogeneity factor, the anisotropic factor and viscoelastic factors can be integrated into the model. Inhomogeneity exists randomly in the initial state in cloth and the effects of inhomogeneity are so small that the behavior of cloth is nearly equal with the same force applied to the same shape of cloth. Global anisotropy affects the total shape of cloth after an external force is applied. Local anisotropy affects the ways how wrinkles propagate. Viscoelasticity states that the deformation of cloth depends on the history of the deformation of cloth.

The Work of Teng et al. and Chen et al.: Finite volume method was developed to model cloth in the work of Teng et al. [129] and Chen et al. [38]. A fabric sheet is discretized into many small structural patches called finite volume (or control volume). By defining the bending and membrane deformations of the patches, the motion equation of the entire fabric sheet can be obtained.

2.3.4   Advantages and limitations of continuum systems

Continuum systems provide a more physically realistic simulation with fewer particles than particle systems do. Although we need to solve a relatively smaller linear system, the computation of the motion equation is expensive. There is a significant amount of time for pre-processing when Finite Element Methods (FEMs) [159] are adopted. The mass and stiffness matrices must be computed during the simulation if the deformable object changes its shape beyond small deformation limits.

2.3.5   Formulation of motion equation

In both particle systems and continuum systems, the formulation of the motion equation can be either energy-based or force-based methods. Energy-based methods calculate energy of the deformable objects. The shape of the deformable objects is obtained when the total energy of all the particles of the deformable objects is a minimum. Force-based methods capture forces exerting upon the particles as a set of partial differential equations. At each time step, we need to compute the particle positions and to move the particles to the new positions accordingly.

Motion formulation for particle systems: In order to formulate the motion equation using force-based approach, the motion equation can be derived by using Newton's second law of motion. The motion equation of a particle system is given by:

$$\mathbf{M\ddot{x} + C\dot{x} + Kx = f} \tag{2.6}$$

where $\mathbf{M}$, $\mathbf{C}$, and $\mathbf{K}$ are the $3N \times 3N$ mass, damping and stiffness matrices, respectively. The vector $\mathbf{x}$ is the 3N-dimensional position vector and the vector $\mathbf{f}$ is the external force vector. The matrices are large but sparse. By rearranging the terms, we obtain

$$\dot{\mathbf{v}} = \mathbf{M}^{-1}(-\mathbf{Cv} - \mathbf{Kx} + \mathbf{f}) \tag{2.7}$$

$$\dot{\mathbf{x}} = \mathbf{v} \tag{2.8}$$

where $\mathbf{v}$ is the velocity vector. A conjugate gradient method [120] can be applied to solve the motion equation. The preprocessing of the inverse of the matrices can be adopted [48] in order to speedup the process. However, this is infeasible for a system with a large number of particles. The inverse of a matrix may consist of a lot of non-zero entries. In [74], $\mathbf{v}$ is approximated by using the velocities of the particles obtained from the previous frame.

Another way to formulate the motion equation is by computing energy of the particles. The total energy of a deformable system is given by: $\Pi = \Lambda - W$, where Λ is the total strain energy and W is the work done by external loads. After that, the task is to minimize energy of the entire system.

Motion formulation for continuum systems: When the deformable object is in the equilibrium state, its potential energy is at a minima. Denote Π as the total potential energy of a deformable system, Λ the total strain energy of the deformable object, and W the work done by external loads on them. Then Π is given by:

$$\Pi = \Lambda - W \tag{2.9}$$

Finite Element Methods (FEMs) [159] are used to obtain the numerical solutions for the continuum models. In FEMs, the continuum models are divided into smaller elements which are joined at discrete nodal points. In order to compute the equilibrium state, the equilibrium equation of each element is needed to solve. The equilibrium equation is in the form of continuous function. The function is discretized before the equation is solved.

2.3.6 Numerical integration for motion equation

We need to solve a set of equations governing the motion of the deformable objects in both particle systems and continuum systems. These equations are deferential equations. Generally, there is no closed form solution for the differential equations. In order to solve the motion equations, numerical methods are used.

There is a variety of numerical methods [112] which are employed to solve the differential equations. These methods are called numerical integration methods. There are two major classes of integration methods: explicit method and implicit method. Given that we have an Ordinary Differential Equation (ODE):

$$X' = F(X) \tag{2.10}$$

By adopting the numerical integration methods to solve the ODE Equation 2.10, we obtain a series of approximate solutions $X_n, n = 1, 2, ...$, to represent the exact solutions $X(t_n)$. We define $h_n = t_{n+1} - t_n$ as the time step at the n-th step. By using the linear multistep formulae, we have:

$$\sum_{i=0}^{k} \alpha_i X_{n-i} + h \sum_{i=0}^{k} \beta_i X'_{n-i} = 0 \tag{2.11}$$

According to the unknowns and the values of β_0, the integration method is classified into two classes: explicit predictors and implicit correctors. In explicit predictors, $\beta_0 = 0$, and X_n is the only unknown variable. In implicit correctors, $\beta_0 \neq 0$, and X_n, X_n' are unknown variables. The explicit methods require that the integration time step must satisfy the Courant condition [159]. This condition states that the integration time step should be small enough so that there is enough time for the information to propagate in the space discretization. Implicit methods are not subject to the Courant condition for stability. Therefore, it is possible to simulate a stiff spring-mass system in large time step [20, 143]. However, we need to trade off the inaccuracy for stability of the system when we use large time step.

2.3.7 Inverse dynamics

Figure 2.4: Large deformation appears near the fixed point in a spring-mass system.

Figure 2.4 shows the phenomenon of super-elongation in a spring-mass model. Some springs have high deformation compared to other springs. The percentage of the elastic deformation rate of these springs exceeds 100%. In the simulation of certain deformable objects, this super-elongation should be prevented. For example, this will not happen in real woven fabrics except for some loose knitted woven fabrics. There is one way to alleviate this problem that is to increase the stiffness of springs. However, this requires increasing the sampling rate, i.e. using a small integration time step so as not to break the Courant condition when explicit integration methods are employed. This will slow down the overall performance. Provot [113] proposed an inverse dynamic procedure to adjust the length of springs when necessary. The order of adjustment is depended on the data structure. Kang et al. [74] suggested using a bucket sort strategy to order the springs according to their length. The order of the length adjustment is based on the result obtained from the bucket sort. The inverse dynamic method is simple. However, the method does not guarantee to converge all the time.

Bridson et al. [33] employed the similar idea to limit the strain and strain rate of the springs. Instead of changing the positions, they modified the velocities of the particles by using the Jacobi iterative method [112].

Discussion: The inverse dynamics method does not always converge. It also makes the system unstable. By changing the positions or velocities of the particles directly without evolving the deformable surfaces dynamically, the continuity condition of the system will be broken. The forces produced by the springs will suddenly change and break the stable condition of the local regions of the deformable surfaces. The global stability of the deformable surfaces will be affected poorly.

2.4   Hybrid techniques

Hybrid techniques integrate both geometrical and physical techniques together. The geometrical techniques control the global shape of the deformable surfaces while the physical techniques enhance the local features of the deformable surfaces. We summarize four hybrid systems as follows.

The Work of Kunii et al.: Kunii et al. [82, 83] represented the cloth surface as a grid with springs connecting the points. Two kinds of energy are defined, metric and curvature. The initial shape of the surface is obtained by using the gradient descent method to find the energy minima. The geometric properties are obtained by applying singularity theory for shape analysis. A sinusoidal curve $f(s) = X sin\frac{n\pi s}{\lambda}$ is used to construct the surface with wrinkles, where X is a small constant, n is a natural number,

31

λ is the length of the curve, s is the parameter for arc-length ($0 \leq s \leq \lambda$), and $f(s)$ is the vertical displacement of the points s. After that, energy minimization is applied again to compute the final shape of the surface.

The Work of Tsopelas: Tsopelas [134] proposed a method to model folds. The garments are treated as thin cylindrical tubes under axial loads and simulated garment folds using thin-walled deformation theory. This process focuses on regions with large curvatures where folds are most likely to appear.

The Work of Dhande et al.: Dhande et al. [49] used a swept surface to model the draping effects of a fabric over a rigid flat surface. They used a *generatrix curve* and a *directrix curve*[2], $\mathbf{r}_1(v, u)$ and $\mathbf{r}_2(v, u)$, to generate a biparametric surface: $\mathbf{r}(u, v) = \mathbf{r}_2(v) + \mathbf{M}(v)\mathbf{r}_1(v, u)$, where M is a transformation matrix. The function $\mathbf{r}_2(v)$ exhibits the blending and shear properties.

The Work of Taillefer: Taillefer [128] proposed a scheme to incorporate kinetic information into Weil's [148] geometrical model so as to model the vertical and horizontal folds of hanging cloths. Forces, such as stretching, bending, body weight and self-repulsion, exerting on each point of the catenary are taken into account during the relaxation process in obtaining the final shape of cloths.

2.4.1 Advantages and limitations

The hybrids techniques are applied only to handle deformable surfaces in some specific situations. In order to handle some complex situations, such as interactions between deformable objects and the environment, much research should be done. By applying the geometrical techniques first and then followed by applying physical techniques for refinement will not work well in this situation. When there is an interaction, the global shape of deformable objects may change drastically. There should be some rules to govern how the global shape should be evolved. This requires the manipula-

---

[2]Generatrix: the point or the mathematical magnitude, which, by its motion, generates another magnitude, as a line, surface, or solid. Directrix: the line along which the generatrix moves in generating a surface. Websters Dictionary

tion from animators when there are interactions between the deformable objects and other objects. The physical techniques can be applied first to compute the rough shape of the deformable objects. After that the geometric techniques are applied to refine the details of the deformable objects. For example, in simulation of cloth, Bridson et al. [33] employed the subdivision method to smooth the final surface of cloth. In the work of Larboulette and Cani [36], wrinkles are added to garments in the post refinement process.

Chapter 3

Related Work on Collision Detection

3.1 Introduction

When two objects are moving towards each other, they will touch or intersect with each other. This phenomenon is called *collision*. Collision detection methods are employed to check whether two objects have collided. If these two objects belong to a larger object, the collision event is called an intra-collision event; otherwise, the collision event is called an inter-collision event. A collision detection method should report collision information of the colliding objects including the collision time, the collision points, and the collision normals. The component of a simulation system that is responsible for detecting and reporting collisions is called *collision detector*.

3.1.1 Motivation

Collision detection has been recognized as one of the bottlenecks in an animation [62]. In the eighties, Hahn found that almost 95% of the computation time was spent in collision detection. Since then, interactive collision detection has been an area of active research. This is due to (1) inherent complexity in the representation of highly deformable surfaces, and (2) stringent requirements for interactive frame rates in the presence of complex geometry and dynamic interactions between objects in a virtual environment.

Solutions to the polyhedral intersections and rigid-body collision detection have been well covered in the computer graphics literature [102, 147, 88, 87, 160, 155, 55, 123, 110, 90, 69, 64, 42, 70, 111, 79, 100, 126]. The classic work in this area is the GJK algorithm [57], the Lin-Canny algorithm [88], RAPID [59] based on space efficient OBB trees and the separating axis theorem [58]. Chung and Wang [40] developed a fast collision detection method based on the separating vector concept. This method is limited to convex polyhedra and, in practice, it has been observed to be less stable in the presence of sharp features. Mirtich [100] proposed a robust polyhedra collision detection algorithm V-Clip which continued the work of Lin, Gottschalk, Manocha and Ponamgi et al. [111]. Alternatively, Klosowski et al. [79] proposed k-DOPs to bound an object by k hyper-planes. A comprehensive coverage on collision detection for geometric models can be found in [89].

Although searching for an efficient solution for the interactive rigid-body collision detection problem is still an active area of interest, the potential to solving the more difficult problems prevalent in clothing and garment simulation is attracting an increasing number of researchers in this area. For example, Hu et al. [68] and Chen et al. [38] have recently applied the finite elements and finite volume methods, respectively, in order to generate mechanically realistic draping and contact dynamics of textiles. This direction is highly motivated by a strong demand in the design and control of human-like virtual actors and character models for interactive 3D environments [155, 139, 144, 20, 143, 142, 156, 44, 138, 157, 158], and more specifically for interactive 3D games [97, 16]. A comprehensive coverage on collision detection for deformable objects can be found in [133].

3.1.2 A typical collision detection pipeline

There are three major layers in a typical collision detection pipeline:

1. **Collection of potential colliding object pairs:** This is the first layer of a collision detector. Some of the objects are far away from each other and they do

not have a chance to collide with each other in the current frame. For these objects, there is no need to compute collision information among them. The noncolliding object pairs should be eliminated as many as possible. The potential colliding objects are passed into the second layer.

2. **Collection of potential colliding primitives (e.g. patches, polygons, triangles):** This is the second layer of a collision detector. The primitives of the objects which are in proximity or have a chance to collide are collected. These primitives are passed into the third layer.

3. **Intrinsic collision detection for primitive pairs:** This is the third layer of a collision detector. It performs exact or approximate collision detection for the primitive pairs and reports collision information of the colliding pairs. We call this layer the *intrinsic collision detection unit*.

In order to improve the performance for these three layers, the temporal and geometric coherence properties are exploited. Based on these two properties, a variety of techniques has been developed. In the first layer, the techniques are ranging from interval sorting [42], spatial partitioning [99], to hierarchical trees [22, 59, 70]. In the second layer, the dominant methods are the hierarchical tree techniques [92, 137, 33]. Other techniques are based on the low curvature approach [140, 114], the voxel-based technique [156] and the image information stored in the image (frame) buffer [138, 10]. All these methods work well in eliminating a lot of non-colliding primitives. However, for collision detection of deformable surfaces, there is still a lot of potential colliding primitives which are required for further processing. Hence the time spent in the third layer (or the bottom layer) contributes a significant amount of percentage in the entire collision detection process.

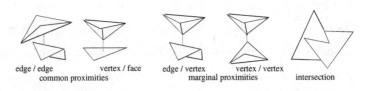

edge / edge   vertex / face   edge / vertex   vertex / vertex
common proximities   marginal proximities   intersection

Figure 3.1: Intersections and proximities in polygonal meshes.

3.1.3 Classification of collision events

The methods for determining whether two objects have collided can be classified into two categories. The first category is that the objects are separated by a distance smaller than a given predefined distance. The second category is that the objects intersect with each other (shortest distance is zero). The former one is called *proximity collision* and the latter one is called *intersection*. Figure 3.1 shows the different collision events: edge–edge, vertex–face, edge–vertex, vertex–vertex and intersection.

3.2 Collision detection for deformable objects

There is a lot of potential colliding pairs (PCPs) when a deformable object interacts with other objects. Efficient methods should be developed to eliminate the non-colliding pairs. There are two approaches for collision detection: object-based collision detection (OBCD) and image-based collision detection (IBCD) [11]. The OBCD methods are generally dependent on the geometrical structure of objects. The computation is done only in the main processor. The IBCD methods attempt to balance the computational load between the main processor and the graphics rendering pipeline.

3.2.1 Object-based collision detection

The object-based collision detection approaches have two representatives: the bounding volume tree approach and the low curvatured surface approach.

Bounding volume tree approach: Liu et al. [93] exploited the intrinsic properties of the iso-oriented bounding boxes of the triangles to detect self-collision. A binary hierarchical structure of an object is constructed. Each leaf node contains a single triangle and each node has a minimum bounding box which encloses all the triangles in the node. The bounding boxes of these two nodes are traversed recursively to detect whether two nodes collide or not. A similar idea is adopted in [137, 33]. This approach can be used for performing inter- and intra-collision detection.

Low curvatured surface approach: Volino et al. [140] addressed the self-

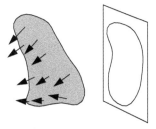

Figure 3.2: Geometrical conditions for free of self-collisions.

collision problem by introducing a constant hierarchical structure based on the geometrical regularity of a surface. The bounding volume is AABB (axis-aligned bounding box). The idea of the approach is that if a surface is deformed a little (see Figure 3.2), i.e. with low curvature[1], the surface hardly intersects itself. The direction is sampled in 3D space, as shown in Figure 3.3. When collision detection is performed, a bottom-up method is employed to merge subsurfaces satisfying the low curvature property. In order to improve the computation, a bitwise-AND operation is used to compute a value

---

[1] A surface is low curvatured if there exists a vector such that the dot product of the vector and the normals of all the points of the surface is non-negative.

bottom-up. A *true* value indicates that the merged surface satisfies the low curvature property.

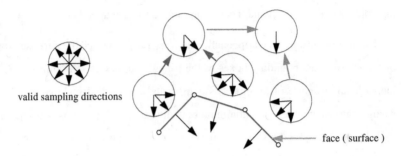

valid sampling directions

face (surface)

Figure 3.3: Sampling directions in space and merging subsurfaces bottom-up.

If the subsurface is convex, then there is no need to check whether there is an intersection along the contour[2]. If the subsurfaces can be merged, then they are treated as a single subsurface. Thus, this method avoids checking a lot of adjacent triangles. The classic AABB tree traversal is adopted for detecting collisions among subsurfaces. The method requires the adjacent information of subsurfaces in order to perform merging.

Later on, Volino et al. [143] improved the above algorithm by replacing the bounding volume with the discrete oriented bounding polytope, such as the six-axe of dodecahedral volume. Readers can find the implementation and the intersection test procedure on discrete bounding oriented polytopes in the paper of Klosowski et al. [79].

Provot [114] refined the curvature method by dynamically constructing the hierarchy of subsurface regions that satisfies a specific smoothness condition. These subsurfaces are called (π, β)-surfaces. Instead of sampling the directions in space, Provot presented another bottom-up method to group the cones formed by the admissible directions of the objects. Each leaf node contains a single triangle. The idea is to group cones recursively so that at each step, the newly created cone is sufficiently large to contain the existing cones in a zone. The triangles containing in a cone satisfy the low

---

[2]In order to perform the contour intersection check, the polygon patches are projected onto a 2D plane and then the 2D polygon intersection algorithm [118, 47] is applied.

curvature property. It is assumed that there is no collision for two adjacent zones if they can be merged together. As the zones are grouped together, bounding boxes are computed for each newly created zone.

These methods are designed for self-collision detection only. They do not take into account the movement of the vertices. As the vertices of the polygonal patches move within a frame, the low curvature properties will no longer be satisfied. These methods are suitable for *interference test*. The assumption about the penetration-free within a low curvatured surface is weak without appropriate justification.

3.2.2   Image-based collision detection

The methods of image-based collision detection have been researched in [121, 103, 8, 14, 149]. Initially, these methods are designed for handling rigid bodies. They do not need much preprocessing for rigid-body collision detection. In the work of [103, 8, 14, 149], graphics hardware is employed for fast rendering of the objects. Depth information, color information, and stencil information are used for determining whether the objects collide or not. In [149], a method is proposed for performing a pre-rendering process of an object into the depth map. The depth map is used for checking whether another object collides with the former object. Vassilev et al. [138] applied a similar technique for performing collision detection between human body and cloth models. The depth map of the human body is computed using graphics hardware. The assumption is that the human body should be convex. In his work, Vassilev reported rates in the order of 33ms per iteration for the collision detection problem involving meshes of up to 3,840 vertices running on a 1.0 GHz Pentium processor. The method does not account for all kinds of collision events. Thus, penetration will happen. Further progress in this area is found in [77, 52, 66].

A human body is generally not convex as a whole. A hierarchical partitioning must be employed when the viewing window is perpendicular to a lateral direction onto the body. Taking a sample through one of the arms may result in multiple ranges

41

that correspond to internal parts of the body and arms. If the non-convex topology is known in advance then it is not difficult to find the depth and the normal maps of the body. However, if the topology is not known in advance and the object is not convex, then it is difficult in general to compute the depth maps in hardware as proposed by Vassilev unless multiple depth buffers are used.

3.3 Approximated collision detection

Liu et al. [93] used bounding boxes to enclose triangles. If the bounding boxes of the triangles collide, then it is assumed that there is collision among the corresponding triangles. Volino et al. [143] suggested that some other large geometrical primitives such as large metaballs can be used. Simplified objects can also be used. When performing collision detection for high complexity objects, the simplified models of the high complexity objects are used.

These methods are fast. However, they report inaccurate collision information. Consequently, undesirable visual effects are produced due to incorrect computation of collision response. For example, two colliding regions may have a large gap between them when they slide relatively upon each other.

3.4 Multiple collisions

Multiple collisions occur because of cyclic collisions. For example, when two triangles collide, their states (for example, positions, velocities or accelerations) are modified so that they do not collide. However, these triangles may introduce new collision events with the other group of primitives. The positions of these primitives are repetitively adjusted and as a result, a cyclic situation may occur. Provot [114] developed a technique that groups colliding objects together in order to solve the problem of multiple collisions. If there is collision for the first time, one more collision detection is carried out after the positions of the objects are altered due to collision response. If there is no collision, the next time frame is advanced; otherwise, the set of objects involved in multiple collisions are recorded. These objects are grouped together to form a zone of impact. The zone of impact acts as a rigid body. Section 4.4 discusses the collision response techniques for the zone of impact in details.

3.5   Collision avoidance

Breen et al. [31] presented a method to avoid multiple collisions. If there is collision, the time step is decreased and let the objects move again so as to find the exact contact point. Since the first exact contact point is computed, multiple collisions can be avoided. There is no interpenetration. Therefore, there is no need to adjust the positions of the triangles. However, this method is expensive.

Liu et al. [93] suggested that the first aligned collision plane is computed for the bounding boxes of the colliding objects. The vertices of the bounding boxes of the objects are allowed to move only on the plane. The new positions of the objects are computed by solving the motion equation with the movement constraint imposing on those vertices. After obtaining the new positions of the objects, collision detection is performed again and the entire process is repeated.

Lafleur et al. [84] subdivided a surface into small pieces of triangles. For each triangle, a thin force field is constructed to create a cell based on the normals at the vertices of the triangle. When a point enters the cell, a force is applied to the point. The force depends on the velocity, the normals and the distance between the point and the surface. The role of the force is to prevent the point from intersecting the surface.

3.6 Intrinsic collision detection: interference test and continuous collision detection

There are two kinds of intrinsic collision detection for two triangles: interference test and continuous collision detection. In the interference test, the triangles are static and the task is to check whether they share a common point. In continuous collision detection, the initial positions and the vertex trajectory information of the triangles are given in a frame. The task is to determine whether they collide within the frame.

Interference test: This method is performed in a discrete manner. Every time the object is frozen in the space and the collision status of objects is computed. If the objects are moving too fast, they may be passing through each other in a single time step. Therefore, the time step should be sufficiently small to in order to avoid passing.

Tomas Möller [101] developed an interference test for two triangles by checking whether they share an interval or not. However, in the implementation of the method, the coplanar check is put at the end. The major problem of this method is that it does not handle numerical errors appropriately. Consider that there are two coplanar triangles. Their distance is around the length of an edge. The method may report that these two triangles collide. Another problem of this method is the discrepancy in the determination of whether two triangles collide.

Continuous collision detection: This approach incorporates the time quantity to perform collision detection. It is done in four-dimension space (i.e. time domain). The intersection test [92] for two moving triangles is generalized into two cases, edge–edge and vertex–triangle. In each case, four vertices are involved. The vertices are assumed to move in constant velocities. Thus, this method is also called *velocity-based* collision detection. In order to detect collision, the time at which the four vertices are coplanar is computed. This requires solving a cubic equation. After that the triangles are moved to the time at which the four vertices are coplanar. Then it is checked whether the two triangles share a common point or not. The method is exact in the sense that the method reports the accurate collision time, collision normal, and collision points. The accuracy is in the order of the maximum of all the floating point numbers obtained in a floating point computation of the corresponding items. A similar approach is adopted in [114, 33].

Hallgren and Halpegama [63] computed the convex polyhedrons which bound the polygonal patches and then perform the Cyrus-Beck algorithm [3] to determine whether or not the patches collide. However, this method does not take into account the movement of the vertices.

3.7   Collision orientation maintenance

When the objects collide, they react accordingly based on the relative collision orientation. The relative collision orientation tells on which side an object is lying with respect to a given object so that a suitable reaction can be computed for the object. As a result, the colliding objects behave consistently.

Volino et al. [141] proposed two methods to compute the collision orientation: collision remanance and orientation consistency tracking. For collision remanance, when there is a collision, in-out orientation check is invoked. This information is maintained in a structure for a certain duration in case the contacting objects move apart several frames later. For orientation consistency tracking, all the collision areas of the scene are traced. All the objects which contribute to each area are grouped independently. There is a collision direction associated with every object in a group. By counting the number of collision pushes in a certain direction of the group, the majority direction is chosen for that group.

Volino et al. [139] of the same group extended the work of [140]. They incorporated a new tracking technique into the original collision detection method. This tracking technique is called *cinematical tracking*. When the objects are moving within

---

[3]Cyrus-Beck algorithm is used to deal with clipping a line segment against a polytope exclusively in computer graphics.

proximity in the first time, they are stored in a record. This information can be used to check whether a crossing has just happened or not. However, numerical errors are not justified in their methods. Without careful treatment, penetration will happen easily. Robust treatments of numerical errors are important in building a robust collision detector.

Baraff et al. [21] proposed the GIA (global intersection analysis) to determine the collision orientation. This method suits to handle features that will intersect with certainty in their motion paths. It does not account for the past collisions.

3.8   Discussion

There are some problems in the low curvature approach and the approach of using conventional hierarchical structure. The low curvature approach eliminates a lot of non-colliding pairs if the surface is low curvature. However, if the surface is not "convex enough", extra time will be spent in performing the 2D intersection test. This will be expensive. Another problem of the low curvature approach is that it does not suit to handle deformable objects which are deforming. The low curvature condition and the "convexity" condition may be broken during the deformation. Thus, the method is suitable only for interference test. The approach of using hierarchical structure can detect all the potential colliding pairs. However, it spends a lot of time in inspecting the adjacent elements of the deformable objects. Much research should be done in this area.

Although these two approaches eliminate many of the non-colliding pairs, there is still a large number of non-colliding pairs and they are passed into the bottom-most layer of the collision detector. Moreover, when there is interaction between deformable objects, the contact area may be large. There will be a lot of potential colliding pairs that is required for further processing. Developing an efficient method for intrinsic collision detection is demanding.

46

Another problem in the current approach is that the topology of the hierarchical structure does not change even though the surface undergoes a drastic evolution dynamically. By adapting the hierarchical structure or the low curvatured surfaces to the shape of the deformable objects, it may be able to improve the overall performance of a collision detector.

Chapter 4

Related Work on Collision Response

4.1 Introduction

Collision events impose collision constraints on the involved colliding regions. These constraints should be satisfied so that the colliding regions will not penetrate each other. The task of enforcing the collision constraints is responsible by the collision response unit. Collision response is a process of correcting the interaction behavior of the objects when they collide. The positions, velocities and accelerations of the colliding objects and the forces exerting on the particles may change accordingly so that they do not penetrate each other and their distance is kept not less than a given distance. When the objects collide, the forces induced by collision are called collision forces. Collision forces include friction forces and repulsive forces. Friction will be present between the colliding regions with rough surfaces. Repulsive forces are used to repel colliding regions.

4.2 Methods for prevention of intersection

There are several methods which are applied in order to satisfy the non-penetration condition for the colliding objects: (1) analytical approach, (2) using repulsion force or penalty force, (3) immediate correction, (4) constraint-based methods, and (5) correction of particle state dynamically.

(1) Analytical approach: Baraff [19] proposed an analytical approach to handle collision response. Contact forces are computed by solving simultaneous equations that reflect all of the forces acting on all the bodies. It is assumed that there is a finite number of local constraints. Each constraint is in the form of

$$\ddot{\chi}_i(t_0) \geq 0 \tag{4.1}$$

where $\ddot{\chi}_i(t_0)$ is a measure of the separation between two bodies in the normal direction at time t. Let f_i be the signed magnitude of the contact force at contact i. Then the system of equations is given by:

$$\ddot{\chi}_i(t_0) \geq 0, f_i \ddot{\chi}_i(t_0) = 0, f_i \geq 0 \tag{4.2}$$

In order to compute the contact forces satisfying these constraints, quadratic programming [17, 18] is used. The computation of the quadratic programming is expensive.

(2) Repulsion force or penalty force: Lafleur et al. [84] proposed to use repulsion force for colliding objects. A thin force field is constructed to create a cell (Figure 4.1) for each colliding triangle based on the normals at its vertices. When a point enters the cell, a force is applied to the point. The role of the force is to prevent the point from intersecting the surface. At the same moment, the triangle is assumed to be immobile. The force depends on the velocity, the normals and the distance between the point and the surface. Another assumption is that the time step is sufficiently small so that the point does not move completely across the cell. Some other constraints are imposed on the dynamic model in order to avoid degenerate cases, for example, minimal area and maximal angle.

Gudukbay et al. [61] suggested creating a potential energy function around the objects. When the objects are moving in proximity, a couple of repulsive forces exerts on the objects in opposite directions. The potential energy function of an object is defined as: $c\ exp(\mathbf{a}(x)/\xi)$, where c and ξ are constants and $\mathbf{a}$ is the implicit function of the object. The repulsive force is given by:

$$\mathbf{f}_c(u, t) = -c((\nabla \mathbf{a}(x)/\xi)exp(-\mathbf{a}(x)/\xi \cdot \mathbf{n})\mathbf{n} \tag{4.3}$$

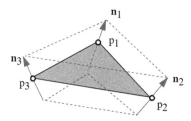

Figure 4.1: Force field (cell) around a triangle.

where $n(u, t)$ is the unit surface normal vector of the object and ∇ is the gradient operator.

Baraff et al. [20] inserted a strong damped spring force to push the colliding objects apart or to enforce the movement constraint for the objects. Another dissipative force (damping force) opposite to the sliding direction is applied.

Bridson et al. [33] applied repulsion force in their simulation of cloth. The repulsion force is limited to a maximum so that it avoids the problems with stiffness. They claimed that their method will not propel the objects outside the overlapping region in a single time step.

Repulsion force should be controlled well. Undue repulsion force will lead to stiffness problems. It also produces undesirable motion such as oscillation or vibration.

(3) Immediate correction: When there is a collision for the objects, the positions of the objects are repositioned immediately so that the objects do not intersect each other. It is pointed out that this will introduce discontinuity in the position. Consequently, the motion will become jumpy and the system will become stiff. This method is not suitable for a multi-step differential equation solvers such as Runge-Kutta methods, suggested in [20].

(4) Constraint-based methods: In the work of Liu et al. [92], the collision planes are computed. The vertices of the concerned bounding boxes are allowed to move only on the collision planes. A vertex may be involved in more than one collision event.

51

In this case, the first collision plane is used. The new positions of the objects are computed by solving the motion equation with the movement constraint imposing on those vertices. This is the constraint condition imposed on the vertices. The motion equation is solved by using the Gauss-Seidel method.

(5) Position, velocity, acceleration and force correction: Eberhardt et al. [50] presented a method to modify the velocity of a particle. Let p_0 be the initial position of a particle and p_1 be the new position of the particle obtained after solving the differential equations. Let R be a ray shooting from p_0 to p_1. If R intersects an obstacle at point p, the surface normal n at p is computed. The scheme is that no velocity is allowed in the opposite direction of n at p. The particle location is adjusted to p_{new}:

$$p_{new} = p + d_{min}n \qquad (4.4)$$

in which $d_{min} > 0$ is the minimal ray length of R. The new velocity is computed as:

$$v_{new} = k_f v_{\parallel} + k_r \|v_{\perp}\| n \qquad (4.5)$$

where k_f and k_r are coefficients which depend strongly on material properties. The vector n is the intersection normal, and $v_{\parallel}$ and $v_{\perp}$ are the perpendicular component and horizontal component of the computed velocity with respect to n, respectively. A similar approach was adopted in [71]. The velocity is computed as $v_{\parallel} - rv_{\perp}$, where r is the restitution coefficient.

Baraff et al. [20] applied position correction to deal with the collision response for deformable objects and rigid objects in their particle system. An arbitrary small valid change of the position of the deformable objects is fed back to the motion system. After that, the motion equation is solved for the new velocity update.

Volino and Thalmann [143] proposed a scheme for computing the correction for the accelerations of particles. The collision force is treated as an external force exerting on the respective particle. By integrating the collision into the motion equation, the new velocity of the particles can be solved.

In another paper of the same group of people [142], they extended the work and

52

focused on the global collision correction. Sometimes, some of the particles are constrained and these particles are expected to behave in a certain way. In the paper, they intended to solve for all collisions so that the effective collision corrections and desired collision corrections are equal.

4.3 Friction handling

Provot [114] applied the Coulomb friction model in the simulation of cloth. The velocity of an object after the collision and the force generated by the impact are unknowns at the collision point. However, the greater the velocity is, the greater the force is generated. When the objects collide, an amount of energy may be dissipated. According to this observation, Provot proposed the following method to approximate the Coulomb friction model with dissipation of energy. Let $\mathbf{v} = \mathbf{v}_{\parallel} + \mathbf{v}_{\perp}$ be the velocity of a particle before collision. The velocity $\mathbf{v}'$ after the collision of the point is given by:

1. if $\|\mathbf{v}_{\parallel}\| \geq \mu_s \|\mathbf{v}_{\perp}\|$, $\mathbf{v}' = \mathbf{v}_{\parallel} - \mu_s \|\mathbf{v}_{\perp}\| \frac{\mathbf{v}}{\|\mathbf{v}_{\parallel}\|} - k_d \mathbf{v}_{\perp}$

2. if $\|\mathbf{v}_{\parallel}\| < \mu_s \|\mathbf{v}_{\perp}\|$, $\mathbf{v}' = -k_d \mathbf{v}_{\perp}$

where μ_s is the friction coefficient and k_d is the dissipation coefficient ($0 \leq k_d \leq 1$). Bridson et al. [33] adopted a similar approach to model friction. A single friction parameter μ is used. The final (kinetic) tangential velocity is modeled as:

$$\mathbf{v}_{\parallel} = max(1 - \mu \frac{\Delta \mathbf{v}_{\perp}}{\|\mathbf{v}_{\parallel}^{pre}\|}, 0) \mathbf{v}_{\parallel}^{pre} \tag{4.6}$$

where $\Delta \mathbf{v}_{\perp}$ is the change in relative velocity in the normal direction. The method is an exact method if an explicit integration method is adopted. However, it is not true if an implicit integration scheme is adopted as the forces exerting on a particle will be spread out and affect the neighboring particles. Jimenez and Luciani [72] proposed to attach a spring between the closest points to model static friction. Let $\mathbf{F}_N$ be the normal force. When the force exerted by the spring is beyond the threshold $\mu_s \|\mathbf{F}_N\|$, the spring is removed.

4.4 Zones of impact

Provot [114] suggested that the colliding regions in multiple collisions can hardly move. These colliding regions form the zone of impart. They are treated as a whole a rigid body. Therefore, the interaction between these objects can be treated as perfectly inelastic and non-sliding. The motion of the "rigid" bodies is computed accordingly. Bridson et al. [33] adopted the similar approach in their simulation of cloth. They corrected a mistake in Provot's formulation of the motion equation of the "rigid" bodies.

This approach modifies the velocities of particles locally. From our observation, if the velocities of particles are adjusted locally too much, instability may occur.

4.5 Discussion

The new positions of colliding objects not only depend on the external forces but also depend on the interaction between objects. Collision is one of the important interaction events. When there is collision, the collision force becomes one of the components in the equation of motion physically. The contribution of the collision force should be integrated into the equation of motion when the equation of motion is solved. A global instability may occur if this is not treated appropriately.

Chapter 5

Image-Based Collision Detection and Adaptive Backward Voxel-based Hierarchical Structure

5.1 Introduction

We have built upon our work started in [8, 13, 14, 10, 11] and developed a novel image-based method to perform collision and self-collision detection tests for deformable surfaces represented by large triangular meshes on the conventional graphics hardware. By exploiting mathematically well-defined smoothness conditions over smaller patches of deformable surfaces and resorting to image-based collision detection tests, we have developed an efficient collision detection method. The collision detection method achieves interactive rates while tracking self-interactions in highly deformable surfaces consisting of a large number of elements. This is ascribed to a viewing process which can be performed by using the Graphics Processing Unit (GPU). By employing the viewing process, the number of potential colliding pairs is improved for low curvatured surfaces. An adaptive backward voxel-based (BVOX) hierarchical structure is proposed for dealing with highly compressed surfaces.

5.1.1   A viewing process for collision detection

Definition 5.1 : A surface intersects itself if and only if there exist two points whose coordinates are the same.

Definition 5.2 : A point of a surface is seen if there exists a point not belonging to the surface such that the line segment formed by these two points does not intersect other points of the surface.

Definition 5.3 : If two or more points have the same coordinates, only one point can be seen.

Corollary 5.1 : A point of a surface can be seen if and only its coordinates are unique.

Proof: If a point of a surface can be seen and its coordinates are not unique. Then there must exist another point q whose coordinates are the same as the coordinates of p. Then q cannot be seen.

Assume that a point of a surface is unique and it cannot be seen. As the point is unique, then we can construct a point p' such that $p' = p + l n$ does not belong to the surface, where l is a positive scalar value and n is a unit vector. Moreover, the line segment formed by p and p' does not intersect other points of the surface.

We show that there exists l and n to fulfill our requirement. If they do not exist, then this implies that there exists $l_0 > 0$, and for $\forall\, l \in (0, l_0)$ p' belongs to the surface. This implies that the surface is, in fact, a solid. This violates that the definition of a surface. $\square$

Theorem 5.1 : A surface does not intersect itself if and only if each point of the surface is seen.

Proof : We prove this to the contrary. Assume that each point of a surface is seen and the surface intersects itself. As there is an intersection, there exist at least two points whose coordinates are the same. This is a contradiction.

Assume that there exists a point **p** of the surface that the point is not seen and the surface does not intersect itself. If the point **p** is not seen, then there exists another point whose coordinates are the same as the coordinates of **p** according to Lemma 5.1. This is a contradiction. □

Corollary 5.2 : If there is an one-to-one mapping between a surface and its image on an image plane, the surface does not intersect itself.

Definition 5.4 : A viewing process consists of two parts. The first part is the projection of a surface onto an image plane. The second part is the inspection process in which each image point is checked for uniqueness.

5.2 Outline and assumption

Our proposed method for self-collision detection is based on the viewing process. An image-based method is adopted for accelerating the viewing process. The surface input to the viewing process is a (π, β)-surface which satisfies a smoothness condition. Our approach of performing self-collision detection for a surface is that the surface is decomposed into a set of (π, β)-surfaces. This is called the *decomposition process*. After that, each (π, β)-surface is projected and inspected. We do not inspect points of a surface. Rather, we inspect the triangles of the surface. Specifically, we inspect the image points of triangles.

The projection process is done in the Graphics Processing Unit (GPU). Each triangle of a (π, β)-surface is rendered into the frame buffer. The rendering of a triangle is done by using a regular scan-line algorithm (e.g. [53]) in OpenGL. The frame buffer consists of a depth buffer, a color buffer and a stencil buffer. Because of the limit size of the frame buffer, the image of the triangles is discretized into pixels. This introduces the aliasing problem which causes some triangles missed. We solve the problems arising due to aliasing (frame buffer sampling) and degenerate projections that may occur in the image-space. We manipulate the pixels with other information carefully in order to collect the potential colliding (triangle) pairs.

The advantage of this image-based method is that irregular regions are handled. There is no need to maintain an adjacent matrix among the subsurfaces. The method can detect the collision events that the purely low curvature approach fails.

When surfaces compress highly in a small volume, the image-based viewing process will be slow. We propose a dynamic backward voxel-based method (BVOX). We will show that the BVOX method suits to perform collision detection for deformable surfaces which are highly compressed. The BVOX method is also used for collecting potential colliding pairs among (π, β)-surfaces.

We have two assumptions. First, we assume that a triangular mesh intersects itself if two non-adjacent triangles intersect[1] [2]. This is not applied to the boundary triangles. In some special (π, β)-surfaces, the assumption is not applicable for the interior triangles, too. For example, a triangular mesh, namely, pre-t-vertex mesh, is created by cutting along the edge at a T-vertex and extra triangles are attached to the vertex. This mesh is a valid (π, β)-surface and there are three interior adjacent triangles that collide. However, this kind of (π, β)-surface is unlikely to happen in a physical simulation. Second, we assume that there are no slim triangles in the decomposition process. If the surface has slim triangles, a preprocessing can be invoked to mark them as unsuitable for the decomposition process. The marking process for slim triangles can also be done at run-time.

The outline of this chapter is as follows: Section 5.3 proposes a method for decomposing a surface into a set of (π, β)-surfaces. The decomposition of the surface into (π, β)-surfaces is based on a breadth-first search. Section 5.4 describes an image-based

---

[1]In AABB tree traversal, usually, the collision of adjacent interior triangles is automatically prevented by checking the non-adjacent triangles ([93]).

[2]Two triangles are adjacent if and only if they share a vertex; otherwise, they are non-adjacent.

method for collecting potential colliding pairs. A multi-viewport arrangement scheme is proposed for placing viewports into a larger rendering window. Section 5.5 develops a BVOX-AABB hierarchical structure. The BVOX-AABB hierarchical structure is used for collision detection among the (π, β)-surfaces. Section 5.6 presents and analyzes the performance of the proposed method. We present the summary and discussion in Section 5.7.

5.3 Decomposition of a surface into (π, β)-surfaces

A constant hierarchy [140] fails to adapt to the shape of cloth. If a single triangle does not satisfy the low curvature condition, two subsurfaces cannot be merged. We extend the work of Provot [114] to decompose a surface into a set of (π, β)-surfaces dynamically each frame. We want to grow each (π, β)-surface as large as possible. The breadth-first search strategy is employed.

Formally, the low curvature condition (or smoothness condition) for a triangular mesh $\mathcal{T} \equiv \{T_1, T_2, \cdots, T_n\}$ is that: *if there exists a unit vector π_s and an angle β_s, such that for all $i \in \{1, 2, \cdots, n\}$, we have $\pi_s \cdot \mathbf{n}_i \geq cos\beta_s$, where $\mathbf{n}_i$ is the unit normal of the triangle T_i and $0 \leq \beta_s < \pi/2$.* Alternatively, we call this surface a (π_s, β_s)-surface. The vector π_s is the surface direction and the value β_s is the surface angle.

A single triangle is by definition a (π, β)-surface. The surface direction is the normal of the triangle and the surface angle is zero. In order to decompose a surface into (π, β)-surfaces, we start with a single triangle and add its edge-adjacent triangles into a queue. At each step, we pick a triangle from the queue and check whether we can merge this triangle into the current (π, β)-surface. If we can, then we update the surface direction and surface angle. Moreover, the edge-shared triangles are added to the queue if they do not belong to any (π, β)-surfaces. If we cannot grow the (π, β)-surface further, the construction of the current (π, β)-surface is finished. We construct another (π, β)-surface by picking another triangle not belonging to a (π, β)-surface

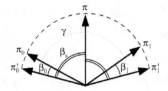

Figure 5.1: Merging two (π, β)–surfaces, (π_0, β_0) and (π_1, β_1).

and repeat the entire process. By doing so, we decompose the surface into a set of (π, β)-surfaces. We use a queue because we want to merge the nearest triangles first.

Figure 5.1 shows the merging of two surfaces, (π_0, β_0) and (π_1, β_1). Let γ be the angle between π_0 and π_1. If $(\beta_0 + \beta_1 + \gamma \leq 2\beta_{max})$, then these two surfaces can be merged into a larger surface with the new surface direction π_s and surface angle β_s, where $\pi_s = (\pi'_0 + \pi'_1)/\|\pi'_0 + \pi'_1\|$, and $\beta_s = (\gamma + \beta_0 + \beta_1)/2$. The threshold β_{max} is used for controlling the quality of the resultant surface and its value is in the interval $[0, \pi/2)$. For example, if $\beta_{max} = 0$, each (π, β)-surface is flat.

5.4   An image-based self-collision detection

By projecting a plane along its normal, we will maximize its image area. It is likely that by projecting a subsurface along its surface direction π, we will maximize its image area. Therefore, the subsurface is orthogonally projected onto a viewport along π (projection direction) when it is rendered. We also compute a projection orientation about the projection direction in order to maximize the area occupied by the subsurface with respect to the viewport dimension. The ideal projection orientation is aligned with the viewport perpendicular to the tight oriented bounding box (OBB) of the subsurface image. However, this is more computationally intensive. We approximate this projection orientation by computing an orientation such that the $AABB$ image of the local $AABB$ of the subsurface aligns with the viewport.

Figure 5.2 shows the steps for computing the projection orientation. Let the local axis-aligned bounding box of the subsurface be $AABB^{local}$. We denote $AABB^{local}$ in

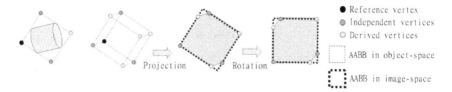

Figure 5.2: Computation of projection orientation for rendering.

the object-space and in the image-space by $AABB^{object}$ and $AABB^{image}$, respectively. In order to compute the projection orientation, we project orthogonally a (reference) vertex of $AABB^{object}$ and the other three independent vertices of $AABB^{object}$ onto the image plane. Then the remaining four vertices of $AABB^{object}$ can be derived by using vector addition accordingly on the image plane. These eight vertices on the image plane are used for computing $AABB^{image}$. After that, we compute a rotation for $AABB^{image}$ in order to align it with the viewport. This rotation is the projection orientation. It is noticed that if the reference point is treated as the origin of the projection, only three independent vertices of $AABB^{object}$ are required for projection.

Each triangle of the original surface is assigned a unique positive integer. When the triangle is rendered, this integer is converted to a color (R, G, B)[3]. We reserve the integer zero as the background color. After a subsurface is rendered, we retrieve the contents of the frame buffer into the main memory and scan the buffer. If the viewport resolution is sufficiently high, each triangle of a subsurface should occupy at least one pixel.

5.4.1 Frame buffer scanning for collecting potential colliding pairs

We assume that the frame buffer stores the pixel color of the incoming fragments with the smallest depth value. Two pixels are adjacent if the distance between them is equal to one. The distance metric used is $d((x_1, y_1), (x_2, y_2)) = \max(|x_1 - x_2|, |y_1 - y_2|)$, where (x_1, y_1) and (x_2, y_2) are the coordinates of two pixels.

---

[3]A similar idea is used in [81, 30].

There are three possible cases resulting from the intersection of two triangles: a point, a line or a plane. Let there be a pair of adjacent pixels such that each pixel belongs to a different triangle. If we know two adjacent pixels which belong to different triangles, then their corresponding triangles may collide.

We want that after two triangles are rendered, they occupy at least one pixel in the frame buffer. However, we may not be able to guarantee that each triangle occupies at least one pixel. This occurs if one of the following three conditions arises.

1. A triangle is co-planar with a larger triangle and the former triangle may lie entirely inside the latter (a plane intersection region). After they are rendered, we do not know whether the fragments of the former one or the latter one will be stored in frame buffer. It is possible that only the fragments of the second triangle are stored. The first one is missed.

2. One of the two triangles just touches the other and the former triangle lies entirely behind the latter (a point or line intersection region).

3. The triangle is either too narrow or too small to occupy a pixel (subsampling).

In order to solve these problems, we render the missing triangles at the same resolution again. We also use the adjacent information (see Section 5.4.3) to construct the potential colliding pairs for the missing triangles.

After the subsurface is rendered, we read the contents of the frame buffer of each viewport and store them into a two-dimensional array. For each pair of adjacent pixels, we inspect the corresponding color indices. If the corresponding triangles of the color indices are not adjacent to each other, the triangles may collide. We collect all these potential colliding pairs and perform intrinsic triangle test for them.

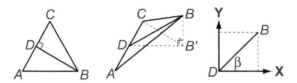

Figure 5.3: Computation of the viewport dimension for rendering.

5.4.2 Intrinsic triangle–triangle intersection test

We collect the potential colliding pairs of triangles from the frame buffer indices. Then we adopt the method developed by Möller [101] for intrinsic triangle intersection test. This method efficiently performs an intrinsic collision test for two triangles if they are not coplanar. If two triangles are co-planar, we project them onto the axis-aligned plane where the areas of the triangle are maximized. This increases the correctness of the computation. Then we perform a two-dimensional triangle–triangle intersection test. This method reports only whether or not there is collision. It does not report other collision information, for example, collision points. In Chapter 6, we will introduce the velocity-based approach for intrinsic collision detection, which accurately reports collision information for dynamics computation.

5.4.3 Dynamic viewport

The area of the projected image of a triangle changes if the orientation of the triangle changes with respect to the projection direction. We want the viewport to be sufficiently large so that each triangle will be likely to occupy at least a single pixel but it should not be too large or this will take longer time to scan the frame buffer. We develop a method to compute the dimension of the viewport dynamically according to the surface angle.

Figure 5.3 illustrates how a viewport dimension is computed for an equilateral triangle $\triangle ABC$. Let ℓ be the length of a side of the triangle, D the middle point of AB and B' the image of B. We need to compute $\overline{DB'}$. Assume $\angle BDB' = \beta_s$ and we

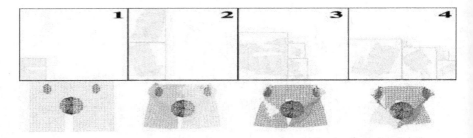

Figure 5.4: An arrangement of the dynamic multi-viewport during the deformation of a cloth piece. (The colors in the viewports are inverted.)

obtain $\overline{DB'} = \sqrt{3/4}\ell cos\beta_s$. If we project DB' further onto the x-axis and the y-axis, respectively, we obtain the minimum longest length of its image $\sqrt{3/8}\ell cos\beta_s$. Before the simulation, we compute ℓ as the average of the shortest edges of the triangles. The rotation angle is simply the surface angle. Therefore, we have $\ell' = \sqrt{3/8}\ell cos\beta_s$. We define $AABB'$ as the image of the $AABB$ on the viewport after the $AABB$ is aligned with the viewport axis. Assume that the dimension of $AABB'$ of the surface is (b_x, b_y). Then the dimension of the viewport is $(b_x/\ell', b_y/\ell')$.

Sometimes, there are triangles not occupying a single pixel when the (π, β)-surface is rendered. We call these triangles as "missing triangles". In order to solve this problem, we propose to use the information of their adjacent triangles to construct their potential colliding pairs. This can be justified as follows. Consider a triangle which does not occupy a single pixel. Then its image should be covered by the images of its adjacent triangles. We assume that the pixels of its adjacent triangles belong to it. In this way, we collect its the potential colliding pairs. Alternatively, a tree traversal or a voxel-based method can be applied to collect the potential colliding pairs for the missing triangles.

We may scale up or down the dimension of the viewport. If the dimension of the viewport is scaled up, it will take longer time to scan the frame buffer. If the dimension of the viewport is scaled down, there will be more missing triangles. There is a risk that we will miss potential colliding pairs if the viewport resolution is too low.

5.4.4 Multi-viewport rendering

We construct dynamic viewports for rendering the (π, β)-surfaces. Our goal is to render not just a single (π, β)-surface at a time but as many (π, β)-surfaces as possible. Figure 5.4 shows the arrangement of viewports of (π, β)-surfaces in a larger rendering window. Each (π, β)-surface is rendered in a dynamic viewport occupying a portion of the rendering window. We treat each viewport and the window as a rectangle. We have a set of small rectangles and we want to assign them in the window in a non-overlapping manner. When they are placed into the window, the translation operations are applied only; no rotations are applied. Each time we place a small rectangle at a location such that the immediate *fragmented space* below the small rectangle is the minimum. We repeat this process until no more rectangles can be placed into the window. This completes one assignment process. We render the corresponding (π, β)-surfaces and perform the frame buffer scanning. The same procedure is applied for the remaining (π, β)-surfaces. The details of the assignment process is discussed next.

5.4.5 Multi-viewport assignment

Given a set of small rectangles, denoted by $R_s = \{r_1, r_2, \cdots, r_n\}$ and a window R (large rectangle) in 2D integer domain. Each small rectangle r_i has width w_i and h_i. Let the window R have width R_w and height R_h, such that $R_w \geq w_i$, $R_h \geq h_i$, for all small rectangles r_i. All variables w_i, h_i, R_w, $R_h \geq 1$, i.e. at least pixel size. The task is to assign the small rectangles into R such that the small rectangles do not overlap and they lie inside R, and the axes of small rectangles align with R. We do not need to put all small rectangles into R at the same time. If no more small rectangles can be added, we restart all over with the remaining small rectangles. This is a 2D rectangle packing problem which is known as an NP-hard problem. The more general packing problem is discussed in [27, 76]. We are not interested in the optimal solution. We want to have an algorithm which arrange the small rectangles as fast as possible but should be reasonably tight.

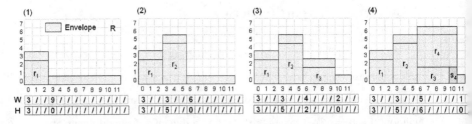

Figure 5.5: An assignment sequence of four small rectangles, $r_1(3, 3)$, $r_2(3, 5)$, $r_3(2, 4)$, and $r_4(5, 4)$, into a large rectangle $R(12, 8)$. In (1), $X(0, 12) = \{0, 3, 12\}$. In (2), $X(0, 12) = \{0, 3, 6, 12\}$. In (3), $X(0, 12) = \{0, 3, 6, 10, 12\}$. In (4), $X(0, 12) = \{0, 3, 6, 11, 12\}$. The fragmented space s_4 of r_4 is equal to 2.

We define an integer Cartesian Coordinate System with respect to the large rectangle. The origin is the lower left corner of the larger rectangle. We define the x-axis along the horizontal direction and the y-axis along the vertical direction.

During the assignment of the small rectangles, we maintain a data structure called the *shifted envelope*. The envelope helps us quickly locate a position to place the small rectangles. The data structure of the envelope has two integer arrays W and H, both of size $R_w + 1$. Intuitively, the array W stores the relative position of the next height change along the x-axis, with respect to the current position in x-coordinate. The array H stores the height of envelope (the maximum y-coordinates of small rectangles) along the x-axis. The initial envelope is a straight line segment starting from the origin of the x-coordinate 0, length R_w, and height of zero, i.e. $(W_0, H_0) = (R_w, 0)$. Denote H_x as the number which is stored in the x-th position of the array H and W_x as the number which is stored in the x-th position of the array W. Figure 5.5 shows the assignment of four viewports.

When the small rectangles are placed, the following two constraints must be satisfied: (1) small rectangles should lie entirely inside the large rectangle; (2) the small rectangles should not overlap one another. In the following, we discuss a method to place a small rectangle $r_i(w_i, h_i)$ into the large rectangle.

We start from the position $(0, H_0)$ and then adjust the y-coordinate when necessary. This is done by adding a non-negative offset α to the y-coordinate. So that α

66

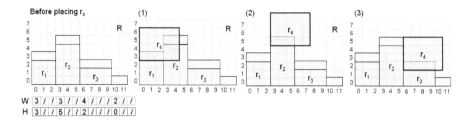

Figure 5.6: Probing positions for the small rectangle $r_4(4,5)$ in $R(12,8)$. $X(0,5) = \{0,3,6,12\}$. In (1), we try to place r_4 at $(0,3)$ at the beginning. During the validation process, α is adjusted to 2, i.e. trying to place it at $(0, 3+2)$, but a part of it lies outside R. In (2), we try to place it at $(3,5)$ but this is invalid. In (3), placing it at $(6,2)$ is possible.

is the minimum value such that when we place the rectangle at $(0, H_0 + \alpha)$, the two constraints are satisfied. Assume that we are at the x-coordinate x. We must check whether we can place the small rectangle at $(x, H_x + \alpha)$. If we can, then the small rectangle should lie entirely inside the large rectangle. Therefore, these two conditions should be satisfied: $R_w \geq x + w_i$ and $R_h \geq H_x + h_i + \alpha$.

We define $X(x, w_i)$ such that it contains the x-coordinates of all the positions that needed to be checked for the small rectangle, starting from coordinate x.

$$X(x, w_i) \equiv \{x'_n < min\{x + w_i, R_w\}$$
$$\mid x'_n = x'_{n-1} + W_{x'_{n-1}}, n \geq 1 \text{ or } x'_n = x, n = 0\} \tag{5.1}$$

The position x should satisfy condition: $x \in X(0, R_w)$. In order to impose the non-overlapping restriction of the placement of the small rectangles in an incremental manner, we have:

$$\forall x' \in X(x, w_i) \ H_x + \alpha \geq H_{x'} \tag{5.2}$$

This condition ensures that the small rectangle $r_i(w_i, h_i)$ does not overlap with the portion behind the envelope. If we fail to place the small rectangle at $(x, H_x + \alpha)$ for any α, we advance W_x units along the x-axis and check the next position $(W_x + x, H_{W_x+x})$. We repeat the procedure until we either find a position to place the small

67

rectangle or run out of the array W. If we run out of the array W, the assignment of the small rectangles is terminated.

Finally, assume that we have found the valid position (x, y) to place $r_i(w_i, h_i)$. We update the boundary of the envelope. An example is shown in Figure 5.6. We have $\exists! x_p$ such that $x_p + W_{x_p} \geq x + w_i$ and $x + w_i > x_p$ are satisfied. The number x_p indicates the starting position of the previous envelope which may contribute to the new envelope. Based on this condition, we update the contents of W and H in the following order:

- W_{x+w_i} to $x_p + W_{x_p} - (x + w_i)$: The previous portion of the envelope, starting from x_p to $x_p + W_{x_p}$, contributes $x_p + W_{x_p} - (x + w_i) > 0$ unit(s) of length to the new envelope.

- H_{x+w_i} to H_{x_p}: At the x-coordinate $x + w_i$, the height is set to H_{x_p}. This is contributed by the previous portion of the envelope. The update is applied when $x' + W_{x'} - (x + w_i) > 0$.

- W_x to w_i: The length of the portion of the new envelope contributed by the small rectangle is w_i.

- H_x to $H_x + h_i + \alpha$: The height is changed from H_x to $H_x + h_i + \alpha$ at x-coordinate x. This is contributed by the small rectangle.

If we place the small rectangle at a position where there is an immediate unfilled space we have fragmentation or wasted space under the small rectangle. In Figure 5.5, s_4 shows the fragmented space in the viewport by the placement of the small rectangle r_4. We compute a position to place a small rectangle such that the fragmented space s_i is the smallest. Assume x is the current possible position, then the next position to be checked is $x + W_x$.

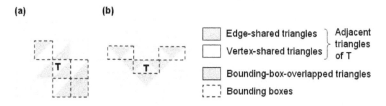

Figure 5.7: A triangle T and its connectivity to neighboring triangles.

5.4.6 Improvement in potential colliding pairs

Figure 5.7 shows a triangle T and its connectivity to its neighboring triangles. It is likely that the number of triangles obtained in an AABB tree that is needed to check against with the triangle T for collision detection is larger than the number obtained in an image-based method. Consider that the resolution of the viewport is sufficiently high that the image of each triangle is clearly seen. We count the number of potential colliding pairs that the triangle T is involved. The image-based method will return nothing for the potential colliding pairs. However, by using an AABB tree, five and two potential colliding pairs will be reported in case (a) and in case (b), respectively.

5.4.7 A method does not work

By having the appropriate setting for the stencil operation upon the stencil buffer[4], we can obtain the number of fragments covering a specific pixel. The determination criterion of the collision status is that if more than one fragment covers the pixel, then there is a potential collision; otherwise there is no collision. This method does not work. Assume that there are two triangles intersecting each other. Owing to the aliasing, the pixels of these two triangles may not overlap.

---

[4]A stencil buffer stores a number for each pixel and it can be used for the purpose of counting.

5.4.8 Clustering and limitations

We can assign the same color index to triangles which are in neighborhood to form clusters. The advantage is that we can lower the image resolution as the region of a cluster is larger than a single triangle. The disadvantage is that if the pixels of two clusters lying adjacent to each other, we need to perform all-pair tests for the triangles of two clusters. Moreover, we also need to make sure that there is no self-collision in each cluster.

If there is a slim triangle or a triangle with small area, we may fail to collect the potential colliding pairs for these kinds of triangles. Owing to aliasing and low resolution, these kinds of triangles may occupy pixels which do not adjacent to the pixels of which the other triangles collide with these triangles. For these kinds of triangles, we should isolate them from the construction of the (π, β)-surfaces or group them with their neighboring triangles in clusters.

Another limitation of the image-based method is that we may miss collisions owing to large deformation of the surfaces. Initially, there are two triangles and their projected distance is larger than the size of a pixel. During the time interval, they move and collide with each other. In this case, their pixels will not adjacent to each other as the projection process is performed only in the beginning of the time interval. Thus, the triangles with large projected speed should be isolated from the construction of the (π, β)-surfaces.

5.4.9 A pipeline of image-based collision detection

The image-based method can record only the image of static deformable surfaces in the frame buffer at an instant. The movement of the deformable surfaces within a frame cannot be captured in the current technique unless some kind of "memory" can be implemented in the image-based method. Thus, in the current approach, we propose that a general image-based method should contain the following six stages: (1) input subsurfaces, (2) filter slim elements (3) filter elements with large projected speed (4) perform projection process, (5) perform inspection process, and (6) output potential colliding pairs. In stages 2 and 3, the elements are isolated if they are not suitable for image-based method.

5.5 Collision detection among (π, β)-surfaces

We construct the Bounding Volume Tree (BVT) for each (π, β)-surface. After that, we perform the classic tree traversal to collect the potential colliding triangle pairs for each pair of (π, β)-surfaces.

5.5.1 Bounding volume trees for (π, β)-surfaces

We adopt a *backward* voxel-based approach to construct a BVT for a surface bottom-up each frame. The voxels are built as follows. Assume that the dimension of the bounding box of the entire surface is (b_x, b_y, b_z). We subdivide the volume of the entire surface until a desired depth is reached. The maximum depth d of the BVT is determined by using the formula: $d = \lceil \log n_t \rceil$, where n_t is the total number of triangles of the surface.

At the bottom level of the BVT, i.e. at depth d, we assign each triangle to a voxel by determining in which voxel the center point of the triangle locates. A voxel containing one or more triangles forms a cluster that becomes the node of the BVT and the triangles form the children of the node. Each node is bounded by an AABB. The coordinates of the center point of a node are the center point of its AABB. This process is repeated for the next level up until we are left with one voxel which is the AABB of the entire surface.

5.5.2 A backward voxel-based method for BVT

Let the dimension of the AABB of the entire surface be $(b_x,\ b_y,\ b_z)$, and name this AABB be $AABB^0$ (i.e. the root of the BVT, at depth $zero$). Let the reference point of $AABB^0$ be $(x_{min},\ y_{min},\ z_{min})$, such that for any vertex $(x,\ y,\ z)$, we have $x \in [x_{min}, x_{min} + b_x]$, $y \in [y_{min}, y_{min} + b_y]$, and $z \in [z_{min}, z_{min} + b_z]$, i.e. $AABB^0$ encloses all the triangles of the surface. We take into account the thickness of the deformable surface. Without loss of generality, we assume that $b_x \geq b_y \geq b_z$.

In the *forward* approach, we recursively decompose the deformable surface along the medial axis of the longest side of $AABB^0$ into voxels, assign the triangles to them, group them and form nodes until a desired subdivision level (depth) is reached. Finally, with respect to $AABB^0$, the number of subdivision levels along the $x-$, $y-$, and $z-$axis, respectively, will be n_x, n_y, and n_z. Thus, along the x-axis, y-axis, and z-axis, $AABB^0$ is cut evenly into 2^{n_x}, 2^{n_y}, and 2^{n_y} pieces, respectively. As we assume that $b_x \geq b_y \geq b_z$, we will have $n_x \geq n_y \geq n_z \geq 0$.

In the backward voxel-based approach, we compute n_x, n_y, and n_z directly for a given depth d and the triplet (b_x, b_y, b_z). We want the result of (n_x, n_y, n_z) to be as close as to the ones obtained from the forward method. In order to subdivide $AABB^0$, we choose one of the three schemes:

1. Divide the $AABB^0$ along one axis, i.e. x-axis;

2. Divide the $AABB^0$ along two axes, i.e. x- and y-axis;

3. Divide the $AABB^0$ along three axes, i.e. x-, y-, and z-axis.

We develop a set of rules to determine which scheme we will adopt. Assume that we can only subdivide $AABB^0$ along the x-axis. Then we must have $b_x \geq 2^{d-1}b_y$. If $b_x < 2^{d-1}b_y$, then we need to decide whether we should adopt scheme (2) or (3). Assume that we adopt scheme (2). Let the number of subdivision along the two axes be n_x and n_y times, respectively. Thus, we have $d = n_x + n_y, n_x, n_y \geq 1$. According to the forward method, we should have:

$$\frac{b_x}{2^{n_x-1}} \ge \frac{b_y}{2^{n_y}} \quad \text{and} \quad \frac{b_y}{2^{n_y-1}} > \frac{b_x}{2^{n_x}} \tag{5.3}$$

By inequalities 5.3_1 and 5.3_2, we have:

$$\frac{b_x}{b_y} \ge 2^{n_x-n_y-1} \quad \text{and} \quad 2^{n_x-n_y+1} > \frac{b_x}{b_y} \tag{5.4}$$

Rearrange the terms, we obtain:

$$2^{n_x-n_y+1} > \frac{b_x}{b_y} \ge 2^{n_x-n_y-1} \tag{5.5}$$

$$n_x - n_y + 1 > \log_2 \frac{b_x}{b_y} \ge n_x - n_y - 1 \tag{5.6}$$

$$n_x - (d - n_x) + 1 > \log_2 \frac{b_x}{b_y} \ge n_x - (d - n_x) - 1 \tag{5.7}$$

$$(\log_2 \frac{b_x}{b_y} + d + 1)/2 \ge n_x > (\log_2 \frac{b_x}{b_y} + d - 1)/2 \tag{5.8}$$

So that we have $n_x = \min\left\{ \left\lfloor \left(\log_2 \frac{b_x}{b_y} + d + 1\right)/2 \right\rfloor, d \right\}$, $n_y = d - n_x$, and $n_z = 0$.

If scheme (2) should be adopted, the condition $\frac{b_y}{2^{n_y-1}} \ge b_z$ should be satisfied. If it is not satisfied, then we adopt scheme (3). In this case, we have $d = n_x + n_y + n_z$ and $n_x, n_y, n_z \ge 1$. According to the forward method, the necessary and sufficient conditions to subdivide $AABB^0$ along x-, y-, and z-axis up to n_x, n_y, and n_z times, respectively, are:

$$\frac{b_x}{2^{n_x-1}} \ge \frac{b_y}{2^{n_y}}, \frac{b_z}{2^{n_z}} \quad \text{and} \quad \frac{b_y}{2^{n_y-1}} \ge \frac{b_z}{2^{n_z}} \tag{5.9}$$

$$\frac{b_y}{2^{n_y-1}} > \frac{b_x}{2^{n_x}} \quad \text{and} \quad \frac{b_z}{2^{n_z-1}} > \frac{b_x}{2^{n_x}}, \frac{b_y}{2^{n_y}} \tag{5.10}$$

By inequalities 5.9 and 5.10, we have:

$$2^{n_x-n_y+1} > \frac{b_x}{b_y} \ge 2^{n_x-n_y-1} \tag{5.11}$$

$$2^{n_x-n_z+1} > \frac{b_x}{b_z} \ge 2^{n_x-n_z-1} \tag{5.12}$$

$$2^{n_y-n_z+1} > \frac{b_y}{b_z} \ge 2^{n_y-n_z-1} \tag{5.13}$$

Take $\log_2$ on sides and rearrange the terms, we have:

$$\left.\begin{array}{l} n_x - n_y + 1 > \log_2 \frac{b_x}{b_y} \geq n_x - n_y - 1 \\[2mm] n_x - n_z + 1 > \log_2 \frac{b_x}{b_z} \geq n_x - n_z - 1 \\[2mm] n_y - n_z + 1 > \log_2 \frac{b_y}{b_z} \geq n_y - n_z - 1 \end{array}\right\} \qquad (5.14)$$

By inequality 5.14, we have:

$$2n_x - (n_y + n_z) + 2 > \log_2 \frac{b_x^2}{b_y b_z} \geq 2n_x - (n_y + n_z) - 2 \qquad (5.15)$$

$$2n_y - (n_x + n_z) + 2 \geq \log_2 \frac{b_y^2}{b_x b_z} \geq 2n_y - (n_x + n_z) - 2 \qquad (5.16)$$

$$2n_z - (n_x + n_y) + 2 \geq \log_2 \frac{b_z^2}{b_x b_y} > 2n_z - (n_x + n_y) - 2 \qquad (5.17)$$

We substituting $d = n_x + n_y + n_z$ into inequality 5.15 to obtain the bound on n_x:

$$2n_x - (d - n_x) + 2 > \log_2 \frac{b_x^2}{b_y b_z} \geq 2n_x - (d - n_x) - 2 \qquad (5.18)$$

By rearranging the terms, we obtain:

$$(\log_2 \frac{b_x^2}{b_y b_z} + d + 2)/3 \geq n_x > (\log_2 \frac{b_x^2}{b_y b_z} + d - 2)/3 \qquad (5.19)$$

Similarly, by substituting $d = n_x + n_y + n_z$ into inequalities 5.16 and 5.17, respectively, we obtain:

$$\left.\begin{array}{l} (\log_2 \frac{b_y^2}{b_x b_z} + d + 2)/3 \;\geq n_y \geq (\log_2 \frac{b_y^2}{b_x b_z} + d - 2)/3 \\[2mm] (\log_2 \frac{b_z^2}{b_x b_y} + d + 2)/3 \;> n_z \geq (\log_2 \frac{b_z^2}{b_x b_y} + d - 2)/3 \end{array}\right\} \qquad (5.20)$$

Therefore, the numbers of subdivision are: $n_x = \min\left\{\left\lfloor\left(\log_2 \frac{b_x^2}{b_y b_z} + d + 2\right)/3\right\rfloor, d\right\}$, $n_y = \min\left\{\left\lfloor\left(\log_2 \frac{b_y^2}{b_x b_z} + d + 2\right)/3\right\rfloor, d\right\}$, and $n_z = d - n_x - n_y$, along the three axes, respectively, at depth d. In order to build the tree bottom-up, we recursively assign nodes to voxels, form new nodes and get to the next level up until we are left with one voxel, i.e. $AABB^0$, which is the root node. We call this tree *BVOX-AABB* (backward voxel-based AABB) tree. Nodes at the leaf level are AABBs of the triangles. These

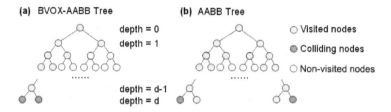

Figure 5.8: Comparison between BVOX-AABB tree and AABB tree.

AABBs enclose the triangles at the beginning and final positions within a frame and they are enlarged by the thickness of the deformable surface. The nodes at the same voxel form a new node and the AABB of the new node is computed. The assignment of a node to a voxel (i, j, k) is determined by using equations:

$$i = \min\left\{\left\lfloor\left(\frac{x - x_{min}}{b_x}\right)2^{n_x}\right\rfloor, 2^{n_x} - 1\right\},$$

$$j = \min\left\{\left\lfloor\left(\frac{y - y_{min}}{b_y}\right)2^{n_y}\right\rfloor, 2^{n_y} - 1\right\},$$

$$k = \min\left\{\left\lfloor\left(\frac{z - z_{min}}{b_z}\right)2^{n_z}\right\rfloor, 2^{n_z} - 1\right\}$$

where (x, y, z) is the center point coordinates of the AABB of the node. A small offset can be added to b_x, b_y and b_z in order to avoid computing the ceiling operation.

The advantage of the BVOX-AABB tree is that the nodes locating in the same spatial neighborhood are likely assigned in the same branches of the tree. This reduces significantly in the traversal time. It adapts to the shape of cloth well. For example, in the beginning, two nodes are far away from each other. After deformation, they are brought near each other. They should be assigned to the same branch of the tree. This is not achievable using the constant hierarchy of AABB tree. Thus, in general, it takes less time to traverse the BVOX-AABB tree than to traverse the constant AABB tree when we perform collision detection. Figure 5.8 shows an example. Consider that there are two objects and each have two nodes which are initially far away from each other. After deformation, these four nodes collide. We consider only the time spent in collecting the potential pairs of these four nodes regardless of the rest of the time spent in checking other nodes. Both of the traversal time spent in the BVOX-ABB tree and the constant AABB tree are $O(d)$. However, the speedup of the BVOX-AABB tree over the constant AABB tree is 4.

5.6 Experiments and results

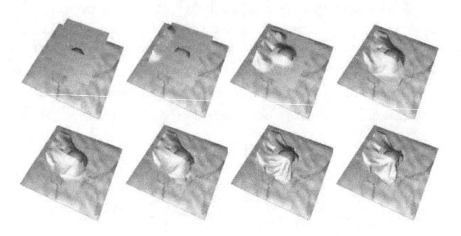

Figure 5.9: Example: Draping of a single cut cloth on three sphere-like tables.

We investigated how the threshold β_{max} affected the performance of the algorithm. We collected statistics for a scene in which a partially cut cloth was animated. After that, we performed performance comparison among three methods: the image-based method, the BVOX-AABB tree and the constant AABB tree in another four example scenes. All the experiments were run on a 1.5GHz Pentium 4 PC with 1GB of main memory and an nVidia geForce 3 graphics card. Double precision was used. In our implementation, we rendered the objects into the pixel buffer (pbuffer). The advantage of using the pbuffer is that we can perform offscreen rendering [4]. The dynamic interaction would be kept to the minimum. If there were collisions for the deformable surfaces, the involved particles would be frozen in the current frame. The movement of these particles would be computed in the next frame.

Figure 5.9 shows a partially cut cloth. We animated it in order to demonstrate the interactions due to self-collision and the collision of the cut cloth with other objects.

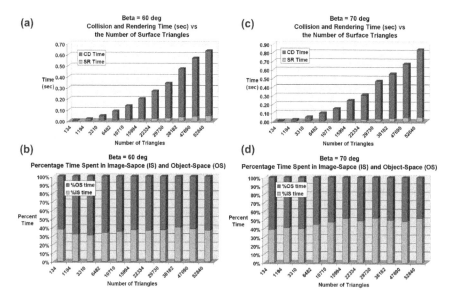

Figure 5.10: Partially cut cloth. $\beta = 60\ deg$ and $\beta = 70\ deg$.

Some particles along the left edge are fixed. As the cloth piece falls under gravity, it collides with a hemisphere. The involved part is stuck while the two regions of the cloth piece in the right hand side still fall onto the area of ground. Finally, these two regions collide with each other at their tips in front of the hemisphere. This serves as a good example for taking performance statistics of our collision detection algorithm. Figure 5.10 shows the performance statistics for this example in the cases $\beta_{max} = 60$ degrees and $\beta_{max} = 70$ degrees. By selecting different β_{max} angles for controlling the smoothness condition in dynamically decomposing the (π, β)-surfaces, we show that the timing characteristics for the collision detection have similar growth rates as the number of triangular elements increases from 134 to 52,840.

The graphs in Figure 5.10(a)(c) show the scene rendering and the collision detection times for surface clusters that maintain a threshold of $\beta_{max} = 60$ degrees and $\beta_{max} = 70$ degrees. As the number of triangles increases, the time patterns for the collision detection are similar in all cases ranging from under 30ms for low triangle counts of about 1000 to around one second for triangle counts in excess of 50,000. In all cases, the rendering times are lower than the collision detection times. However, we must emphasize again, that the image–space collision computation is emulated in software using the data extracted from the color buffer. This contributes to IO transfers and main memory checks. The multi-viewport setup algorithm is also software emulation which contributes to the collision detection time. If these operations are supported in hardware, we expect the image-space computations to be drastically reduced.

The interesting feature of this algorithm is the impact of the threshold angle β_{max} on the distribution and computational loads for the object-space and image-space, respectively. We note that the distribution of computations across the object-space and the image-space shifts towards the object-space by approximately 10%, as seen in Figure 5.10(b)(d). This means that as β_{max} increases the image-space load also increases and the object-space load decreases. The main reason is that as β_{max} increases, the viewport sizes also increase making the image-space the dominant computational load for collision detection. This result is positive on two accounts. First, as β_{max} increases the relative curvature of the surface patch is allowed to vary more than for lower β_{max} values. Thus, the bounding volume tree decreases in size as large regions can be accommodated. Second, the load is taken up by the image–space tests that can be further optimized by hardware support or parallelizing the process.

In the following, we performed the comparisons between three methods: (1) image-based method, (2) BVOX-AABB tree, and (3) AABB tree. We implemented the AABB tree which was proposed in [93, 137]. We stored the nodes in a linear array so that we could update the tree without traversing it. We set $\beta_{max} = 60$ deg. We constructed four example scenes in which the complexity of the cloth piece could be adjusted. Figure 5.11 shows the snapshots from the scenes. Usually, the performance of the methods depends on the configuration of the scenes. Therefore, we tracked their performance for the entire simulation sequence in the four example scenes. We plotted the following graphs: (a) total collision detection time in each frame, (b) detailed profile of the image-based method, (c) number of (π, β)-surfaces (PIBs) and percentage of missing triangles, (d) BVT (bounding volume tree) traversal time, (e) BVT update time, (f) number of bounding box tests, and (g) the number of potential colliding triangle pairs. We define the potential colliding triangle pairs (PCPs) as the pairs which will be tested using the intrinsic triangle collision detection.

In Scene one, a rectangular piece of cloth (44,688 tri.), which has short fringes at two boundaries, falls on a solid sphere (1,600 tri.) with a long leg sticking out onto the area of ground. When the cloth piece drapes on the sphere, the sides are pulled back together and wrinkles arise. Figure 5.12 shows the statistics collected for the three methods. In the beginning, the image-based method is almost four times faster than the AABB and the BVOX-AABB methods. In the end, when the cloth piece deforms drastically, the image-based method becomes slower. The BVOX-AABB turns out to be the fastest in the end of the simulation. The ranges of the collision detection time of the image-based, the BVOX-AABB, and the AABB methods are 0.4-0.7(sec), 0.45-1.85(sec), and 0.65-1.85(sec), respectively.

In Scene two, a cylindrical piece of cloth (45,600 tri.) falls on a hemisphere (1,600 tri.) and then onto the area of ground. The upper part of the cloth piece is cut into three rectangular pieces. During the simulation, the cloth piece collides with the hemisphere and is compressed itself along the axial direction. When the cloth piece is compressed, a lot of self-collision occurs. Figure 5.13 shows the statistics collected for the three methods. In the beginning, the image-based method is the fastest. As the cloth piece is compressed, the image-based method becomes slower. The BVOX-AABB method has stable performance, in this case. The ranges of the collision detection time of the image-based, the BVOX-AABB, and the AABB methods are 0.35-2.7(sec), 0.9-1.3(sec), and 0.9-2.3(sec), respectively.

In Scene three, a rectangular piece of cloth (46,524 tri.) with a long fringe in the middle falls on the facing part. Two rows of the middle vertices are fixed during the simulation. In this experiment, we do not have complex wrinkle patterns. However, it shows clearly how the long fringe collides with another part of the cloth piece. It demonstrates that the proposed image-based method can handle irregular shape of the cloth piece. Figure 5.14 shows the statistics collected for the three methods. As the cloth piece does not deform much, the image-based method performs stably. The image-based method is the fastest during the entire simulation. The ranges of the collision detection time of the image-based, the BVOX-AABB, and the AABB methods are 0.35-0.5(sec), 0.5-1.75(sec), and 0.6-1.9(sec), respectively.

In Scene four, a "net" (45,056 tri.) falls on a sphere (1,600 tri.) in the beginning of the simulation. The net is a rectangular piece of cloth with rectangular holes. At frame 400, the sphere is removed. After that, the net continues to fall onto the area of ground (800 tri.). Figure 5.15 shows the statistics collected for the three methods. In the beginning, the collision detection time of the image-based, the BVOX-AABB, and the AABB methods, are 0.45, 1.75, and 1.9 (sec), respectively. In the end, the collision detection time of the image-based, the BVOX-AABB, and the AABB methods, are 0.8, 0.45, and 0.8 (sec), respectively. The ranges of the collision detection time of the image-based, the BVOX-AABB, and the AABB methods are 0.45-0.8(sec), 0.4-1.75(sec), and 0.6-1.9(sec), respectively.

When the cloth piece does not deform much, the AABB and the BVOX-AABB methods spend a lot of time in the traversal (see graphs (d) and (f)). The image-based method suits to handle deformable surfaces which have large "low curvature" regions. When the cloth piece is quite flat, there is a lot of AABBs overlapping. Most of the corresponding triangles do not collide. The image-based method successfully skips these non-colliding triangle pairs (see graphs (g)) as they are far away. When the cloth piece deforms drastically, the cloth surface is decomposed into a lot of small (π, β)-surfaces (graphs (c)) for collision detection. This will take a longer time to scan the frame buffer as well as to construct the BVTs. In order to perform collision detection for these subsurfaces, we need to perform BVT traversal for all pairs of the subsurfaces. This increases the time significantly. However, the BVOX-AABB method performs quite stably in this situation.

When we render the (π, β)-surfaces into the frame buffer, we may have some "missing" triangles which do not have a pixel in the frame buffer. However, the percentages of the missing triangles are relatively not high. The percentages are 0-6%,

0-8%, 0-3.5%, and 0-0.4% for scene one, two, three, and four, respectively. Currently, We render these triangles in the same resolution so as to collect the PCPs. Other schemes are also recommended as stated in this chapter.

Graphs (b) show the time spent in four essential components in the image-based method: (1) decomposing the cloth surfaces into (π, β)-surfaces, (2) rendering the (π, β)-surfaces, (3) reading the frame buffer (FB) into the main memory, (4) scanning the frame buffer. The process of scanning the frame buffer takes over than 50% of the time. Consider that a $n \times m$ viewport. It requires to carry out around $8mn$ inspection operations for this viewport. An inspection operation is that a pixel is checked against one of its neighboring pixels. After the inspection operation is taken, it indicates whether the corresponding two triangles are adjacent. This is an expensive process. The decomposition process is the second highest (except in Scene two)). In Scene two, there are more viewports (over one thousand) that were read from the frame buffer. Many small (π, β)-surfaces consisting of a few triangles were obtained. This increased the amount of time spent in the reading process. Hence, the timing of the reading process is higher than the timing of the decomposition process.

The BVOX-AABB tree outperforms the constant hierarchy AABB tree. It takes about twice the time to update a BVOX-ABB tree comparing to a AABB tree (see graphs (e)). However, the traversal time spent in BVOX-AABB is much faster than the constant AABB one (see graphs (d)). Usually, it takes fewer number of bounding box tests in the BVOX-AABB tree than the constant AABB tree (see graphs (f)). (The traversal time is proportional to the number of bounding box tests.) When the cloth piece deforms drastically, the traversal speedup is around three.

Finally, we increased the complexity of the cloth piece and collected the performance statistics. Similar graph patterns are obtained in all the cases. Figure 5.16 shows the average total collision detection (CD) time of the animation. In Scene one, three and four, the imaged-based method is the fastest. In Scene two, the BVOX-AABB method is the fastest. In all cases, the AABB tree method is the slowest. The average total CD time is proportional to the number of triangles of the cloth piece. In Scene

81

Two, the surface of cloth is highly compressed along the axial direction. There is a lot of (π, β)-surfaces consisting of a few triangles. The overhead, including rendering and scanning process, in the image-based method is high in this case.

5.7 Summary and discussion

We proposed an image-based method for performing efficient collision detection by (1) utilizing object–space decomposition and culling of large surfaces into (π, β)-surfaces and (2) performing image space inspection for arbitrary deformable surfaces.

We acquire the image-space information using the multiple dynamically adjustable viewports that represent the projections of overlapping regions of a surface in the object space. The scanning process is performed to collect all the potential colliding triangle pairs by using the image-space information. After that, collision tests are invoked for the potential colliding pairs in the object space. The robustness of this collision detection method is ensured by (1) Automatic segmentation of a general surface into (π, β)-surface patches. This guarantees local convexity as a basic requirement for hardware-based collision tests. (2) Aliasing detection and subpixel sampling together with tracking the influence of all the neighboring pixels of the current pixel in the image-space. This takes into account the active tracking of the source triangles in the image buffers. This allows the proposed method to detect the collision events that the purely low curvature approach (without projection) fails to detect. The proposed method is also capable of the collecting the the potential colliding pairs for a subsurface if the deformation of the subsurface is less than half of a pixel distance.

The image–space loading increases with the increase of the threshold angle β_{max} as the viewport size becomes the dominant bottleneck in the computational process. A good balance between the threshold angle, viewport processing and the boundary volume tree is the key to an efficient and robust collision detection algorithm that makes use of the image buffers. However, this also depends on the hardware support for reading, writing and scanning the image buffers efficiently. Currently, the scanning process of the image buffers is emulated in software. In the future, we believe that if the scanning process can be entirely done in hardware, a significant improvement in the collision detection speed can be achieved.

The proposed BVOX-AABB method suits to collision detection if the cloth piece is highly compressed. It automatically allocates the neighboring triangles in the same branches of the tree. Thus, it significantly reduces the traversal time. The BVOX-AABB approach consumes a large amount of memory. However, the memory used in this part can be reused by other objects once the BVOX-AABB of an object is built.

The extension of our image-based method to handle very large deformable surfaces is straightforward. If the surface is discretized into many triangles, it is likely that the computed viewport dimension becomes too large. In this case, the computed viewport of subsurfaces may not fit into our predefined maximum rendering window. Instead of using a single large viewport, we divide the viewport into smaller viewports. These smaller viewports overlap at the boundary. The width of the boundary is the size of the scanning area. Once the width of the boundary is defined, we compute the optimal number of smaller viewports and then compute their dimensions. At each frame, we only render the corresponding triangles to their assigned viewports. This can be done by setting the orthogonal projection matrix or by setting the viewing volume. We also note that the (R, G, B)-triple (with 8-bit each) can support $(2^{24}-1)$ triangle indices (i.e. #triangles). For many practical applications, this range is sufficient.

If the surface does not fit into the main memory, then we can load only a part of its triangles from secondary storage. We can still perform the decomposition and the image-based collision detection method for the loaded triangles. After this stage, we can obtain some of the (π, β)-surfaces of the original surface. We can then repeat this process for the remaining triangles of the original surface. Finally, we obtain a set of (π, β)-surfaces. We adopt the image-based method to collect potential colliding pairs for the set of (π, β)-surfaces. The final task is to perform only collision detection among the (π, β)-surfaces.

Two further extensions of this work under investigation are the following:

1. *Direct extraction of subsurfaces.* Currently, a surface is decomposed into a set of (π, β)-surfaces at each frame. This step is done in the object space. Alternatively, the image information can be used to decompose the surface. For example, we can render the surface and then collect all the triangles which contribute at least one pixel in the frame buffer. Then the surface can be decomposed into two subsurfaces consisting of: (1) a set of triangles that appear in the frame buffer, and (2) a set of triangles that do not appear in the frame buffer. We can repeat this subdivision with the triangles that do not appear in the frame buffer. This approach may create a smaller number of subsurfaces. Depth buffer can be used for eliminating triangles that are far away. Moreover, if multi-frame buffers are supported, the number of required renderings can be dramatically reduced.

2. *Time-domain extensions for collision detection.* The image-based approach is based on static interference tests for the potential colliding triangles. The static interference test by itself is fast and requires less computational overhead. The distance information between triangles are stored in the frame buffer. If the relative movement of the cloth piece is small, our current method can be extended to handle collision detection in the time domain directly by simply replacing the intrinsic collision detection unit with a velocity-based collision detection unit. However, due to potential undersampling, collision events may be missed as a triangle could potentially pass through another completely in a single frame. No matter how small the time step, such collision events may be difficult to detect. In order to handle this problem, the method can be extended to take into consideration the relative motion of the triangles and establish an intermediate checkpoint based on the relative velocities of the vertices of the triangles. The velocities of the pixels can be stored in a velocity buffer. We need to detect collision among "moving pixels" or in "pixel soup".

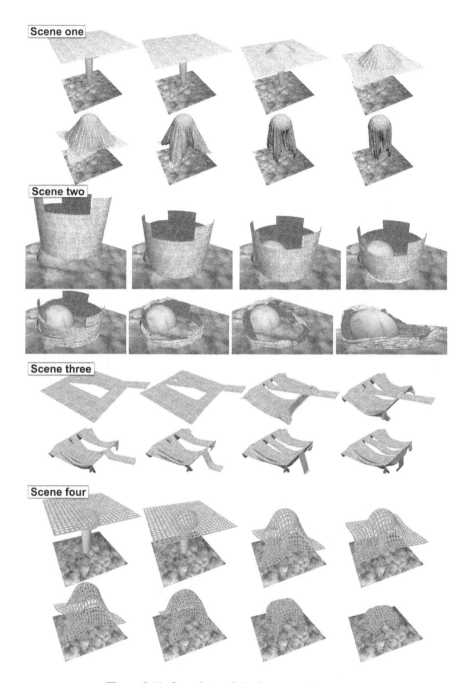

Figure 5.11: Snapshots of the four example scenes.

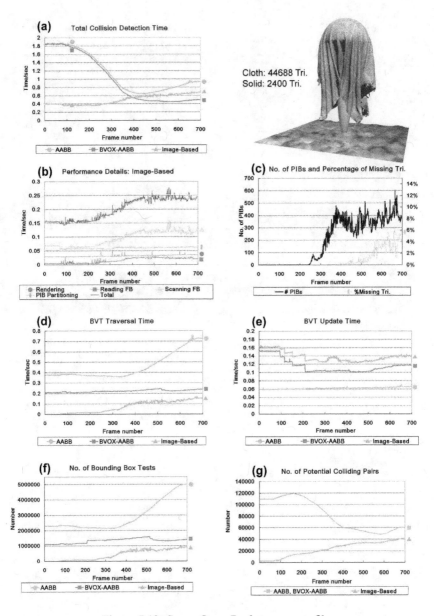

Figure 5.12: Scene One : Performance profiles.

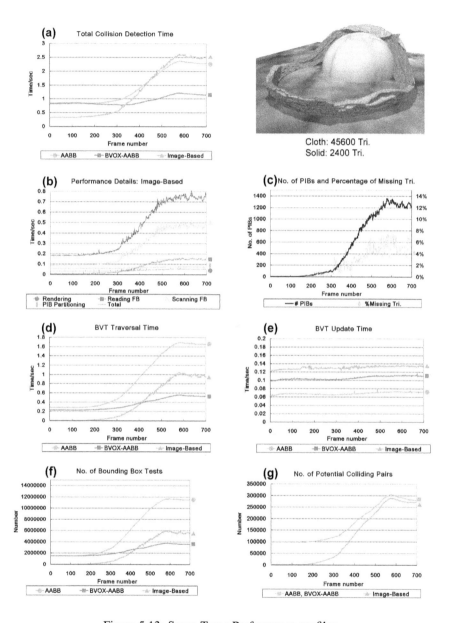

Figure 5.13: Scene Two : Performance profiles.

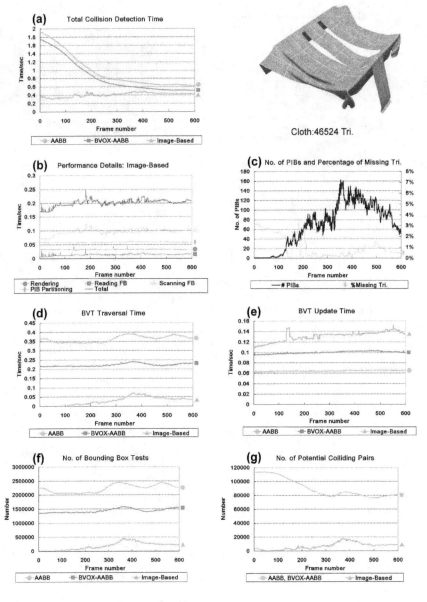

Figure 5.14: Scene Three : Performance profiles.

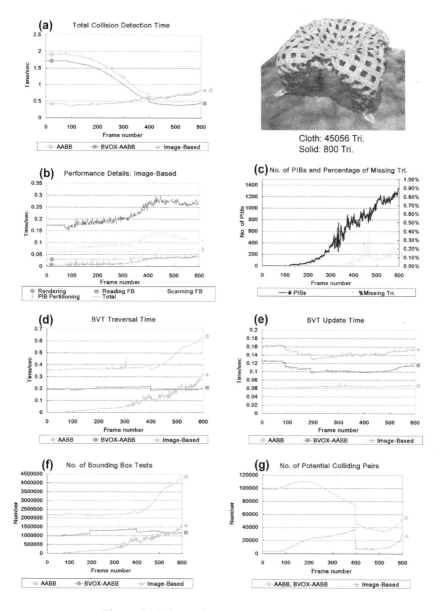

Figure 5.15: Scene Four : Performance profiles.

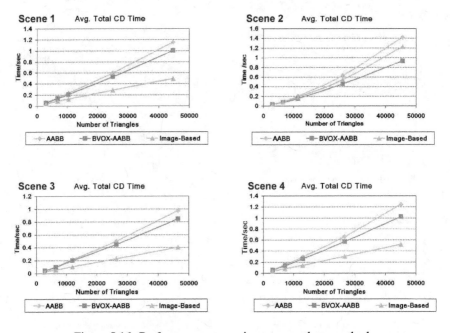

Figure 5.16: Performance comparison among three methods.

Chapter 6

An Architecture for The Intrinsic Collision Detection Unit

6.1   Introduction and motivation

The intrinsic collision detection unit plays an important role in a simulation system. It not only informs us whether a PCP collides or not, but also provides us with collision information about each colliding feature pair: collision time, contact points, collision normal and collision orientation. We assume that the PCPs are collected and then these PCPs are passed into the intrinsic collision detection unit for further processing. In this chapter, we propose an architecture for the intrinsic collision detection unit (or intrinsic test unit) so that intrinsic collision detection can be performed accurately, efficiently and robustly, for the *potential colliding feature pairs* (PCP). The problems induced by numerical errors are addressed.

In the simulation of deformable surfaces, there is a lot of potential colliding features which are required for further processing. Hence the time spent in the intrinsic collision detection unit contributes a significant amount of percentage in the entire collision detection process. This motivates us to investigate heuristic techniques to improve the performance for this unit. As the simplest form of the primitives with finite area is triangle, our focus will be on developing a system performing collision detection for triangles as fast as possible. Another issue that is the kind of models that we use in our collision detection method – approximate or exact. From our investigation, exact collision detection is much appropriate to our system requirement. Although approximate collision detection is faster than the exact collision detection, it does not preserve the geometry details of the objects. By employing an exact collision detection, we could observe the shape of the underneath objects when a very flexible surface covers on them. This is impossible to achieve by employing an approximate method. Moreover, an exact method improves the accuracy of the motion of the objects when they interact with each other.

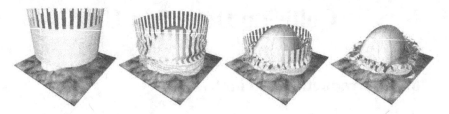

Figure 6.1: A column with fringes falls on the upper part of an ellipsoid. A large number of contact points due to inter-collisions and self-collisions.

Figure 6.1 shows a typical scene in which the complexity of a deformable surface — column-strip — is around 20, 000 triangles. When the column-strip falls onto the area of ground, there is a lot of self-collision events. The regions at the base of the column-strip blend themselves in several layers naturally and pack inside a small volume. In such a small volume, there is a lot of triangles in proximity and there are thousands of contact points[1]. All these contact points should be reported so that the proper action can be taken in order to prevent the colliding pieces from further penetration. Conventionally, we could apply the static interference test to perform collision detection and then adopt the backtracking mechanism to narrow the distance between objects iteratively by halving the traveling distance of the vertices (or particles) each time. However, it will be too slow to do so, especially, in such a complex interactive environment. The simulator will be stalled if there is a lot of collision events occurring in a single frame. This problem is illustrated in Figure 6.2. The figure shows that there

---

[1]The number of contact points is counted as the number of colliding feature pairs.

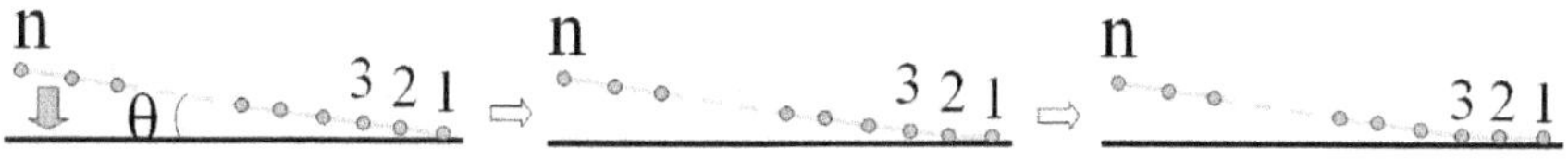

Figure 6.2: A side view that a rectangular surface falling onto a plane with angle θ.

is a rectangular surface and the surface slightly tilts with respect to a plane with an angle θ. There are n particles along one side of the surface and the right-most particle lies on the plane. Assume that we want to generate a simulation for the surface falls onto the plane. Now, if the angle is sufficiently small, it will take $(n-1)$ frames to complete this simulation even though the particles could hit the plane in one time step. The second problem of employing the static interference test is due to the *passing through problem* when dealing with arbitrary thin surfaces. One part of a surface can pass through another part of a surface within a single time step. Collision events will be undetected in this case. In order to avoid these two problems, we employ the velocity-based collision detection [92] for deformable surfaces.

By employing the velocity-based method, we need to tackle the following two problems. First, we need to solve one polynomial equation for each feature pair. In total, there are fifteen polynomial equations (six for point–triangle and nine for edge–edge) for each triangle pair. This is rather expensive to solve them. Second, it is difficult to track collision orientation when the features are near. The features may be determined lying on the wrong sides owing to a numerical error and a fault collision event will be reported. We address the first problem by developing heuristic rules to eliminate the pairs that do not collide so that we need not to solve the polynomial equations or not even to compute the coefficients of the polynomial equations. The second problem is addressed by tracking the history of the PCPs. We will propose an alternative approach in Chapter 7 for robust computation of collision orientation.

6.2 Outline

The outline of this chapter is given as follows. Section 6.3 presents optimization methods for performing deformable triangle collision detection in the time domain. The velocity-based collision detection is employed for the intrinsic collision detection. We propose a combination of heuristic methods to improve the collision detection process. A method is proposed for computing the shortest distances of all the feature pairs of two triangles by avoiding unnecessary computation. A front-end polynomial coefficient check is proposed for determining the non-colliding pairs. Section 6.4 develops an architecture for storing and retrieving the information of potential colliding pairs quickly. This information is kept in a hash structure. We present two cache schemes depended on the demand level of memory. Section 6.5 proposes a method which maintains stable collision status for previously colliding pairs. Section 6.6 shows that, under certain condition, the absolute relative error is bounded between a root of a cubic equation and the corresponding root of the truncated equation. In Section 6.7 the performance statistics are detailed. We compare the proposed method with other six methods. We present the summary and discussion in Section 6.8. A future research direction is discussed for implementing the proposed method in a parallel machine.

6.3 Deformable triangle collision detection

We develop a set of heuristic methods in order to perform collision detection for two deformable triangles in this section.

6.3.1 A pipeline of collision detection for a feature pair

Figure 6.3 shows the collision detection pipeline for a feature pair. We assume that the vertices of the triangles move with constant velocities within a frame. Our task is to compute the first contact time for each of the potential colliding feature pairs in a certain time interval **I**. We employ a hybrid-method based on the blind distance check combined with the coefficient check to prune off many of the non-colliding feature pairs. We construct equations for each of the remaining potential colliding feature pairs. The solutions of the equations are computed and then verified. The smallest valid solution is the first contact time of the pair.

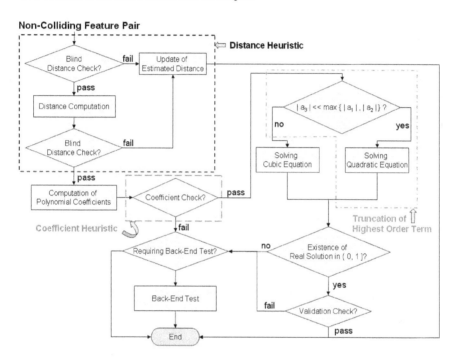

Figure 6.3: The collision detection pipeline for a feature pair.

6.3.2 Collision detection for a feature pair

We maintain the estimated distance $\tilde{d}(F0, F1)$ for each feature pair $(F0, F1)$. The estimated distance $\tilde{d}(F0, F1)$ should not be larger than the exact shortest distance $d(F0, F1)$ of $(F0, F1)$. In the following, we assume that the thickness of a feature F is $2\varepsilon_F$.

We compute the total maximum non-oriented displacement[2] of the features. Let $\|\mathbf{u}_{F0}\|$ and $\|\mathbf{u}_{F1}\|$ be the maximum non-oriented displacements of $F0$ and $F1$, respectively. By using these values, we define the condition of the blind distance check as follows:

$$\tilde{d}(F0, F1) \leq \|\mathbf{u}_{F0}\| + \|\mathbf{u}_{F1}\| + \varepsilon_{F0} + \varepsilon_{F1} \tag{6.1}$$

If the inequality (6.1) is not satisfied, this feature pair will not collide in the interval **I**. This is due to that the sum of the total maximum non-oriented displacement and one-half of their total thickness is smaller than their estimated distance. The estimated distance is updated by using a lazy scheme and then we are done. The lazy scheme is given by:

$$\tilde{d}(F0, F1) \leftarrow \tilde{d}(F0, F1) - (\|\mathbf{u}_{F0}\| + \|\mathbf{u}_{F1}\|) \tag{6.2}$$

If the inequality (6.1) is satisfied in the first time, we compute the shortest distance of this feature pair and then check the condition again. If it is not satisfied, we update $\tilde{d}(F0, F1)$ using the lazy scheme, Equation 6.2, and we are done.

If the inequality (6.1) is satisfied again, we proceed to solve the polynomial equation of the feature pair (see Section 6.3.4). After obtaining the solutions, we verify them (see Section 6.3.6). The smallest valid solution t_c in the interval **I** is the current collision time of the feature pair and the smallest collision time among all the feature pairs is the collision time of the triangle pair.

The reason why we compute the shortest distance in the first time when the inequality (6.1) is satisfied is justified as follows. In the first time that the inequality (6.1) is satisfied, alternatively, we could employ one of the two schemes: (1) computing the shortest distance, checking the condition and then solving the polynomial equation when necessary; (2) solving the polynomial equation alone.

We analyze the cost taken in each scheme. Let $(1 - \rho)$ be the probability of that the condition is satisfied (Ineq. 6.1). Assume that the cost of checking the condition

---

[2]Maximum non-oriented displacement of a feature is the maximum non-oriented displacement of its vertices.

is C_{cond}, the cost of computing the shortest distance is C_{short}, and the cost of solving a polynomial is C_{poly}. By adopting scheme (1) and scheme (2), the costs are $C_{short} + C_{cond} + (1 - \rho)C_{poly}$ and C_{poly}, respectively. If $C_{short} + C_{cond} + (1 - \rho)C_{poly} < C_{poly}$, i.e. $C_{short} + C_{cond} < \rho C_{poly}$, we employ scheme (1); otherwise, we employ scheme (2). The values of C_{short}, C_{cond} and C_{poly} can be obtained from empirical analysis. However, the value of ρ is not known. We know only the past history of whether the condition was satisfied. Therefore, we need to guess the value of ρ from the history of the corresponding feature pair.

The estimated distance is updated by using the lazy scheme each frame. The exact shortest distance of the feature pair is not known. Although the inequality (6.1) is satisfied, it does not mean that $\tilde{d}(F0, F1) \geq d(F0, F1)$. It is possible that $d(F0, F1)$ is much larger than $\tilde{d}(F0, F1)$. If $\tilde{d}(F0, F1)$ is updated by computing the exact distance $d(F0, F1)$ in this situation, the condition may not be satisfied for a certain number of subsequent frames. By employing scheme (1), we can save time if we need not to solve the equation.

If the features are far away from each other in the previous frame, the probability that the condition not satisfied is higher than the probability that the condition is satisfied. From this point of view, it will be productive to adopt scheme (1). However, once the two features collide, it is likely that they will be on contact each other for a while. In this case, scheme (2) should be employed.

6.3.3 Shortest distances of feature pairs

We will compute the shortest distance in two cases: edge–edge and point–triangle. We discuss each of them below.

Shortest distance between two edges

Let the two edges be $\overline{p_0 p_1}$ and $\overline{q_0 q_1}$. Assume that $\mathbf{p}$ and $\mathbf{q}$ are the two points on the two supporting lines of the two edges, respectively. Formally, we have:

$$
\begin{aligned}
\mathbf{p} &= \mathbf{p}_0 + u(\mathbf{p}_1 - \mathbf{p}_0) \\
\mathbf{q} &= \mathbf{q}_0 + v(\mathbf{q}_1 - \mathbf{q}_0)
\end{aligned}
\tag{6.3}
$$

We define $D^2 \equiv (\mathbf{p} - \mathbf{q}) \cdot (\mathbf{p} - \mathbf{q}) = ((\mathbf{p}_0 - \mathbf{q}_0) + u(\mathbf{p}_1 - \mathbf{p}_0) - v(\mathbf{q}_1 - \mathbf{q}_0))^2$ which is the square of the distance between $\mathbf{p}$ and $\mathbf{q}$. By setting $\frac{\partial(D^2)}{\partial u}$ and $\frac{\partial(D^2)}{\partial v}$ as zero, we obtain a linear system of u and v. There is a unique solution for u and v when the supporting lines of the two line segments are not parallel. If both of $\mathbf{p}$ and $\mathbf{q}$ belong to the edges, then they are the nearest points of the two edges. If one of them do not belong to the edges, the two nearest points will be that one point lies on an edge (including endpoints) and the other point is an endpoint of another edge.

If the edges are parallel, we reduce the 3-D problem to an 1-D problem by projecting $\overline{p_0 p_1}$ and $\overline{q_0 q_1}$ onto a line parallel to both of them orthogonally. If their images overlap, then the shortest distance is simply the shortest distance of the two supporting lines and the distance d equals to $\| (\mathbf{p}_0 - \mathbf{q}_0) - \frac{(\mathbf{p}_0 - \mathbf{q}_0) \cdot (\mathbf{q}_1 - \mathbf{q}_0)}{(\mathbf{q}_1 - \mathbf{q}_0)^2} (\mathbf{q}_1 - \mathbf{q}_0) \|$. If they do not overlap, then the two nearest points are the two endpoints (one from each edge) of the edges whose images are the nearest.

Shortest distance between a point and a triangle

Let $\mathbf{p}$ and $Tq(\mathbf{q}_0, \mathbf{q}_1, \mathbf{q}_2)$ be the point and the triangle, respectively, and $\mathbf{q}_0$, $\mathbf{q}_1$ and $\mathbf{q}_2$ be the vertices of Tq. Assume that $\mathbf{q}$ is a point on the supporting plane of Tq and $\mathbf{q} \equiv \mathbf{q}_0 + u(\mathbf{q}_1 - \mathbf{q}_0) + v(\mathbf{q}_2 - \mathbf{q}_0)$. As the triangle does not degenerate into a line segment or a point, we have a unique solution for u and v. We solve for u and v such that $\mathbf{q}$ is a point of T closest to $\mathbf{p}$.

The edges of Tq are extended and the regions can be classified into three types as shown in Figure 6.4: (1) Triangle (denoted by T); (2) Major regions denoted by R.

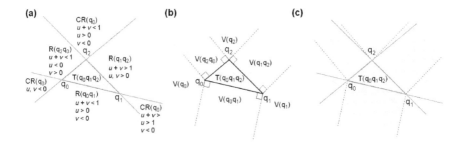

Figure 6.4: Simple regions and generalized Voronoi regions of a triangle. In (a), we have the simple regions partitioned by the supporting lines of the edges of the triangle $Tq(\mathbf{q}_0, \mathbf{q}_1, \mathbf{q}_2)$. In (b), we have the generalized Voronoi regions of the triangle. In (c), the boundaries of the simple regions and generalized Voronoi regions are drawn together.

Each is formed by one edge and two extended lines; and (3) Cross regions denoted by CR. Each is formed by one vertex and two extended lines.

If $\mathbf{q}$ lies inside the triangle, then the shortest distance is the distance between $\mathbf{p}$ and $\mathbf{q}$. If $\mathbf{q}$ lies in one of the major region, then the shortest distance is from $\mathbf{p}$ to the edge facing the major region. If $\mathbf{q}$ lies in a cross region CR, then the shortest distance will be either from $\mathbf{p}$ to one of the two edges forming the cross region. Let $\mathbf{q}_e$ be the common vertex of the two edges. If the dot product between the two vectors emitting from $\mathbf{q}_e$ along the two edges is non-negative, then $CR(\mathbf{q}_e) \subseteq V(\mathbf{q}_e)$. Therefore, the shortest distance is from $\mathbf{p}$ to $\mathbf{q}_e$. If the dot product between the two vectors emitting from $\mathbf{q}_e$ along the two edges is positive, then the dot product of $(\mathbf{p}, \mathbf{q}_e)$ and one of the two edges must be non-negative. In this case, the shortest distance is from $\mathbf{p}$ to that edge.

Computation of shortest distances of all feature pairs

We need to compute the shortest distances of all the feature pairs of two triangles. We observe that there are some common terms which appear in the computation of the shortest distances of these pairs. Moreover, there are some terms which can be derived by performing a finite number of addition and subtraction operations on the already

		Points	
Common Terms	$\mathbf{p}_0$	$\mathbf{p}_1$	$\mathbf{p}_2$
$(\mathbf{q}_1 - \mathbf{q}_0)^2$	$(\mathbf{p}_0 - \mathbf{q}_0) \cdot (\mathbf{q}_1 - \mathbf{q}_0)$	$(\mathbf{p}_1 - \mathbf{q}_0) \cdot (\mathbf{q}_1 - \mathbf{q}_0)$	$(\mathbf{p}_2 - \mathbf{q}_0) \cdot (\mathbf{q}_1 - \mathbf{q}_0)$
$(\mathbf{q}_2 - \mathbf{q}_0)^2$	$(\mathbf{p}_0 - \mathbf{q}_0) \cdot (\mathbf{q}_2 - \mathbf{q}_0)$	$(\mathbf{p}_1 - \mathbf{q}_0) \cdot (\mathbf{q}_2 - \mathbf{q}_0)$	$(\mathbf{p}_2 - \mathbf{q}_0) \cdot (\mathbf{q}_2 - \mathbf{q}_0)$
$(\mathbf{q}_1 - \mathbf{q}_0)(\mathbf{q}_2 - \mathbf{q}_0)$			

Table 6.1: This table shows the terms required in the computation of the shortest distance between the triangle $T_q(\mathbf{q}_0, \mathbf{q}_1, \mathbf{q}_2)$ and the points $\mathbf{p}_0$, $\mathbf{p}_1$, and $\mathbf{p}_2$, respectively. The common terms are listed on the left-most column.

		Points	
Common Terms	$\mathbf{q}_0$	$\mathbf{q}_1$	$\mathbf{q}_2$
$(\mathbf{p}_1 - \mathbf{p}_0)^2$	$(\mathbf{q}_0 - \mathbf{p}_0) \cdot (\mathbf{p}_1 - \mathbf{p}_0)$	$(\mathbf{q}_1 - \mathbf{p}_0) \cdot (\mathbf{p}_1 - \mathbf{p}_0)$	$(\mathbf{q}_2 - \mathbf{p}_0) \cdot (\mathbf{p}_1 - \mathbf{p}_0)$
$(\mathbf{p}_2 - \mathbf{p}_0)^2$	$(\mathbf{q}_0 - \mathbf{p}_0) \cdot (\mathbf{p}_2 - \mathbf{p}_0)$	$(\mathbf{q}_1 - \mathbf{p}_0) \cdot (\mathbf{p}_2 - \mathbf{p}_0)$	$(\mathbf{q}_2 - \mathbf{p}_0) \cdot (\mathbf{p}_2 - \mathbf{p}_0)$
$(\mathbf{p}_1 - \mathbf{p}_0)(\mathbf{p}_2 - \mathbf{p}_0)$			

Table 6.2: This table shows the terms required in the computation of the shortest distance between the triangle $T_p(\mathbf{p}_0, \mathbf{p}_1, \mathbf{p}_2)$ and the points $\mathbf{q}_0$, $\mathbf{q}_1$, and $\mathbf{q}_2$, respectively. The common terms are listed on the left-most column.

computed terms. In order to improve the overall performance, we compute all the terms in the point–triangle cases explicitly and use these terms to derive the terms for the edge–edge cases. Tables 6.1 and Table 6.2 show only the terms in point–triangle cases. A common term appears in the computation of the cases in the same row. For example, the term $(\mathbf{q}_1 - \mathbf{q}_0)^2$ appears in the cases of point–triangle. The points are $\mathbf{p}_i$ and the triangle is $T_q(\mathbf{q}_0, \mathbf{q}_1, \mathbf{q}_2)$, where $i = 0, 1$ and 2.

6.3.4 Computation of collision time for a deformable triangle pair

Denote $\mathbf{x}_i(t)$ as $\mathbf{x}_i + t\mathbf{w}_i$ and $\vec{\mathbf{x}}_{ij}(t)$ as $(\mathbf{x}_j + t\mathbf{w}_j) - (\mathbf{x}_i + t\mathbf{w}_i)$. We define $\mathbf{n}(t)$ and $D(t)$ as follows:

$$\mathbf{n}(t) \equiv \vec{\mathbf{x}}_{k2}(t) \times \vec{\mathbf{x}}_{34}(t) \tag{6.4}$$

$$D(t) \equiv \mathbf{n}(t) \cdot \vec{\mathbf{x}}_{l1}(t) \tag{6.5}$$

We are interested in only the normalized interval $\mathbf{I} = (0, 1]$ for time t. The vectors $\mathbf{x}_i$ and $\mathbf{w}_i$ denote the position and velocity of a vertex i in $\mathbf{I}$.

In the velocity-based collision detection method, the collision of two triangles could occur in two ways: point–triangle and edge–edge. In point–triangle cases, we denote the point as $x_1(t)$ and the triangle as $(x_2(t), x_3(t), x_4(t))$. This is done by setting $k = l = 3$. The vector $n(t)$ is the normal of the supporting plane of the triangle and the number $\frac{D(t)}{\|n(t)\|}$ is the perpendicular distance from the point x_1 to the plane. In edge–edge cases, we denote the first edge as $\overline{x_1(t)x_2(t)}$ and the second edge as $\overline{x_3(t)x_4(t)}$. This is done by setting $k = 1$ and $l = 3$. Assume that two edges are not parallel[3]. Then $n(t)$ is perpendicular to the supporting lines of the two edges and $\frac{D(t)}{\|n(t)\|}$ is the distance between these two lines.

Computing the time at which four points are co-planar is equivalent to solving t for the following polynomial equation of time t:

$$D(t) = 0 \qquad (6.6)$$

By expanding $D(t)$ and organizing the terms, and we obtain:

$$
\begin{aligned}
& t^3 (\vec{w}_{k2} \times \vec{w}_{34} \cdot \vec{w}_{l1}) \\
+\ & t^2 ((\vec{x}_{k2} \times \vec{w}_{34} + \vec{w}_{k2} \times \vec{x}_{34}) \cdot \vec{w}_{l1} + \vec{w}_{k2} \times \vec{w}_{34} \cdot \vec{x}_{l1}) \\
+\ & t ((\vec{x}_{k2} \times \vec{w}_{34} + \vec{w}_{k2} \times \vec{x}_{34}) \cdot \vec{x}_{l1} + \vec{x}_{k2} \times \vec{x}_{34} \cdot \vec{w}_{l1}) \\
+\ & \vec{x}_{k2} \times \vec{x}_{34} \cdot \vec{x}_{l1} \hspace{4cm} = 0
\end{aligned}
\qquad (6.7)
$$

In the following, we assume that the coefficient $(\vec{w}_{k2} \times \vec{w}_{34} \cdot \vec{w}_{l1})$ of the third-order term of Equation (6.7) is non-zero. Therefore, Equation (6.7) is a cubic equation with respect to a time variable t.

We further define:

$$
\begin{aligned}
a_3 &\equiv \vec{w}_{k2} \times \vec{w}_{34} \cdot \vec{w}_{l1} \\
a_2 &\equiv (\vec{x}_{k2} \times \vec{w}_{34} + \vec{w}_{k2} \times \vec{x}_{34}) \cdot \vec{w}_{l1} + \vec{w}_{k2} \times \vec{w}_{34} \cdot \vec{x}_{l1} \\
a_1 &\equiv (\vec{x}_{k2} \times \vec{w}_{34} + \vec{w}_{k2} \times \vec{x}_{34}) \cdot \vec{x}_{l1} + \vec{x}_{k2} \times \vec{x}_{34} \cdot \vec{w}_{l1} \\
a_0 &\equiv \vec{x}_{k2} \times \vec{x}_{34} \cdot \vec{x}_{l1}
\end{aligned}
$$

---

[3]In order to detect whether two edges are parallel or not, we solve the equation by letting $n(t) = 0$.

Therefore, Equation (6.7) becomes:

$$a_3 t^3 + a_2 t^2 + a_1 t + a_0 = 0 \qquad (6.8)$$

Solving the cubic equation is expensive. Therefore, before solving the cubic equation (6.8), we perform the coefficient check (see Section 6.3.5) to determine whether there is any real root in the interval. The coefficient check is a low cost operation. If the coefficient check passes, then we solve the cubic equation. A solution t only indicates that the two features are coplanar. They do not necessarily collide. Therefore, we must perform a validation check at time t for them. If their shortest distance is under a certain threshold, then they collide.

We keep the smallest valid solution t_c which is known as the current collision time for the feature pair. Therefore, the interval of interest becomes $(0, t_c]$. Solutions outside the interval $(0, t_c]$ are ignored when the collision detection for the remaining feature pairs is performed. This technique of shrinking the interval of interest is also employed in [85, 115].

If the technique of shrinking the interval of interest is applied, the blind distance check of Condition 6.1 becomes:

$$\tilde{d}(F0, F1) \le t_c \|\mathbf{u}_{F0}\| + t_c \|\mathbf{u}_{F1}\| + \varepsilon_{F0} + \varepsilon_{F1} \qquad (6.9)$$

6.3.5 A front-end coefficient check

The function $D(t)$ is a continuous function of t. If there exist t_0 and t_1 in the interval, such that $d(t_0)d(t_1) \le 0$, then the equation $D(t) = 0$ exists at least one real solution in the interval $[t_0, t_1]$. One way to determine the existence of the interval $[t_0, t_1]$ is to compute the extrema of $D(t)$ in the interval of interest $(0, 1]$. This may need to solve the quadratic equation $D'(t) = 0$. An alternative way is to determine that $D(t) \ne 0$ for all t in $(0, 1]$. Based on that we obtain the following conditions.

1. $|a_0| > |a_3| + |a_2| + |a_1|$.

2. $a_0 a_1 < 0$ and $\mid a_1 \mid > 2 \mid a_2 \mid + 3 \mid a_3 \mid$ and $a_0 (a_0 + a_1 + a_2 + a_3) > 0$

3. $a_0, a_1 > 0$ and $a_0 + a_1 > \mid a_3 \mid + \mid a_2 \mid$

4. $a_0, a_1 < 0$ and $a_0 + a_1 < -(\mid a_3 \mid + \mid a_2 \mid)$

5. $a_0, a_1, a_2 \geq 0$ and $a_0 + a_1 + a_2 > \mid a_3 \mid$

6. $a_0, a_1, a_2 \leq 0$ and $a_0 + a_1 + a_2 < - \mid a_3 \mid$

7. All a_i have the same sign.

If one of them is satisfied, there are no real roots in $(0, 1]$. In cases (1-2), the distance between the point and the triangle is too large for them to collide within a single time step. In cases (3)-(6), the point and the triangle could be close but they are moving apart. In case (7), the point and the triangle are moving apart. If all these tests fail, we solve the cubic equation (6.8). In practice, by checking conditions (1)-(4), we can filter a lot of non-colliding feature pairs.

In the simulation of deformable surfaces, the deformation rate is small. For example, in the simulation of cloth, the deformation rate does not exceed 20% [114, 33]. Usually, we have the relation that $|a_3| \leq |a_2| \leq |a_1|$. When the time step size is small, in the order of 0.02 second or less, we will usually have $|a_3| \ll |a_2| \ll |a_1|$. Therefore, the probability that a cubic equation does not have real roots in $\mathbf{I}$ is high for randomly distributed a_i. Readers are referred to Appendix C.3 for the probability of the existence of real roots of linear, quadratic and cubic equations in the interval $(0, 1]$.

Now, we assume that $t_c \in (0, 1]$ is the current minimum collision time for a triangle pair. The interval of interest is $(0, t_c]$ when we perform collision detection for its remaining feature pairs. The conditions of the coefficient check become:

1. $\mid a_0 \mid > \mid a'_3 \mid + \mid a'_2 \mid + \mid a'_1 \mid$.

2. $a_0 a'_1 < 0$ and $\mid a'_1 \mid > 2 \mid a'_2 \mid + 3 \mid a'_3 \mid$ and $a_0 (a_0 + a'_1 + a'_2 + a'_3) > 0$

3. $a_0, a'_1 > 0$ and $a_0 + a'_1 > \mid a'_3 \mid + \mid a'_2 \mid$

4. $a_0, a_1' < 0$ and $a_0 + a_1' < -(| a_3' | + | a_2' |)$

5. $a_0, a_1', a_2' \geq 0$ and $a_0 + a_1' + a_2' >| a_3' |$

6. $a_0, a_1', a_2' \leq 0$ and $a_0 + a_1' + a_2' < - | a_3' |$

7. a_0 and all a_i' have the same sign.

where $a_i' = a_i t_c^i$, for $i = 1, 2,$ or 3. If one of the above conditions is true, we have $| a_3' t^3 + a_2' t^2 + a_1' t + a_0 |> 0$ for $t \in (0, t_c]$ and it implies that there are no real roots in $(0, t_c]$.

The coefficient check can help us eliminate equations that do not have a real root in the interval of interest. However, it may add cost to the collision detection pipeline. Assume that the blind distance check is satisfied. There are two schemes and we have to employ the scheme which is the lowest cost.

- Scheme (1): Performing coefficient check and then solving the cubic equation when necessary. The cost is given by:

$$C_{cubic\_eq} = C_{compute\_coef} + C_{coef} + \rho_{coef} C_{eq} \qquad (6.10)$$

- Scheme (2): Solving the cubic equation directly. The cost is given by:

$$C_{cubic\_eq} = C_{compute\_coef} + C_{eq} \qquad (6.11)$$

where

C_{cubic_eq}	the cost of solving a cubic equation,
$C_{compute\_coef}$	the cost of computing the equation coefficients,
C_{coef}	the cost of coefficient check,
C_{eq}	the cost of computing the roots of the equation, and
ρ_{coef}	the probability of passing the coefficient check.

The scheme with the lowest cost C_{cubic_eq} is chosen. If the cost is the same, we choose the second scheme. The values of $C_{compute\_coef}$, C_{coef} and C_{eq} can be obtained by using the empirical analysis. However, we do not know the exact value of ρ_{coef}. We have to guess ρ_{coef} from the history. If there exists a solution in the previous frame, we will adopt scheme (2); otherwise, adopt scheme (1).

6.3.6 Validation of collision time

After obtaining the coplanar time t, we need to verify it. We move the two features to their new positions accordingly at time t and check whether they are in proximity within a certain threshold. We choose the threshold to be the half of the sum of their thickness, i.e. $\varepsilon_{F0} + \varepsilon_{F1}$.

There are two methods which are not reliable for verifying whether or not two features colliding. The first method is that it projects the features onto an axis-aligned 2D plane which maximizes their image areas or lengths. This method will lead to discrepancy when deciding whether they are close enough or not as the projected distance between them depends on their orientation with respect to the axes. This leads to inconsistent result. The second method is that it checks whether two triangles intersect. However, the computed collision points may not lie on the triangles due to numerical errors.

A reliable method is to check the shortest distance between the features. If the shortest distance is not larger than $\varepsilon_{F0} + \varepsilon_{F1}$, then the feature pair has a collision. The shortest distance validation method is also suggested in [85, 33].

6.3.7 Collision/contact points and collision normal

The collision points of two features are their closest points. In a point–triangle case, the two collision points are the point itself and the point $\mathbf{p}_0 + u(\mathbf{p}_1 - \mathbf{p}_0) + v(\mathbf{p}_2 - \mathbf{p}_0)$ on the triangle. In a edge–edge case, the two collision points are $\mathbf{p}_0 + u(\mathbf{p}_1 - \mathbf{p}_0)$ and $\mathbf{q}_0 + v(\mathbf{q}_1 - \mathbf{q}_0)$.

The collision normal $\mathbf{n}_{F_0 F_1}$ between two features F_0 and F_1 is defined such that the contact point of F_1 lies on the positive side of a plane W. The plane W passes through the contact point of F_0 [4] and its normal is $\mathbf{n}_{F_0 F_1}$.

6.3.8 Updating particle positions

In a simulation step, we will move all the vertices to the new positions in the end of the frame. The update scheme for a particle i is given by:

$$\mathbf{x}_i \mapsto \mathbf{x}_i + t_{c_i} \Delta \mathbf{x}_i \qquad (6.12)$$

where t_{c_i} is the collision time of the particle i. If the particle does not participate in any collision events, t_{c_i} is equal to 1.

6.3.9 Fault collision events and amendments

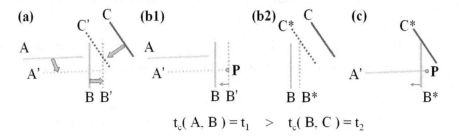

$$t_c(\text{ A, B }) = t_1 \quad > \quad t_c(\text{ B, C }) = t_2$$

Figure 6.5: Instantaneous change of the orientation of contact points due to collision after position update.

In a simulation step, we will move all the vertices to the new positions in the end of the frame. The orientation of the contact points may change instantaneously after the positions of the particles are updated. This happens when a feature collides with more than one feature. Figure 6.5 shows three features A, B and C. Figure 6.5(a) shows the new positions and the trajectories of the three features if there is no collision. The features A, B and C will move to their new positions A', B' and C', respectively, in the

---

[4]Owing to numerical errors, the contact point of F_1 may lie on the negative side.

end of the interval. Assume that we will perform first the collision detection for the pair (A, B) and then another pair (B, C). Figure 6.5(b1) shows the situation in which A and B collide at time t_c(A, B) = t_1. If there is no other collision, A and B will move to A' and B', respectively. Figure 6.5(b2) shows the situation in which B and C collide at time t_c(B, C) = t_2. If there is no other collision, B and C will move to B* and C*, respectively. After performing the collision detection for all the pairs, we have to update the positions of the features. Figure 6.5(c) shows their final positions. In this case, if $t_1 > t_2$, the contact point $\mathbf{p}$ of A lies on the wrong side of B after the update is carried out. In the following frames, if $\mathbf{p}$ moves along the direction $\mathbf{n}$ and collides with the feature B, a fault collision event will be reported. In order to avoid reporting this kind of fault collision events, we propose to use the history of the orientation information to resolve this problem. Assume that in the previous frame we had D^{prev} and $\mathbf{n}^{prev}$ and in the current frame, we have $D^{cur}(t)$ and $\mathbf{n}^{cur}(t)$. Based on that, we adopt the following strategy :

1. if ($\mathbf{n}^{prev} \cdot \mathbf{n}^{cur}(0) \geq 0$ and $D^{prev}D^{cur}(0) \geq 0$) or ($\mathbf{n}^{prev} \cdot \mathbf{n}^{cur}(0) \leq 0$ and $D^{prev}D^{cur}(0) \leq 0$), then the current orientation is consistent with the one in the previous frame. We are done.

2. if ($\mathbf{n}^{prev} \cdot \mathbf{n}^{cur}(0) < 0$ and $D^{prev}D^{cur}(0) > 0$) or ($\mathbf{n}^{prev} \cdot \mathbf{n}^{cur}(0) > 0$ and $D^{prev}D^{cur}(0) < 0$), then the orientation is inconsistent with the previous frame. This may be due to the update of the particle position or numerical errors. If $D^{prev} \frac{D^{cur}(t)}{dt}\Big|_{t=0} > 0$, the two features will move apart. As the two features are lying on the wrong side, we should ignore the first root obtained from the equation.

   If $D^{prev} \frac{D^{cur}(t)}{dt}\Big|_{t=0} < 0$, there is a tendency that the two features will penetrate further[5]. Therefore, we should report the collision time as $t = 0$. However, we should prevent this from happening. We will discuss this further in Section 6.3.10 for ghost particle pulling.

---

[5]This might not be true that, owing to numerical errors, the two features penetrate each other. However, as long as we consider the issue of collision, we avoid reporting fault collision event.

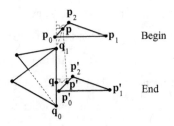

Figure 6.6: A non-contact collision event.

The flipping of triangle orientation increases the difficulty in constructing a robust collision detector. The problem could be ameliorated by calling the collision detection iteratively. However, this will slow down the entire process. If the time is a major consideration and the simulator can afford for small penetration by calling the collision detector once per frame, the above strategy provides a robust mechanism to track the orientation of two features.

6.3.10 Ghost particle pulling and backend collision detection

Owing to numerical errors, we may miss the collisions occurring near the end of the interval $(0, t_c]$ if we consider the solutions obtained from the cubic equations alone. In some situation, as shown in Figure 6.6, the shortest distance of the two features is much smaller than the allowance threshold in the end of the frame. The triangle moves from $(\mathbf{p}_0, \mathbf{p}_1, \mathbf{p}_2)$ to $(\mathbf{p}_0', \mathbf{p}_1', \mathbf{p}_2')$. Let $F0$ and $F1$ be $\overline{p_0 p_2}$ and $\overline{q_0 q_1}$, respectively. In the beginning, the shortest distance, $\|\mathbf{p} - \mathbf{q}_1\|$, between $F0$ and $F1$ is larger than $\varepsilon_{F0} + \varepsilon_{F1}$. In the final position, the shortest distance $\|\mathbf{p} - \mathbf{q}\|$ is smaller than $\varepsilon_{F0} + \varepsilon_{F1}$. In this case, the coplanar equation does not have any real roots in the interval of interest. (It can be observed that the shortest distance occurs somewhere in-between during $F0$ is moving from the beginning position to the final position.)

This case can be caught by performing the backend collision test if there are no valid solutions in $(0, t_c]$. We employ the backend test if $\|\frac{d(1)}{\mathbf{n}(t_c)}\|$ is in the interval $[0, \varepsilon_{F_0} + \varepsilon_{F_1}]$. In the backend test, we only perform the validation check for the feature pair at time $t = t_c$.

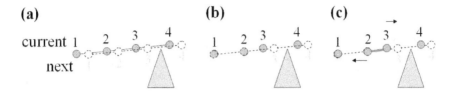

Figure 6.7: Ghost particle pulling.

Another reason to perform the backend test is to ameliorate the problem of ghost particle pulling. Consider that there are regions which collide in the beginning of the frame. The particles of the colliding regions will be stopped moving while the particles of the surrounding regions will be still moving. Now, excess forces will be produced and they will pull some particles towards or repulse some other particles away from the colliding particles in the subsequent frames. This will result in an unnatural motion. We call this phenomenon *ghost particle pulling*. Figure 6.7 shows four particles connected by springs. The spring between particle (2) and particle (3) is compressed unnaturally due to the edge (1,2) colliding with the triangle almost in the beginning of the frame. The spring will store too much energy in the end of the frame. Later on, these two particles will repel each other and lead to a sudden oscillation or vibration state in this local region. We should catch this kind of abnormal collision events and adjust the velocities of the participated particles so as to perform a relative sliding motion as soon as possible. By employing the backend test and using a relatively large threshold in the validation process, we can ameliorate the problem of ghost particle pulling.

6.3.11 Collision detection for previous colliding pairs

Consider two unbreakable features F_0 and F_1. If they collided in the previous frame, they should not penetrate each other in the current frame at the contact points. Moreover, their relative orientation at the contact points should be the same. Let the collision normal be $\mathbf{n}_{F_0 F_1}$ and the velocities of the two contact points of these two features be $\mathbf{v}_{F_0}$ and $\mathbf{v}_{F_1}$. Usually, we should have

$$\mathbf{n}_{F_0 F_1} \cdot \left(\mathbf{v}_{F_0} - \mathbf{v}_{F_1}\right) \leq 0 \qquad (6.13)$$

This implies that the two features will move in the opposite directions relatively with respect to the collision normal and this will avoid penetration. If Condition 6.13 is not guaranteed in a simulator, we should report to the simulator that there is an immediate collision. In Appendix B.4, we detail the method that we apply in order to make sure that Condition 6.13 is always satisfied. There are three approaches to handle the previous colliding pairs: shortest distance check, immediate collision check and departure collision detection.

Shortest distance check: If Condition 6.13 is guaranteed, the two features can only behave in two ways: separate or contact. As they do not penetration each other in both cases, we do not need to invoke full collision check for them. What we need to know is whether they are in contact or not. We compute their shortest distance. If the shortest distance is larger than a certain threshold in the end of the frame, the two features are not in contact.

Immediate collision check: If Condition 6.13 is not guaranteed, we could employ this method. This method requires the prior knowledge about the roughness properties of the surfaces. If the friction coefficient between two features are sufficiently large that they will not slide on each other but they either stick on each other at the contact points or move apart. Let the velocities of the two contact points be $\mathbf{v}_p$ and $\mathbf{v}_q$, respectively, and the collision normal be $\hat{\mathbf{n}}$. If $\mathbf{n}_{F_0 F_1} \cdot \left(\mathbf{v}_{F_0} - \mathbf{v}_{F_1}\right) > 0$, then the two features will penetrate each other in the beginning of the frame. If $\mathbf{n}_{F_0 F_1} \cdot \left(\mathbf{v}_{F_0} - \mathbf{v}_{F_1}\right) \leq 0$, we perform the departure collision detection.

Conveniently, it might be easier to perform a threshold check for the velocities. That is if the speeds of the particles are smaller than a threshold, the velocities are reset to zero. When the speed of the particles is small that the features might, in fact, penetrate each other further slowly. But owing to numerical errors, the collision detector may not detect the penetration. Although it would happen in this way, we do not adopt this thresholding scheme. The slow movement of the particles exhibits an important interaction property between the objects by its nature.

Departure collision detection: If the immediate collision check fails, it implies that the features are separating in the beginning of the frame. We have to solve the cubic equation[6]. However, we should discard the smallest root if the root is corresponding to a fault collision event.

6.3.12 Piecewise continuous collision detection

This is an extension to the regular velocity-based collision detection. Assume that a feature collides at time t_c. The particles of the features should not move beyond time t_c in the interval of interest. Therefore, the particles are at positions $\mathbf{x} + t_c \Delta \mathbf{v}$ for time $t \geq t_c$.

6.4 An architecture for the intrinsic collision detection unit

We propose an architecture for the intrinsic collision detection unit. Caching technique has been widely used in collision detection [18, 42, 99]. We store the collision information in cache so that we could retrieve the information quickly later. The underlying data structure of the cache which is implemented as a hash table.

Unlike convex objects, there is comparatively a large number of triangle pairs which are in proximity when deformable surfaces are in contact with one another. These triangle pairs are called potential colliding triangle pairs. Every pair is checked further for determining whether there is a collision in $(0, 1]$. These potential triangle

---

[6]If we bring the features exactly to their contact time t in the previous frame, then $D(t)$ would be zero. Therefore, we have a trivial root 0 and need to solve a quadratic equation instead. However, $D(t)$ may not be zero due to numerical errors.

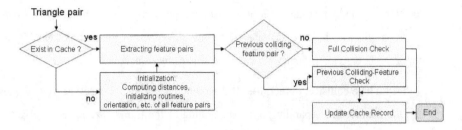

Figure 6.8: The architecture for the intrinsic collision detection unit.

pairs are likely to be checked in the next frame because of the temporal coherence properties of the objects. By maintaining the estimated distance between feature pairs, we can adopt the blind distance check efficiently (Section 6.3.2). There are common values which are computed repetitively for the same pair. Figure 6.8 shows the architecture of our proposed method. We cache the common values in order to speedup the entire collision detection process. For instance, we record in the cache the shortest distance of all (fifteen) feature pairs of the triangle pair, the collision points, the collision normal, the collision status and the collision orientation of all feature pairs, and the pointers of the triangle pair. The cache also helps us resolve the following three major problems:

1. When a triangle collides with another triangle at time t_c, we will bring them close to each other accordingly. In the next frame, we may need to solve the cubic equation for the triangle pair. Owing to numerical errors, a small perturbation will make the two features lying on the wrong side (that is inconsistent collision orientation). We will lose track of the orientation and thus produce a wrong collision normal.

2. As the features lie on the wrong side, we will incorrectly compute a fault collision time.

3. Owing to numerical errors, we will probably miss the collision event. Inevitably the two features will pass through each other.

112

In order to solve these problems, we need to track the history of these triangle pairs. We have to cache the information of the current colliding triangle pairs. So that we can apply the techniques described in Section 6.3.9 to correct the orientation of colliding feature pairs.

In our simulation, there is a lot of potential colliding pairs. During the simulation, many potential colliding pairs in the previous frame will become obsolete while many triangle pairs will be collected as the potential colliding pairs. In some situations, many potential colliding pairs will remain the same for a long time. Therefore, the three operations applied upon the data structure should be: (1) fast insertion of records, (2) fast removal of records, and (3) fast searching for records. The desirable running time of each operation is $O(1)$. An all-pair matrix matches all the requirements of the three operations. However, constructing an all-pair matrix requires $O(n^2)$ memory space. This is feasible for a low complexity scene. However, for a high complexity scene, this will be infeasible and will waste a lot of memory.

If a triangle T_0 is in proximity with another triangle T_1, T_0 is likely in proximity of the neighborhood of T_1. Assume that the bounding volume of a triangle overlaps with at most k triangles. Then there are $O(k^2)$ pairs of triangles in proximity for the pair (T_0, T_1). The total number of potential colliding pairs is at most $O(k^2 n)$, where n is the total number of the triangles in the scene. The factor k^2 is relatively much smaller than n, in general. As our sampling space is small but the universal space is huge, we choose to use hash table as the internal structure of cache.

6.4.1 Hashing

We need to identify a pair of potential colliding triangles in the hash table. We assign a unique id (identifier) to each triangle (e.g. explicitly assigning a unique integer or using the *memory address* of the storage of the triangle). We employ the multiplicity method to compute a key which is in the range of the hash table. Let $id0$ and $id1$ be the identifiers of these two triangles. The key generation function $h(id0, id1)$ is defined as follows:

$$h(id0, id1) = \lfloor M(f(id0, id1)A \bmod 1) \rfloor \qquad (6.14)$$

where the function $f(id0, id1)$ maps to an integer[7], M is the size of the table and A is an irrational number [80]. There are two common methods to resolve hashing collisions: chaining and open addressing. In our implementation, we employ chaining for resolving hashing collisions. We will encounter problems by using open addressing. In open addressing, we do not have any clues to stop the searching process if the records do not exist. The number of probes will be the size of the table for each searching operation.

6.4.2 Managing records

There are three types of records and each type of records requires different operations:

1. **New records:** New records are that the corresponding triangle pairs were not in the set of the PCPs in the previous frame. When new records are inserted, we compute the shortest distances of all the feature pairs of the corresponding triangle pairs and then perform collision detection.

2. **Existing records:** The triangle pairs of the existing records were in the set of the previous PCPs and they also appear in the set of the current PCPs. We perform the collision detection for the corresponding triangle pairs. We employ the shortest distance check for the feature pairs colliding in the previous frame.

3. **Old records:** The old records are not in the set of the PCPs. They should be removed from the cache and the occupied memory should be released back to the memory pool.

---

[7]Preferably, $f(id0, id1)$ should return a unique integer for different pairs of $(id0, id1)$. The computation of this function should be fast.

6.4.3   Two cache schemes

Since there is a lot of PCPs, a large amount of memory is required for storing all the information of the PCPs. The data structure of a hash table is just an array of pointers. Therefore, the memory space required by a hash table is much smaller than the memory space required for storing all the individual records. We develop two cache schemes according to the demand level of memory: (1) *mixed-cache scheme* and (2) *separated-cache scheme*. In the mixed-cache scheme, all the potential colliding pairs are stored in one cache. In the separated-cache scheme, the colliding triangle pairs and the non-colliding triangle pairs are maintained separately. In both schemes, we assume that we have enough memory to store all the current colliding triangle pairs all the time.

Mixed-cache scheme: All the records of the potential colliding pairs are stored in one cache and chaining is used to resolve for hashing collisions.

Separated-cache scheme: We adopt this scheme when the memory is limited. In this cache scheme, we need two hash tables. We assume that we have enough memory to store all the records of the current colliding triangle pairs but do not need to store all the records of the non-colliding triangle pairs. We have two major structures. One maintains the records of the colliding pairs and the other maintains the records of the non-colliding pairs. We have a free record pool. When a new triangle pair is visited, we check its collision status. If the triangles collide, we must find a record storage to store the pair. We start by searching for a free record from the free record pool. If there are no free records, we will get one from the non-colliding record pool and we prefer to get one from the existing records which have been already checked. For an existing record, we check its collision status and migrate it to the corresponding structure when necessary. The old records are released back to the free record pool.

115

6.5 Maintaining stable collision status in the presence of numerical errors

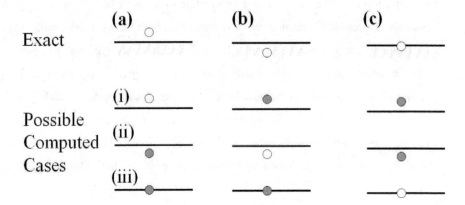

Figure 6.9: Exact and possible computed cases.

Owing to numerical errors [7], the shortest distance that we obtain will not be exactly the same as the one obtained from the arithmetic computation. This is due to the finite representation of a number in computer. Figure 6.9, shows the possible computed situations that we will obtain corresponding to three cases. We want to know the maximum absolute error that we will obtain when we compute the shortest distance of a feature pair at the final stage.

Let us recall the stages that we need to get through in order to compute the shortest distance and then perform the verification for a potential colliding feature pair:

1. Compute of the coefficients of the polynomial equation

2. Solve the cubic equation

3. Move particles to their colliding positions

4. Compute the shortest distance

5. Verify the result

At each stage, there is numerical error for each computed terms and error will be propagated to the next stage. Assume that the maximum absolute error is ϵ_s obtained in the final stage. Then if we use the threshold $\varepsilon_{F_0} + \varepsilon_{F_1}$ to determine whether there is a collision, we should use $\varepsilon_{F_0} + \varepsilon_{F_1} + \epsilon_s$ as the threshold in the implementation. For details of obtaining the value of ϵ_s, a reader is referred to Appendix F.

Now assume that there are two features collided in the previous frame. If it is guaranteed that the features do not pass through each other, we only need to perform stages (3), (4) and (5). Now errors are introduced in stages (3) and (4). Assume that the maximum accumulated absolute error is ϵ_d, then the threshold should be $\varepsilon_{F_0} + \varepsilon_{F_1} + \epsilon_d$ in the implementation. For details, please refer to Appendix F.

In the backend test, we invoke the same stages as what we did for the colliding feature pairs in the previous frame. Therefore, the threshold is $\varepsilon_{F_0} + \varepsilon_{F_1} + \epsilon_d$ in the implementation.

For simplicity, an elegant way for implementing the thresholding scheme is to replace these two threshold values by a single value $\varepsilon_{F_0} + \varepsilon_{F_1} + \max\{\epsilon_s, \epsilon_d\}$. The thresholding scheme is important for maintaining a stable collision status; otherwise, ghost particle pulling will occur easily.

6.6 Absolute relative error bounds between two roots of a cubic and the truncated equation

In our computation, $|a_3|$ is relatively much smaller than $|a_1|$ or $|a_2|$ most of the time. This is due to that w_i are small in magnitude compared to the length of the edges of the triangles and the small time step is used. If $|a_0| \geq |a_1| + |a_2| + |a_3|$ and $|a_3| \ll max\{|a_1|, |a_2|\}$, we solve the truncated equation instead of the cubic one (i.e. discarding the third order term). There are three reasons to do that: (1) when the magnitude of a_3 is relatively much smaller than the magnitude of other coefficients, error in the solutions of the cubic equation is large due to numerical errors, especially, in single precision. If single precision is used, it is possible that some roots cannot be computed because of overflow; (2) the accuracy of solutions obtained from the truncated equation is sufficiently high for our need; (3) the computation of the truncated equation is faster than the computation of the cubic equation. Assume that $a_3 = 1$. If $t \in (0, 1]$ is a root of the cubic equation and t' is the corresponding root of the truncated equation, then $|\frac{t'-t}{t}|$ is $O(\sqrt{\frac{1}{max\{|a_1|,|a_2|\}}})$ and $O(\frac{1}{(max\{|a_1|,|a_2|\})^2})$, in the worst and the best cases, respectively. A reader is referred to Appendix E.2.6 for details.

6.7 Experiments and results

We compared the performance of seven intrinsic collision detection methods including our proposed method. Figure 6.10 shows the block diagrams of these methods. All the methods would perform the backend test when it was necessary. In methods (2)–(5), we did not employ cache for storing the information of PCPs. Therefore, in practice, these four methods may lead to penetration. The description of all the methods is given below :

1. **Cache :** This is the method that we proposed in this chapter.

2. **ND :** The fifteen cubic equations are computed. The validation check for the solutions is performed in an ascending order. If there is no any valid solution, the shortest distances of all their feature pairs are computed one by one in the backend test.

3. **NDCoef :** It is the same as **ND** except that the coefficient check is performed before solving the cubic equations. The interval of interest is kept as $(0, 1]$.

4. **NDCoefAllFTD :** It is the same as **NDCoef** except that the shortest distances of all the feature pairs are computed in the backend test for no valid solutions.

5. **BD:** First, the point–triangle tests are performed and then the edge–edge tests are performed. In the point–triangle cases, the distance between the point and

118

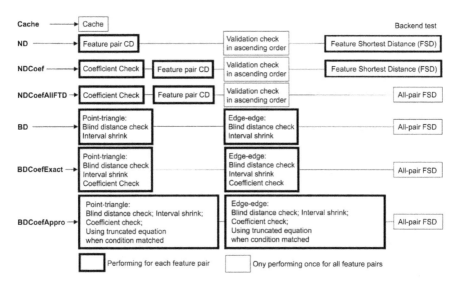

Figure 6.10: Block diagrams of seven collision detection methods for deformable triangle pairs.

the supporting plane of the triangle is computed in the beginning of the frame. After that the blind distance check is performed. The polynomial coefficients are computed and the cubic equation is solved when necessary. In the edge–edge cases, if two end-points of an edge lying on the same side with respect to the other triangle, the blind distance check is employed. These two edges are interchanged and the same test is performed if the previous test is passed. The cubic equation is solved if the blind distance check is passed.

6. **BDCoefExact:** It is the same as **BD** except that the coefficient check and the shrinking of the interval of interest are employed.

7. **BDCoefAppro:** It is the same as **BDCoefExact** except that the third order term of the cubic equation is truncated if $|\frac{a_3}{\max\{|a_1|,|a_2|\}}| < 5 \times 10^{-4}$. A quadratic equation is solved for the coplanar time.

We used the deformable triangular mesh to model cloth. We implemented the internal dynamic structure of cloth as the spring-mass model proposed by Provot [113].

The dynamic response was kept to a minimum. We did not compute collision forces. The image-based method was employed as the front-end collision detector to collect the potential colliding triangle pairs (PCPs). The piecewise continuous collision detection was not employed. All the floating point operations were performed in double precision. The hash table size was 20k. The experiments were run on a computer with 1.5GHz Pentium 4 CPU, 1GB of main memory, and an nVidia geForce graphics card.

Owing to numerical errors, the configurations of the scenes will be different if each experiment is performed independently for each method. In order to make sure that we would have the identical configurations of the scenes, we employed the **Cache** method as a guidance. When we advanced the objects to the new positions for other methods, the positions of the objects were obtained from the **Cache** method.

The total collision detection (CD) time is the sum of timings of collecting the PCPs and timings of performing the triangle-triangle collision detection. We categorize timings of different parts of the collision detection process as follows:

$$
\begin{aligned}
\text{The total CD time} \quad = \quad & \text{Total time of collection of PCPs} \\
& + \text{Cache management time} \\
& + \text{Feature-feature CD time} \\
& + \text{Computation of collision normal time} \\
& + \text{Computation of contact points time}
\end{aligned}
$$

We performed four experiments and our focus was on the performance of the intrinsic test unit in the process of self-collision detection. In the experiments, we collected the timing information for two items: cache management time and feature-feature CD time. The timings of management was not collected for the other six methods. We plotted three kinds of graphs:

1. Graphs (a) shows the total tri/tri collision detection time.

2. Graphs (b) shows the normalized tri/tri collision detection time.

120

3. Graphs (c) shows the total number of potential colliding feature pairs.

The normalized tri/tri collision detection time is the total tri/tri CD time divided by the total number of PCPs and the total number of potential colliding feature pairs is equal to the number of PCPs times fifteen.

Method	Avg. Total Tri/Tri CD Time (sec)	Avg. Total Normalized Tri/Tri CD Time (usec)
Cache	0.144	8.71
ND	1.24	75.1 (8.62)
NDCoef	0.577	34.9 (4.01)
NDCoefallFTD	0.371	22.4 (2.57)
BD	0.336	20.3 (2.33)
BDCoefExact	0.167	10.1 (1.16)
BDCoefAppro	0.165	9.98 (1.15)

Table 6.3: Experiment 1: Average total tri/tri CD time and average normalized tri/tri CD time. Complexity : cloth (23k tri.), solid (800 tri.). Total number of PCPs in the entire simulation: 26.4 million.

Method	Avg. Total Tri/Tri CD Time (sec)	Avg. Normalized Tri/Tri CD Time (usec)
Cache	0.0347	9.41
ND	0.269	72.8 (7.74)
NDCoef	0.130	35.3 (3.75)
NDCoefallFTD	0.0818	22.1 (2.35)
BD	0.0964	26.1 (2.77)
BDCoefExact	0.0426	11.5 (1.22)
BDCoefAppro	0.0417	11.3 (1.20)

Table 6.4: Experiment 2: Average total tri/tri CD time and average normalized tri/tri CD time. Complexity : cloth (26.8k tri.), solid (6.4k tri.). Total number of PCPs in the entire simulation: 3.68 million.

Figure 6.12 shows the snapshots from the first experiment. In the first experiment, a piece of column-liked cloth falls onto the area of ground. The bottom part is squeezed and folds are produced. Self-collisions occur in these regions. It can be noticed that the PCPs near the bottom part of cloth are the same throughout the simulation. As more folds are created, more PCPs are produced. Figure 6.13 shows the snapshots from the second experiment. In the second experiment, a fringy cloth falls on the top region of a smooth solid hemisphere. When the piece of cloth collides with the hemisphere, the colliding regions are stuck. The fringes start to move closer to each other and then squeeze each other. This results a lot of self-collisions. This also leads to complicated

Method	Avg. Total Tri/Tri CD Time (sec)	Avg. Normalized Tri/Tri CD Time (usec)
Cache	0.0653	7.69
ND	0.61	72.1 (9.38)
NDCoef	0.305	35.9 (4.67)
NDCoefallFTD	0.193	22.8 (2.96)
BD	0.137	16.1 (2.09)
BDCoefExact	0.0683	8.04 (1.05)
BDCoefAppro	0.0678	7.98 (1.04)

Table 6.5: Experiment 3: Average total tri/tri CD time and average normalized tri/tri CD time. Complexity : cloth (20.4k tri.), solid (7.2k tri.). Total number of PCPs in the entire simulation: 16.1 million.

Method	Avg. Total Tri/Tri CD Time (sec)	Avg. Normalized Tri/Tri CD Time (usec)
Cache	0.0275	9.97
ND	0.203	73.6 (7.38)
NDCoef	0.35	35.0 (3.51)
NDCoefallFTD	0.22	22.1 (2.22)
BD	0.0807	29.3 (2.94)
BDCoefExact	0.0369	13.4 (1.34)
BDCoefAppro	0.0370	13.5 (1.35)

Table 6.6: Experiment 4: Average total tri/tri CD time and average normalized tri/tri CD time. Complexity : cloth (26.6k tri.), solid (2.4k tri.). Total number of PCPs in the entire simulation: 1.93 million.

interaction between fringes. There are more than four fringes interacting with each other at the same time. Some fringes are frozen due to collisions. Figure 6.15 shows the snapshots from the third experiment. In the third experiment, a piece of column-liked cloth with long fringes falls on an ellipsoid and onto the area of ground. Initially, the size of the piece of cloth is stretched by 5%. In the beginning of the simulation, the piece of cloth shrinks a little bit and this distorts the shape of the fringes. This makes the fringes appear to be in the shape like a wave-form. After that, they start to fall downwards. Near the area of ground, they are compressed themselves gradually. This generates many self-collisions. Figure 6.16 shows the snapshots from the fourth experiment. In the fourth experiment, a net with holes falls on a scepter with a long leg. The holes are arranged in grid pattern. In the beginning of the simulation, the piece of cloth falls on the head of the scepter and sticks on it. The outer regions of the piece of cloth are pull towards the center while they are falling. These regions are compressed gradually and many self-collisions happen.

The performance statistics of the methods are summarized in Tables 6.3-6.6. The numbers inside the parentheses are computed as the timing of the corresponding item divided by the timing that is obtained from the **Cache** method. From the result, it shows that the cache method outperforms the other methods. In the first experiment, the cache method takes around 8.7 usec to perform collision detection for a PCP while the **ND** method takes almost 75 usec to do it. The methods of the fastest to the slowest are **Cache, BDCoefAppro, BDCoefExact, BD, NDCoefAllFTD, NDCoef,** and **ND**. We have similar results for the rest of the experiments. The coefficient check method improves the performance significantly in both **ND**-class and **BD**-class methods. Over 97% of the equations which do not have any real solutions in the interval were pruned off by employing the coefficient check. From the timing information of **NDCoefAllFTD** and **NDCoef**, it is over 30% faster if the optimized method is adopted to compute the shortest distances of all feature pairs compared to computing them individually.

6.8   Summary and discussion

We have presented an efficient architecture for the intrinsic collision detection unit. The velocity-based collision detection is employed for deformable triangles. The accurate collision information: collision time, collision normal, and collision points can be computed. We proposed a reliable method to handle orientation information of the feature pairs. This orientation information help us avoid reporting fault collision events. Before solving the cubic equation, we should perform the low cost method to determine whether there exists a root in the interval. We have shown that under certain condition the absolute relative error between roots of cubic equation and its truncated equation is bounded by a function of the equation coefficients. We cache the computationally intensive information. Depending on the memory usage, we proposed two caching schemes. Both schemes require that there should be enough memory to store the colliding triangle pairs.

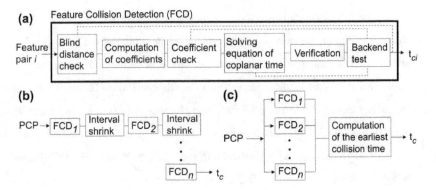

Figure 6.11: An architecture for parallel implementation for feature collision detection (FCD).

In the separated-cache scheme, we had experimented methods to determine whether the old records should be removed or kept, for example, applying the similar techniques (e.g. aging) developed in the field of database. However, we did not observe any significant performance improvement. Therefore, we did not report the result in this thesis.

We had implemented cache for storing feature pairs required for solving cubic equations. So that if the same feature pairs are checked again in different potential colliding pairs, we can skip the computation of the cubic equations. This approach requires a huge amount of memory to store all the feature pairs individually. From our study, we observed that this approach does not have significant improvement over the **Cache** approach. In most cases, the performance of this approach is worse than the **Cache** approach.

The current implementation of collision detection for a PCP is carried out in serial. We want to exploit the parallelism of collision detection in order to improve the performance (Figure 6.11(c)). For each triangle pair, we perform collision detection for the fifteen pairs of features in parallel. After that the smallest collision detection time is the collision time of the triangle pair. However, in this kind of method, we cannot employ the interval shrinking scheme. We should conduct further investigation to compare the performance of these two paradigms.

124

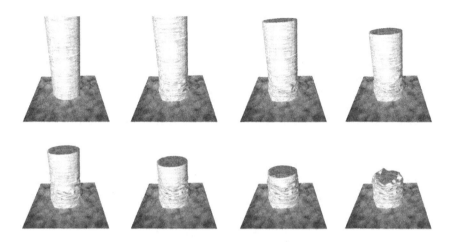

Figure 6.12: Experiment one: A piece of column cloth (23.4k tri.) falls on an area of ground.

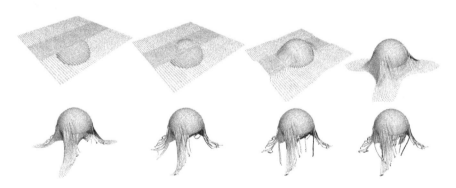

Figure 6.13: Experiment two: A piece of fringy cloth (26.8k tri.) falls on a hemisphere (6.4k tri.).

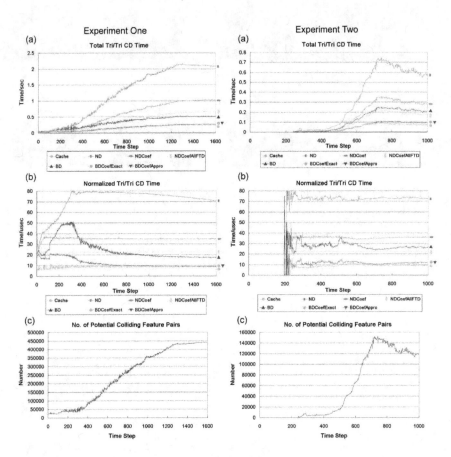

Figure 6.14: Results of Experiment one and Experiment two.

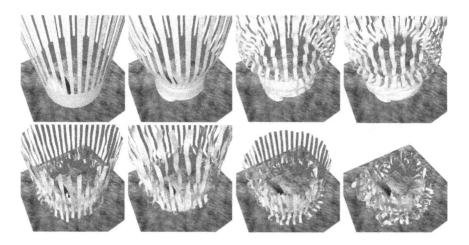

Figure 6.15: Experiment three: A piece of column cloth (20.4k tri.) with long fringes falls on an ellipsoid (6.4k tri.) and a floor (800 tri.). Initially, the cloth piece is stretched by 5%.

Figure 6.16: Experiment four: A net (26.6k tri.) falls on a hemisphere (1.6k tri.) with a long leg.

127

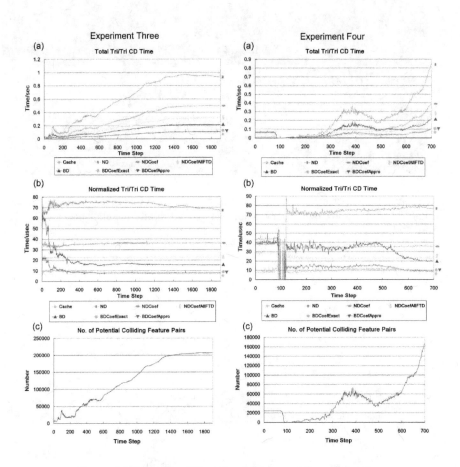

Figure 6.17: Results of Experiment three and Experiment four.

Chapter 7

Dynamic Interaction between Deformable Surfaces and Nonsmooth Objects

7.1 Introduction

In this chapter, we propose a decomposition scheme for self-collision detection, a variety of methods improving the accuracy in computing collision orientation, and techniques for handling some problems in the dynamics of deformable surfaces. A $(\pi, \beta, \mathbf{I})$ decomposition scheme for self-collision detection is proposed. Unlike the image-based method developed in Chapter 5, this scheme can be applied in the time domain. We address the problem of computing the dynamic interaction between deformable surfaces and objects with sharp features in the presence of collision, friction and stiction. This problem is highly common in 3D models of real environments such as terrains with natural features. The interaction of deformable surfaces with such objects poses a significant challenge to the current collision detection methods. Furthermore, the dynamic response due to the interaction of a large number of sharp features with folding materials for real applications such as cloth modeling, draping and design is an open problem.

7.1.1 Challenges and motivation

Collisions are inevitable when deformable surfaces interact with themselves and with other objects. The added complexity of deformable surfaces is the result of the large increase in the number of contact points that must be computed. Furthermore, in order to prevent penetration, we need to maintain the relative orientation of surface patches in the proximity of a collision.

A closed orientable 2-manifold surface can collide only with itself on the same side. If we know the position of an object with respect to the surface in advance, finding the relative orientation with respect to the surface is relatively easy. We can determine the side of the surface that has the potential to interact with the object in the beginning and the relative orientation will not be changed throughout the simulation. For example, the boundary of a rigid body B can be represented by a closed orientable 2-manifold mesh. When an object A collides with B, A can collide only with the boundary of B from the exterior space of B. Another example is that if an object is inside a sphere in 3D, the object can collide only with the interior of the sphere.

In the case of an orientable 2-manifold surface with boundary, both sides of the surface can interact with the surface itself or with other objects. This requires the computation of the relative orientation at run-time, but because of the presence of large numbers of numerical errors and degenerate cases, it is generally not possible without careful treatment, to reliably determine the relative orientation.

7.1.2 Contributions

The techniques provide new mechanisms for high performance collision detection and for the dynamic response of deformable surfaces in highly compact 3D environments consisting of a large number of objects with sharp features. Our main contributions consist of providing practical solutions to three critical problems: self-collision detection in the presence of highly deformable 2-manifold surfaces; robust treatment

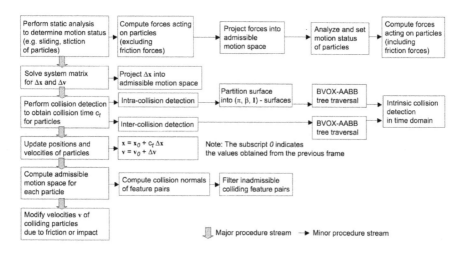

Figure 7.1: System pipeline. The value of c_t is equal to 1.0 if the particle is not involved in any collision events.

for collision orientation; motion constraints for penetration avoidance; dynamic response due to contact, friction and stiction.

7.2 Outline

Figure 7.1 shows the pipeline of our system. We assume that a deformable surface is an orientable 2-manifold which will change its shape due to its dynamic behavior. Its representation can be decomposed into a triangular mesh up to any level of resolution. In order to minimize neighborhood searches and to improve the geometric proximity locally, we introduce a new kind of surface, namely $(\pi, \beta, \mathbf{I})$-surface.

In order to detect self-collision, surfaces are decomposed into a set of $(\pi, \beta, \mathbf{I})$-surfaces and then a backward-voxel AABB scheme is adopted for collision detection for each pair of $(\pi, \beta, \mathbf{I})$-surfaces. It is important to note that the $(\pi, \beta, \mathbf{I})$-surface decomposition is done at run-time, at every frame. This is because the surface decomposition is time dependent as the surface configurations and proximity features change at every time step. This decomposition results in a significant reduction of the number of potential colliding pairs.

We aim to resolve all collision events and avoid regions of surfaces passing through each other in one time step. Therefore, the velocity-based collision detection is adopted in the intrinsic collision test. We use an improved *intrinsic collision detection* to handle the colliding feature pairs that have come in contact in the past frame and the newly colliding ones.

The collision normals of objects with sharp features are often not uniquely defined [73] at the corners. As the number of contact points increases in the neighborhood of sharp features, the non-penetration constraint can be easily broken without careful treatment. We solve this by systematically constructing a penetration-free motion space for the current colliding *features* (vertex, edge, and triangle). By constraining their movement inside the motion space, it is guaranteed that they will not penetrate each other in the next frame. This avoids the direct computation of repulsion forces that is usually necessary for intersection avoidance. Subsequently, the full collision detection check for the corresponding features is reduced to checking only inside the motion space.

We handle friction and stiction by considering the kinematic and dynamic factors involving the velocities and the forces acting on the particles. The results of our experiments show that this method handles sliding and stiction robustly.

The following sections are organized as follows: Section 7.3 describes a new self-collision detection method, robust treatments of numerical errors and the methods for computing the admissible colliding feature pairs. Section 7.4 proposes a method for computing the penetration-free motion space. Section 7.5 describes the motion formulation of the deformable surface. Section 7.6 details the performance of the proposed method. We present the summary and discussion in Section 7.7.

7.3 Collision detection for a surface

In this section, we discuss a method for performing self-collision detection for an orientable 2-manifold deformable surface in the time interval $\mathbf{I} = [0, I_{max}]$. Without loss of generality, we assume that $I_{max} = 1$. The trajectory of a vertex i (or particle) within a frame is described by $\mathbf{x}_i + t\Delta\mathbf{x}_i$, $t \in \mathbf{I}$. The terms and definitions can be found in Nomenclature in the beginning of this thesis.

7.3.1 The canonical cone of a triangle

As the vertices of the triangle move in the time interval $\mathbf{I}[0, I_{max}]$, the normal $\mathbf{n}(t)$ of the triangle changes accordingly. We want to compute a canonical cone $C(\pi_s, \beta_s)$ such that the cone contains $\mathbf{n}(t)$, i.e. $\frac{\pi_s \cdot \mathbf{n}(t)}{|\pi_s||\mathbf{n}(t)|} \geq cos\beta_s$ for all $t \in \mathbf{I}$. The angle β_s is in $[0, \frac{\pi}{2})$. For an optimal solution, β_s should be the smallest among all the possible canonical cones. This will be expensive to compute even if π_s is constant. This requires a quartic equation. Therefore, instead of computing the smallest canonical cone, we compute a cone which is an approximation of the optimal solution.

The normal of a triangle changes from $\mathbf{n}(0)$ to $\mathbf{n}(I_{max})$. The deviation of $\mathbf{n}(t)$ from the space spanned by $\mathbf{n}(0)$ and $\mathbf{n}(I_{max})$ will be small if the deformation of the triangle is not too large. Thus, we choose π_s as $\frac{\mathbf{n}(0)}{|\mathbf{n}(0)|} + \frac{\mathbf{n}(I_{max})}{|\mathbf{n}(I_{max})|}$. We must verify the condition that π_s is a valid axis of the canonical cone. The condition states as: $\forall t \in \mathbf{I}, \pi_s \cdot \mathbf{n}(t) > 0$. If this condition is not satisfied, we will assume that the triangle does not have a valid canonical cone. On the other hand, if the condition is satisfied, we proceed to compute β_s. Let the angle between the cone axis and the triangle normal be $\beta(t)$, i.e. $\cos\beta(t) \equiv \frac{\pi_s \cdot \mathbf{n}(t)}{|\pi_s||\mathbf{n}(t)|}$. We want to compute the largest $\beta(t)$ but this will require solving a quartic equation. Therefore, we compute an upper bound β_m of $\beta(t)$. Let $\mathbf{n}_{max} \in \{\mathbf{n}(t_0) : |\mathbf{n}(t_0)| \geq |\mathbf{n}(t)|, \ t_0 \in \mathbf{I} \text{ and } \forall \ t \in \mathbf{I}\}$. We have

$$\pi_s \cdot \mathbf{n}(t) = |\pi_s||\mathbf{n}(t)| \cos\beta(t) \leq |\pi_s||\mathbf{n}_{max}| \cos\beta(t) \tag{7.1}$$

By rearranging the terms in the above inequality, we have $\frac{\pi_s \cdot \mathbf{n}(t)}{|\pi_s||\mathbf{n}_{max}|} \leq \cos\beta(t)$. We set

Figure 7.2: Merging two surfaces (π_0, β_0) and (π_1, β_1) into a larger one (π_s, β_s).

$\beta_m = \max\{\arccos \frac{\pi_s \cdot \mathbf{n}(t)}{|\pi_s||\mathbf{n}_{max}|} : \forall\, t \in \mathbf{I}\}$. As both $\pi_s \cdot \mathbf{n}(t)$ and $\frac{\pi_s \cdot \mathbf{n}(t)}{|\pi_s||\mathbf{n}_{max}|}$ are positive, we will have $\beta_m \in [0, \frac{\pi}{2})$. We set β_s as $\beta_m(t)$.

7.3.2 Decomposition of a surface into (π, β)-surfaces

We decompose a surface into a set of (π, β)-surfaces by adopting the breadth-first search method as proposed in Chapter 5. This is done at each time step. In Chapter 5, the static case is considered and the canonical cone of a triangle is $C(\mathbf{n}(0), 0)$. In the time domain, the canonical cone of the triangle is $C(\pi_s, \beta_s)$ as described in Nomenclature.

The decomposition process is that a seek triangle with a valid canonical cone is appended to a queue and the canonical cone $C(\pi_0, \beta_0)$ of the current (π, β)-surface S is marked as non-initialized. Then, we pick a triangle T with the canonical cone $C(\pi_1, \beta_1)$ from the queue. If $C(\pi_0, \beta_0)$ is not initialized, we set it as $C(\pi_1, \beta_1)$. On the other hand, if $C(\pi_0, \beta_0)$ has been initialized, we check whether we can merge T into S. If T can be merged into S, we update the canonical cone of S as the smallest cone containing both $C(\pi_0, \beta_0)$ and $C(\pi_1, \beta_1)$ and T becomes a member of S. After that, we append the edge-adjacent triangles of T to the queue if they do not belong to any (π, β)-surfaces. We repeat this breadth-first search process until we cannot merge any more triangles. As a result, we have constructed one (π, β)-surface. For the remaining triangles, we begin with a new seed and repeat the entire process. Consequently, we obtain a set of (π, β)-surfaces of the original surface and a set of isolated triangles.

In order to control the quality of the resultant surface after the merging operation, we restrict that the surface angle of the resultant surface should not be larger than a threshold value, namely *maximum surface angle* β_{max}. We adopt the same scheme developed in Chapter 5 to perform the merging operation for two cones. The merging operation is described as follows. Consider two surfaces (π_0, β_0) and (π_1, β_1) in Figure 7.2. Let γ be the angle between π_0 and π_1. If $(\beta_0 + \beta_1 + \gamma \leq 2\beta_{max})$, then these two surfaces can be merged into a larger surface with the new surface axis π_s and surface angle β_s, where $\pi_s = (\pi_0' + \pi_1')/\|\pi_0' + \pi_1'\|$ and $\beta_s = (\gamma + \beta_0 + \beta_1)/2$.

7.3.3   Properties of a $(\pi, \beta, \mathbf{I})$-surface

In the time interval $\mathbf{I}$, a $(\pi, \beta, \mathbf{I})$-surface exhibits the following six properties:

1. **Restriction of interior vertex[1]:** Let the image plane be perpendicular to the surface axis π. Project the surface onto the image plane along π. Then, the image of an interior vertex does not move across or touch the images of the edges surrounding it.

   Justification: Assume that e is an edge of a triangle T and a vertex p of T moves across this edge. Let $\mathbf{n}(t)$ be the normal of T and π_s be the surface axis. Then there exists $t \in \mathbf{I}$ s.t. $\pi_s \cdot \mathbf{n}(t) \leq 0$. This implies that T should not be a member of the surface.

2. **No collision for edge-adjacent triangles:** Edge-adjacent triangles do not collide.

   Justification: Let T_0 and T_1 be two edge-adjacent triangles. Denote $H_e(T_0, T_1)$ as the half-supporting plane containing triangle T_0 such that the boundary of $H_e(T_0, T_1)$ contains the shared-edge of both triangles.

   The necessary and sufficient condition for T_0 and T_1 to collide is that the non-shared vertex of T_1 passes through or touches $H_e(T_0, T_1)$. At this moment, there exists $t \in \mathbf{I}$ s.t. $\mathbf{n}_{T_0}(t) \cdot \mathbf{n}_{T_1}(t) \leq 0$. However, this violates the condition of a $(\pi, \beta, \mathbf{I})$-surface.

---

[1] The vertex is interior with respect to the $(\pi, \beta, \mathbf{I})$-surface.

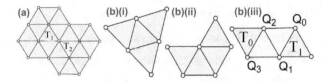

Figure 7.3: Properties of $(\pi, \beta, \mathbf{I})$-surface. (a) No collision for interior vertex-adjacent triangles. T_1 and T_2 do not collide; (b) Four edge-adjacent triangles.

3. **No collision for interior vertex-adjacent triangles:** If two vertex-adjacent triangles are interior with respect to the same $(\pi, \beta, \mathbf{I})$-surface, they do not collide.

   Justification: If they collide, there must be a vertex which moves across an edge surrounding it (Figure 7.3(a)). This is impossible as stated in "restriction of interior vertex".

4. **Restriction on interior triangles:** There is no collision for interior triangles colliding at the same side.

   Justification: Assume that there are two colliding interior triangles T_0 and T_1. When these two triangles approach and then collide, there exists at least one triangle adjacent to them and its image degenerates into a line. If there is no such a triangle adjacent to T_0 or T_1 degenerating into a line, the images and T_0 and T_1 will not touch or move across each other. This is a contradiction.

5. **Restriction on four edge-connected triangles:** For four edge-connected triangles, if all their vertices are interior, then two non-adjacent triangles do not collide with each other.

   Justification: A set of edge-connected triangles is defined as that any two triangles of the set can be reached from one triangle to another by traversing the edge-adjacent triangles. As can be seen in Figure 7.3(b), four edge-connected triangles admit of only three possible topologies: Figure 7.3(b)(i) and (ii) show the first two topologies, in which each pair of triangles shares a vertex. These two topologies do not consist of two non-adjacent triangles. Figure 7.3(b)(iii) shows the third topology, in which, due to the restriction imposed by the interior

136

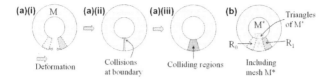

(a)(i) M (a)(ii) (a)(iii) (b) M* Triangles of M*

R_0 — R_1

Deformation | Collisions at boundary | Colliding regions | Including mesh M*

Figure 7.4: Collision with a $(\pi, \beta, \mathbf{I})$-surface. (a) As surface M deforms, collisions may occur at the boundaries or its interior regions; (b) If surfaces M and M^* belong to a larger surface, the first contact point will be detected. In this case, the triangles of M^* will not belong to the same $(\pi, \beta, \mathbf{I})$-surface as the ones that R_0 and R_1 belong to.

vertex, triangles T_0 and T_1 will not collide. If they collide, then there is at least one triangle T attaches at Q_0, Q_1, Q_2 or Q_3 that the image of T will degenerate into a line. This is not allowed.

Assume that the vertices of the triangles are not interior. Then, two non-adjacent triangles will not collide unless there are some triangles whose images are slim. This is also true for five edge-connected triangles.

6. **A condition for the collision of vertex-adjacent triangles:** If two vertex-adjacent triangles are interior with respect to the original surface and they collide with each other, then these collision events will be detected in the inter-collision detection process.

   Justification: According to the result of "no collision for interior vertex-adjacent triangles", one of the triangles must be exterior with respect to the $(\pi, \beta, \mathbf{I})$-surface. In fact, if these two triangles collide, they must collide at an edge or a vertex which is exterior. Thus, the edge or the vertex must belong to either isolated triangles or triangles of another $(\pi, \beta, \mathbf{I})$-surface. The result follows.

According to these properties, we can safely skip collision detection for interior adjacent-triangles of a $(\pi, \beta, \mathbf{I})$-surface. In fact, we will detect the first collision event for a closed orientable 2-manifold mesh[2]. Figure 7.4(a) shows how collisions can occur in a $(\pi, \beta, \mathbf{I})$-surface of a 2-manifold mesh with boundary. Figure 7.4(b) shows

---

[2]Readers can prove this according to the condition of a $(\pi, \beta, \mathbf{I})$-surface and the fact of non-penetration motion. The detail is given in Appendix G.

that if the cavity is filled with mesh M^*, the first collision event will be detected for the regions.

The proposed method fails if there are two triangles of a $(\pi, \beta, \mathbf{I})$-surface colliding at different sides. Consider that a surface is flat and convex initially. This kind of collision happens due to:

1. **Surface undergoing a large inplane deformation:** In this case, the smaller the local deformation of the surface is, the larger the original distance[3] between the two triangles is.

2. **Surface undergoing out of plane deformation:** In this case, the smaller the local curvature of the surface is, the larger the original distance between the two triangles is. The surface will form a loop.

If the surface is sufficiently stiff for limiting inplane deformation [4], the first case can be ignored. In the second case, we monitor the change of the surface angle when the merging process is performed. In the merging process, the surface angle in the lateral direction along the curve connecting the two triangles will reach $\frac{\pi}{2}$ quickly. This prevents the two triangles from being assigned to the same $(\pi, \beta, \mathbf{I})$-surface. Therefore, we skip the self-collision detection for a $(\pi, \beta, \mathbf{I})$-surface.

7.3.4 Robust intrinsic collision detection

We perform full collision detection for the potential colliding triangle pairs if they do not collide in the previous frame. For the pairs colliding in the previous frame, we perform the distance check. In the full collision detection test, the velocity-based method is employed for vertex–triangle and edge–edge cases. We also perform the backend test at the end of the frame. If the shortest distance between the two features

---

[3]This distance is measured before the surface is deformed.
[4]For general garment materials, it is common that the inplane deformation is small.

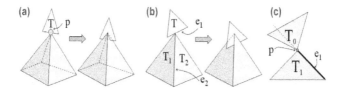

Figure 7.5: Illegal configurations of colliding feature pairs. (a) a vertex p sliding upon a triangle T; (b): an edge e_1 sliding upon another edge e_2; (c) a vertex p of a triangle T_0 sliding upon a triangle T_1 along e_1. In all cases, penetration will occur after a small displacement.

is less than the threshold (i.e. thickness of features) $\epsilon_c(> 0)$, then the two features collide.

As we compute the penetration-free motion space for the previous colliding vertices, the corresponding feature pairs cannot penetrate each other in the current frame. During the current frame, these kinds of feature pairs may take two possible actions: contact or separate. In order to determine whether they separate or not, we need to invoke only the shortest distance check. If the distance between these two features is larger than the threshold $\epsilon_s(\geq \epsilon_c)$, they are not longer in contact. The threshold ϵ_s is chosen to be larger than ϵ_c due to numerical errors.

7.3.5   Determining admissible colliding feature pairs

When we perform the velocity-based collision detection for the feature pairs, some colliding features may be in an illegal configuration. In an illegal configuration (Figure 7.5), the features will penetrate or pass through the surface if the features slide upon each other with a small displacement. We have such illegal configurations because we perform collision detection for the feature pairs without considering the geometry of the entire surface. We should ignore all the colliding feature pairs which are in such illegal configurations. We define a colliding feature pair to be *admissible* if and only if the two features do not penetrate each other or intersect the surface as they slide upon each other with a small enough displacement. According to this, we employ a geometry-based method that allows us to determine whether the colliding features are admissible for the two cases vertex-triangle and edge-edge. In the case of vertex-triangle, let p and T be the vertex and the triangle, respectively. The adjacent vertices of p must lie on the same side with respect to the triangle. In the case of edge-edge, let the two edges be e_1 and e_2. Assume that T_1 and T_2 are the two triangles to be checked. Let W be the plane formed by the collision normal and the middle point of the two points of the shortest distance of the two triangles. Then, their *third vertices*[5] must lie on the opposite sides with respect to W.

7.3.6 Robust computations of collision orientation in the presence of numerical errors

Collisions may happen on both sides of a deformable surface. Due to the resolution and smoothness of triangles, degenerate cases and the ubiquitous problem of numerical errors, it is difficult to determine the *relative orientation* (or orientation in short) of the colliding regions. The main issue is to develop an efficient method for determining the side of the regions that interacts with other objects at run-time. Several challenges become apparent in this problem. In the case of vertex-triangle, (1) when a vertex and a triangle are nearly coplanar, the determination of the direction of approach for the feature pairs is difficult; (2) when a vertex slides from a triangle to another triangle, the approaching direction can be inconsistent with the orientation as shown in Figure 7.6. In the case of edge-edge, (1) if two edges collide and they are nearly parallel to each other, the cross-product of their representative vectors is not reliable in the computation of the collision normal; (2) when an edge slides over another edge and then collides with a new edge, the approaching direction is inconsistent with the orientation. We propose two methods to compute the orientation and two methods to correct the orientation based on the determined configuration in the previous frame and the geometric constraint.

---

[5]The third vertex of a triangle is the vertex which does not belong to the colliding edge.

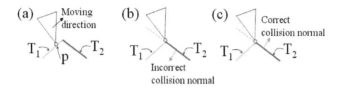

Figure 7.6: Hazard of relying solely on moving direction to determine collision normal. (a) vertex p is sliding from triangle T_1 to T_2; (b) incorrect collision normal is obtained by using the moving direction; (c) correct collision normal is obtained by using history.

- **Sliding in a determined configuration:**

  - **Vertex-triangle:** Assume that a vertex slides from one face to another face across an edge. In this case, the orientation should be consistent.

  - **Edge-edge:** Assume that both a vertex and an edge collide with a triangle simultaneously. Then, the orientation should be the same in both vertex-triangle and edge-edge configurations.

- **Geometric correction:**

  - **Vertex-triangle:** Assume that the adjacent vertices of p lie on the same side of the triangle. Before the collision event, p must lie on the side as these vertices do.

  - **Edge-edge:** Let the two edges be e_0 and e_1. Assume T_0 and T_1 are the two triangles involved. Let a plane be formed by the collision normal and the middle point of the two shortest distance points of the two triangles. Then, their third vertices must lie on the opposite sides with respect to the plane.

In order to obviate the possibility of a numerical error leading us to a wrong conclusion, we must verify whether the collision normal $\mathbf{n}$ is correct. For this purpose, the two triangles of the colliding regions are displaced rigidly with a small distance, the first triangle along the negative direction $(-\delta\mathbf{n})$ and the second along the positive direction $(\delta\mathbf{n})$, where δ is a small positive value. The two colliding regions may be determined as having the status of an intersection status before the displacement, it is not

141

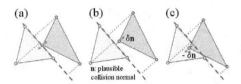

(a)   (b)   (c)

δn

n: plausible
collision normal

Figure 7.7: Verification of collision normal. (a) two colliding triangles; (b, c) compute the square of the distances between the vertices and the collision plane after moving the triangles with a small displacement δn or $-\delta$n, and sum them up. For the case with the larger change (i.e. b) of the sum before and after displacement, its collision normal is more reliable than the one of another case.

reliable to check during the displacement whether an intersection has occurred. This happens due to numerical errors. Instead, we propose a distance verification method (Figure 7.7) that compute the sum of the square distances (i.e. $\sum d_i^2$) between the vertices i of both triangles and the collision plane. If the collision normal is correct, the change in the sum will be larger than that obtained from the incorrect collision normal (i.e. $-\mathbf{n}$).

7.3.7 Collision detection among $(\pi, \beta, \mathbf{I})$-surfaces.

The surface is first decomposed into a set of $(\pi, \beta, \mathbf{I})$-surfaces (or simply (π, β)-surfaces if $I = [0, 1]$). Then, the backward voxel-based AABB (BVOX-AABB) scheme is adopted to collect the potential colliding pairs among (π, β)-surfaces and the *isolated triangles* (triangles with invalid canonical cones).

7.4 Penetration-free motion space for colliding pairs

When two unbreakable features F_1 and F_2 are in contact, they should not penetrate each other. In order to prevent the features from passing through each other, we impose the sufficient non-penetration constraint on the movement of their vertices. Assume that the collision normal of the first feature pair is $\mathbf{n}_c$ (i.e. $\mathbf{n}_c$ pointing to the space containing the contact point of F_2 just before collision). We impose a restriction on the current frame: the vertices of the first feature should not move in the direction of $\mathbf{n}_c$ while the vertices of the second feature should not move in the direction of $-\mathbf{n}_c$. After obtaining the new velocities of the vertices by solving the motion equation, we adjust the vertex velocities in order to satisfy this constraint. In order to solve this problem for the general case, we propose to compute a *constrained velocity cone* (CVC). This cone encloses all the possible velocity vectors of a vertex. The projections of the velocity vectors outside the CVC must be computed onto the CVC. For example, the CVC of the first feature is $C(-\mathbf{n}_c, \frac{\pi}{2})$. we need to compute their projections onto the CVC.

We associate each colliding vertex p with a collision constraint $\mathcal{Z}(C(\mathbf{n}, \beta), N)$, where $C(\mathbf{n}, \beta)$ is the CVC. For each collision event with collision normal $\mathbf{n}_c$, the vertices of the first feature is under a constraint $\mathcal{Z}(C(-\mathbf{n}_c, \frac{\pi}{2}), -\{\mathbf{n}_c\})$ while the vertices of the second feature is under a constraint $\mathcal{Z}(C(\mathbf{n}, \frac{\pi}{2}), \{\mathbf{n}_c\})$. However, a vertex may be involved in more than one collision event. Each collision event imposes one collision constraint $\mathcal{Z}_i$. This means that the combined collision constraint of m $\mathcal{Z}_i$'s is equal to $\mathcal{Z} = \mathcal{Z}_1 \cap \mathcal{Z}_2 \cdots \cap \mathcal{Z}_m$. If there are too many collision constraints, the motion space will be greatly reduced and the movement of the particles will be almost nil. The impact zone would be adopted [114, 33] [6] by treating the involving features as a rigid body. We did not observe this in our experiments.

We have proven that colliding feature pairs under the CVC constraint will not penetrate each other. Consider that there are two colliding features. They lie on the opposite sides of their collision plane. As the vertices of each colliding feature are not allowed to move across the collision plane, penetration is impossible.

7.5 Dynamic response

We need to constrain the particles so that the colliding features will not penetrate each other. We cannot afford to perform an analytical approach [19] based on the

---

[6]In our system, we have not implemented this method.

information of global collisions [9] in order to compute the contact forces. This kind of method is suitable for a scene which has a small number of contact points.

In order to provide an interactive response, the constraints are applied by the adjustment of force and velocity. When a vertex is subject to constraint $\mathcal{Z}$, the forces that act on the particle are modified before solving the motion equation. This forces the particle to lie inside its constrained motion space. If the net force acting on the particle is $\mathbf{F}$, $\mathbf{F}$ becomes $\mathbf{F} \cdot \mathcal{Z}$ after adjustment. Similarly, let $\mathbf{v}$ be the velocity of a vertex. Then, the velocity after adjustment is $\mathbf{v} \cdot \mathcal{Z}$. For an explicit integration scheme, the result will be the same whether the projection is done before or after solving the motion equation. For an implicit integration scheme, however, it is not true as the forces are spread out and affect other particles simultaneously. Thus, it will be more accurate to project the forces into the space of the collision constraint beforehand.

7.5.1 Friction and stiction

By employing the Coulomb's friction model, Bridson et al. [33] proposed to adjust the velocities of the particles after the motion equation was solved without considering the force distribution. If it uses an explicit integration method, the method is exact. This is not true if it uses an implicit integration scheme as the force acting on the particle will be spread out and affect other particles. In order to handle the cases of sticking or sliding, we propose to perform a static analysis and adjust the forces acting on the particles before solving the motion equation.

Kinetic energy of the new colliding feature pairs will be dissipated due to impact and friction. We apply the method proposed by Provot [114] to modify the velocities $\mathbf{v}$ of these particles. The velocity $\mathbf{v}'$ of a colliding particle after collision is computed as follows:

$$\mathbf{v}' = \begin{cases} \mathbf{v}_T - \mu_d |\mathbf{v}_N| \frac{\mathbf{v}}{|\mathbf{v}_T|} - k_c \mathbf{v_N} & \text{if } |\mathbf{v}_T| \geq \mu_d |\mathbf{v}_N| \\ -k_c \mathbf{v}_N & \text{otherwise} \end{cases} \tag{7.2}$$

where k_c is the coefficient of restitution ($0 \leq k_c \leq 1$), μ_d is the dynamic friction coefficient, $\mathbf{v}_T$ and $\mathbf{v}_N$ are the tangential velocity and the normal velocity of $\mathbf{v}$, respectively.

The energy of a particle performing sliding motion in the previous frame is dissipated mainly due to friction. In this case, we do not modify its velocity directly. Rather, we will first modify the forces exerting on the particle. Let $\mathbf{F}$ be the sum of the forces exerting on the particle excluding the friction force. If $\mathbf{F}$ is inside the admissible motion space $\mathcal{Z}$ of the particle, there is no friction. In the following, we assume that $\mathbf{F}$ is not inside $\mathcal{Z}$ and denote the static friction coefficient as μ_s.

1. **Sticking Particle:** If $|\mathbf{F}_T| \leq \mu_s|\mathbf{F}_N|$, the particle will, due to static friction, continue sticking on the surface. If $|\mathbf{F}_T| > \mu_s|\mathbf{F}_N|$, the particle will start to move upon the surface. In this case, the net force becomes $\mathbf{F}_T - \mu_d|\mathbf{F}_N|\frac{\mathbf{F}_T}{|\mathbf{F}_T|}$ due to dynamic friction.

2. **Sliding Particle:** If $\mathbf{v}$ is inside $\mathcal{Z}$ and $|\mathbf{F}_T| > \mu_d|\mathbf{F}_N|$, it is likely that the particle is moving away from the contact region but the distance between the particle and the contact region is not larger than the total thickness of features ϵ_c. Therefore, the net force becomes $\mathbf{F}_T - \mu_d|\mathbf{F}_N|\frac{\mathbf{F}_T}{|\mathbf{F}_T|}$.

   If the velocity is not inside $\mathcal{Z}$, the velocity becomes $\mathbf{v} \cdot \mathcal{Z}$. Let m be the mass of the particle. If $|\mathbf{F}_T| \leq \mu_d|\mathbf{F}_N|$ and $|(|\mathbf{F}_T| - \mu_d|\mathbf{F}_N|)h/m| \geq |\mathbf{v}_T|$, the particle will start to stick on the surface as the particle does not have a sufficient amount of energy to move beyond the time interval. Otherwise, the particle will keep on sliding because either the tangential force or its velocity is sufficiently large. The net force of the particle becomes $\mathbf{F}_T - \mu_d|\mathbf{F}_N|\frac{\mathbf{v}_T}{|\mathbf{v}_T|}$.

7.6 Experiments and results

First, we check our method for handling friction and stiction by comparing the motion of cloth with different friction parameters. Then we investigated how the proposed method is affected by the threshold β_{max}. We evaluated the best value for β_{max}.

The timings spent in different components of the proposed were analyzed. Third, we performed six animations to compare the performance of the proposed method with another two exact methods. Finally, another four animations in which complex interactions of deformable surfaces were demonstrated. These four animations were used for checking the robustness of the computation of collision orientation. Without other specification, we performed experiments on a 1.5GHz Pentium 4 PC with 1GB of main memory. Double precision was employed.

In a typical simulation, the surface would have some relatively flat regions as well as some highly deformed regions. Thus, we designed an example scene as shown in Figure 7.8(a). A rich deformation pattern of cloth could be obtained as it was in motion under the effect of the gravity and stochastic wind loading. The cloth model consisted of 19,200 triangles and 9,801 particles, and the rigid bodies consisted of 5,472 triangles and 2,827 particles. There were in total 2,400 frames and the time step was $\frac{1}{90}$ seconds.

We checked our friction model and compared the motion of deformable surfaces with different friction parameters. Figure 7.8 shows the snapshots from the experiment. Figure 7.8(a) shows the snapshots of the deformable surface with low friction and Figure 7.8(b) shows the snapshots of the deformable surface with high friction. It can be noticed that the deformable surface with low friction, it slides over the surface of the hemisphere and then onto an area of ground. However, if the friction force is sufficiently large, the deformable surface is stuck on the surface of the hemisphere.

We investigated how the proposed method is affected by the threshold β_{max} and evaluated the best value for β_{max}. We collected the statistics information of scene (a). In Figure 7.9(a), we varied the maximum surface angle β_{max} from 30 to 89 degrees. The larger β_{max} is, the shorter the time spent in self-collision detection. When β_{max} becomes larger, there will be more triangles that can be merged into a single (π, β)-surface. The number of (π, β)-surfaces will decrease. However, the speedup increases little when β_{max} becomes too large. The average self-collision detection time changes from 0.8 seconds to 0.26 seconds per frame. We have the best performance when β_{max} is 85 degrees. In this case, the average time per frame is 0.23 seconds. The detailed profile of timings in different components of the self-collision detection process is plotted in Figure 7.10. From 30 to 89 degrees, the traversal time becomes shorter while the decomposition time becomes longer. This allows us save on time spent in checking the non-colliding adjacent triangles during the BVOX-AABB tree traversal.

We tracked the performance of the proposed method frame by frame for different β_{max}. Figure 7.9(b) plots performance in the three cases with different β_{max}. Initially, when the surface is quite flat, the timing in self-collision detection is similar in all cases. However, when the surface starts to deform (as shown in Figure 7.8), the cases with larger β_{max} perform better. This result is consistent with what we saw in Figure 7.9(a). The timings in the total self-collision detection of the entire animation sequence in these three cases are 1910 (30 deg), 700 (60 deg), and 540 (85 deg) seconds, respectively. Figure 7.9(c) plots the graphs for the time spent in the entire collision detection process including cloth-rigid and cloth-cloth for the three cases. The case with $\beta_{max} = 85deg$ performed best. The timings in the total collision detection of the entire animation sequence in these three cases are 2070 (30 deg), 860(60 deg), and 780 (85 deg) seconds, respectively. The results show a significant improvement in performance and the robustness of the collision detection method with respect to other methods as we describe as follows.

After we had evaluated the best value for β_{max}, we performed experiments for another six examples and compared the performance of our method and the other two methods: BVOX-AABB tree and constant AABB tree [137]. The BVOX-AABB tree and the constant AABB tree are exact as they are able to collect all the colliding triangle pairs. In these experiments, almost every triangle of the surfaces participated into collision events. The threshold β_{max} was set as 85 deg. The time step in animation (1) was 0.033 seconds and for the rest animations, the time step was 0.02 seconds. For cloth-rigid collision detection, we adopted the tree traversal scheme. We did not perform collision detection for two triangles if they were adjacent to each other in these three methods. The velocity-based collision detection was employed in the intrinsic collision detection. For each experiment, we exported the vertex positions. Then, we

Animation	Cloth	Cloth Subdivision	Solid	Self-CD per frame (sec)			Cloth-Rigid-CD per frame (sec)			DYN (sec)	CGM (sec)
	#particles /triangles	#particles /triangles	#particles /triangles	(π, β, I)	BVOX-AABB	AABB	(π, β, I)	BVOX-AABB	AABB		
1. Slope	720/1,170	38,689/74,880	1,654/3,104	0.023	0.021	0.031	0.052	0.051	0.052	0.002	0.16
2. Nails	8,905/15,392	129,697/246,272	9,013/17,808	0.16	0.20	0.41	0.37	0.42	0.65	0.029	2.24
3. Sliding	8,181/16,000	128,721/256,000	3,118/5,968	0.22	0.28	0.56	0.43	0.48	0.75	0.028	2.25
4. Tiles	9,331/18,000	145,321/288,000	15,580/29,120	0.12	0.25	0.28	0.35	0.52	0.56	0.014	2.13
5. Draping	12,221/24,000	192,881/384,400	7,254/14,500	0.19	0.30	0.42	0.44	0.60	0.71	0.048	3.32
6. Windy	8,181/16,000	128,721/256,000	8,882/33,600	0.12	0.20	0.27	0.29	0.37	0.43	0.032	2.23

Table 7.1: Summary of the experimental results. Average time spent in the three tasks per time step: CD: collision detection; DYN: updating collision normal, collecting admissible colliding feature pairs, computing admissible motion space, and applying velocity adjustment due to new collisions; CGM: average time spent in analyzing the status of particles and using conjugate gradient method. *In animation 6, the number of primitives (particles/triangles) of the bumpy ground is not counted.

performed a post-refinement process to smoothen out the deformable surfaces by applying Loop's subdivision scheme [3]. Table 7.1 shows the summary of the time spent in self-collision detection, cloth-rigid collision detection, dynamic response computation and solving the system matrix, and the number of particles and triangles of the objects. Overall, the best performance was that of our proposed method. Next is the BVOX-AABB method. Last is the AABB tree method.

Figures 7.11 and 7.12 show the snapshots from six animations. Each animation had stochastic wind blowing on the deformable surfaces. In Animation (1), a net slips over the head of a nail, then it slips on a bumpy slope, collides with a small nail and then falls onto an area of ground covered with sharp crests. In Animation (2), a large net falls over scepters. Each scepter has a long leg sticking out onto an area of bumpy ground. Near the end of the animation, the net collides with itself. In Animation (3), a rectangular cloth falls on a hemisphere and then it slips on a rough surface. In the end, it falls onto an area of ground covered with sharp crests. In Animation (4), a long ribbon slips over bumpy tiles. Two rows of tiles of twelve tiles are placed symmetrically in a slightly sloppy way. Between each pair of tiles is a small gap. In the middle of the two rows is a large gap. Near the end of the animation, the ribbon collides with itself before disappearing into the large gap. In Animation (5), a rectangular cloth falls over two tables, one with a smooth surface (low friction) and another with a rough surface (high friction). In the beginning, it falls onto both tables. One part of the cloth slips over the smooth table. Another part sticks onto the other table. Wrinkles form in a natural way. In Animation (6), 80 needles are placed on the surface of a hemisphere. They form a spiral pattern. The height of the needles is gradually decreased from the outer region to the inner region. The needles are removed one by one from the outer region to the inner region during the animation. Finally, there is one needle left at the top of the hemisphere. The ridges formed by the edges of the triangles show clearly underneath the deformable surface. The wind loading factor was high in Animation 6.

Finally, we conducted another four examples to test the robustness of the computation of collision orientation. Collision orientation was computed at run-time. Figure 7.13 shows a cape and nine rings. In the beginning, nine rings slip downwards on the surface of the cape. They slide closely upon the cape. In the middle of the animation, one ring interacts with the cape in a windy environment and the other rings drop onto the area of bumpy ground. First, the ring lies on the cape when a portion of the cape lies on a smooth surface. Then, the ring is blown in the right direction and hit onto the cape near the waist of the mannequin. After that, the ring falls onto the area of bumpy ground. During the animation, collision orientation between the ring and cape was correctly computed.

Figure 7.14 shows a multi-ribbon consisting of nine long ribbons. The nine ribbons interact with each other on both sides of their surfaces while they falls onto obstacles. In the end of the animation, the multi-ribbon is trapped into the obstacles and the nine ribbons entangle together. The collision detection method employed in this animation is the piecewise continuous collision detection. The zoom-in views of the multi-ribbon can be found in Figure 7.15

In the third and fourth examples, the experiments were run on a computer with 3.0GHz Pentium 4 CPU, 1GB of main memory. It should be noticed that collision detection was performed in the time domain by using our proposed heuristic rules combined with our cache architecture.

In the third example, we have two rectangular pieces of cloth with different sizes. Figure 7.16 shows the snapshots. The larger one is placed at the bottom relatively to the smaller one. The two pieces are displaced by 5 units in the normal direction of the cloth surfaces. The larger one has 31,250 triangles and 15,876 vertices and the smaller one has 20,000 triangles and 10,201 vertices. There is a scepter sticking out of the area of ground. The head of the scepter is a hemisphere with a rough surface. In the beginning, the two pieces of cloth fall on the head of the scepter stably. Wrinkles appear in both pieces naturally. The smaller one stacks on top of the larger one. The wrinkles of the smaller piece of cloth appear in the wrinkles of the large piece of cloth. Some of the wrinkles are overlapped closely. The outer regions of both pieces of cloth continue falling downwards. A rich pattern of wrinkles is produced. After both pieces are draped stably and hanging on the head of the scepter, a stochastic wind loading is activated. There are 2,500 frames. On average it takes 0.82 seconds and 3.8 seconds in collision detection (including both inter-collision and intra-collision) and evaluation of the motion equation, respectively. On average there are 125,000 potential colliding pairs (i.e. 1,875,000 feature pairs). Therefore, on average, it takes 6.56×10^{-6} seconds to perform collision detection for one potential colliding pair.

In the forth example, we have two rectangular pieces of cloth with different sizes and a net with rectangular holes. Figure 7.17 shows the snapshots. Similar draping patterns are obtained as in the third example. The pieces of cloth are placed from bottom to top in the order that the larger rectangular piece of cloth, the smaller rectangular piece of cloth, and then the net. Between two neighboring pieces of cloth, the distance is 5 units in the vertical direction. The larger rectangular one has 31,250 triangles and 15,876 vertices, the smaller rectangular one has 20,000 triangles and 10,201 vertices, and the net has 7,200 triangles and 4,185 vertices. There are 2,500 frames. On average it takes 1.23 seconds and 4.2 seconds in collision detection and evaluation of the motion equation, respectively. On average, there are 212,000 potential colliding pairs (i.e. 3,180,000 feature pairs). Therefore, on average, it takes 5.8×10^{-6} seconds to perform collision detection for one potential colliding pair.

7.7 Summary and discussion

In this chapter, we have introduced a new surface called $(\pi, \beta, \mathbf{I})$-surface in order to achieve robust collision detection between deformable surfaces. The decomposition of a surface into a finite set of $(\pi, \beta, \mathbf{I})$-surfaces also allows for the efficient and robust self-collision detection of an orientable 2-manifold surface. This is because we have shown that for a surface that maintains the $(\pi, \beta, \mathbf{I})$-properties self-collisions are not possible. Therefore, self-collision detection is skipped for each $(\pi, \beta, \mathbf{I})$-subsurface.

We have proposed a variety of methods for determining the validity of the colliding feature pairs and two methods for computing the relative orientation of colliding regions. In order to prevent the surface penetration of the colliding pairs, the scheme of penetration-free motion space was proposed. By restricting the movement of the particles inside the motion space, for a suitable time step, we can guarantee that there will be no penetration during the subsequent time step of the motion of the objects.

We have also proposed a method to handle friction and stiction by checking the particle velocities and incorporating the friction formulation into the motion equation when the conditions arise. Some problems still require further research:

- Computing the accurate collision orientation is still difficult for arbitrary deformable surfaces. We are investigating an image-based method to compute collision orientation. This method is suitable for the penetration case, the non-penetration case, or degenerate cases. Thus, it can tolerate numerical errors up to a certain degree. We render both colliding regions and their local neighbors onto an image plane and check the pixels which are covered by both of them. The determination of the orientation is based on the priority list: (1) all pixels belonging to one region S; (2) all pixels of a surface are surrounded by the pixels of another surface S; and (3) majority of pixels belonging to S. The collision normal with respect to S should be consistent with the viewing direction. By using *NV_occlusion_query* [1], we can retrieve the number of pixels for each region without needing to read the content of the image buffers.

- The original surface may contain holes or narrow regions. The proposed method may fail to detect the first contact time for this kind of surface. We investigate a method to fill the holes or the cavities with some ghost surfaces to the original surface and these surfaces form a composite surface. When we perform the decomposition process for collision detection, we use the composite surface instead of the original surface.

- Although the proposed method prevents penetration, it excludes some possible motion. For example, the method does not allow two colliding edges to "rotate" about each other. In order to solve this problem, the motion-space should be expanded.

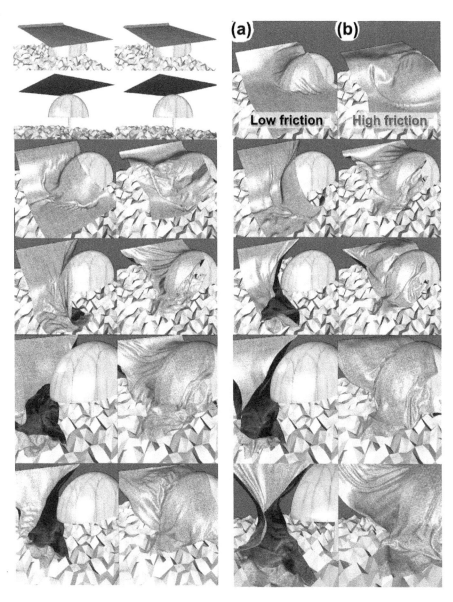

Figure 7.8: Example one: Complex interactions between cloth and rigid bodies. (a) low friction coefficient; (b) high friction coefficient. The particles along the thick lines (indicated in the upper left picture) are fixed during the simulation.

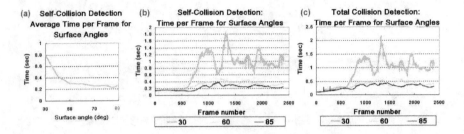

Figure 7.9: Example one: Overall performance.

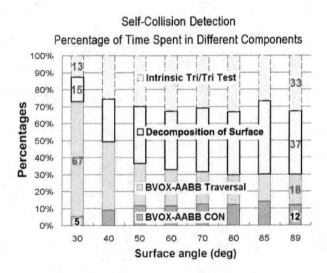

Figure 7.10: Example one: Percentage of time spent in different components of the proposed method. Intrinsic Tri/Tri Test: time domain triangle/triangle collision detection; Decomposition of surface: decomposing a surface into $(\pi, \beta, \mathbf{I})$-surfaces; BVOX-AABB Traversal: traversing BVOX-AABB trees to collect potential colliding triangle pairs; BVOX-AABB CON: construction of BVOX-AABB trees for $(\pi, \beta, \mathbf{I})$-surfaces. The numbers (in the bars) indicate the percentage of the corresponding item contributing to the self-collision detection process.

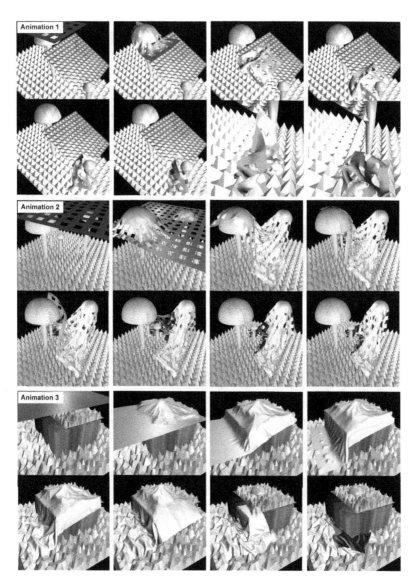

Figure 7.11: Animations 1, 2 and 3. The stiffnesses of the springs in animations 1, 2 and 3 are 1000, 1500 and 2000, respectively.

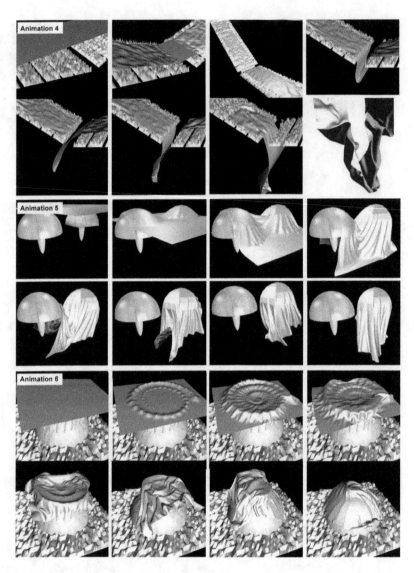

Figure 7.12: Animations 4, 5 and 6. The stiffnesses of the springs in animations 4, 5 and 6 are 1000, 2000 and 2000, respectively. In Animation 6, the ridges formed by the edges of the triangles are clearly shown underneath the deformable surface.

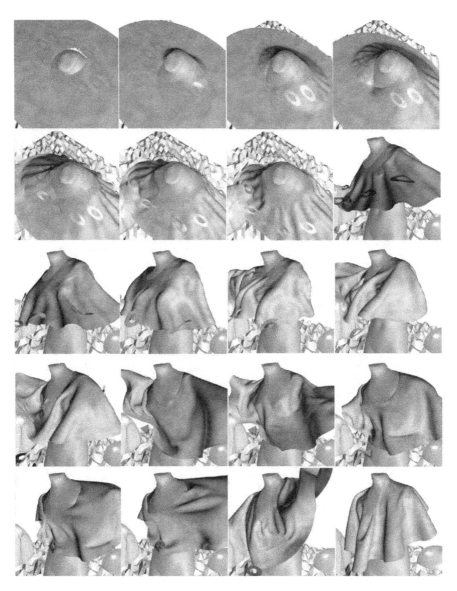

Figure 7.13: Snapshots: nine rings slip over a cape in a windy environment. The small triangle points to a small ring interacting with the cape near the waist of the mannequin. (Robustness computation of collision orientation.)

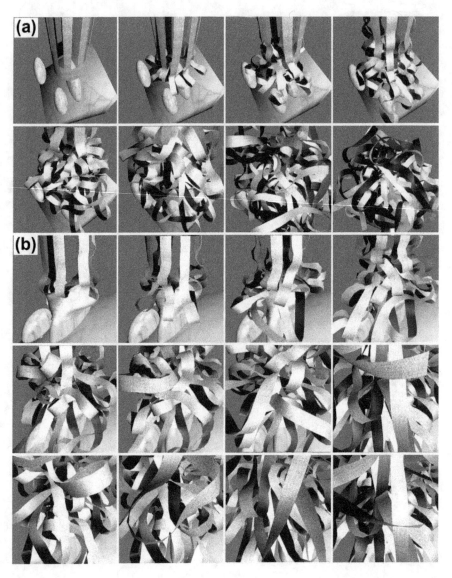

Figure 7.14: Snapshots: a multi-ribbon consisting of nine long ribbons fall onto obstacles. (a) shows the far view; (b) shows the close-up view. (Robustness computation of collision orientation.)

Figure 7.15: Zoom-in view: a multi-ribbon consisting of nine long ribbons fall onto obstacles. There is complicated interaction among nine ribbons. Some parts of the ribbons are lying on the other parts of the ribbons. (Robustness computation of collision orientation.)

Figure 7.16: Snapshots for two rectangular pieces of cloth: draping and fluttering in a windy environment. There is wind blowing on the cloth pieces. The zoom-in view of the image (*) is shown in the middle in the last row. The image at the lower right corner shows the wireframe of (*). (Robustness computation of collision orientation.)

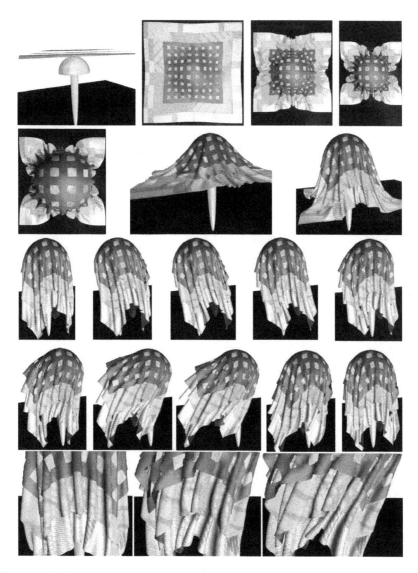

Figure 7.17: Snapshots for two rectangular pieces of cloth and a net with rectangular holes: draping and fluttering in a windy environment. There is wind blowing on the cloth pieces. The images at the bottom row are zoom-in views of a portion of the cloth pieces captured from the scene. (Robustness computation of collision orientation.)

161

Chapter 8

Handling Deformable Surfaces with Irregular and Sharp Features

8.1 Introduction and motivation

If a deformable surface consists of sharp features, the aspect ratio[1] of the elements (or triangles) of the features is large. The elements of a large aspect ratio aversely affect the condition number[2] of the system [28], leading to poor system convergence. An intuitive way of ameliorating this problem is to increase the mesh resolution[3] by performing triangulation or resampling, but even after these processes, sharp features will still remain. Not only is increasing mesh resolution not entirely effective against poor system convergence, it can lead to problems in integration evaluation and collision detection. In integration evaluation, increases in the number of particles increases the size of the system matrix. This means that it will take longer time to evaluate the motion equation. Similarly, in collision detection, increases in the number of elements increases in the number of potential colliding pairs at each frame, with the result that it takes longer to check for collisions.

---

[1]The aspect ratio of an element is the ratio of its maximum to its minimum width [28].

[2]The condition number associated with a numerical problem is a measure of that quantity's amenability to digital computation, that is, how well-posed the problem is. Quoted from http://www.brainyencyclopedia.com/encyclopedia/c/co/condition_number.html. Last visit on 29 Sep. 2004.

[3]Owing to the interaction between deformable surfaces and other objects, the elements of the deformable surfaces are required to be uniformed.

According to the Courant condition, the time step is inversely proportional to the mesh dimension. We need to use a smaller time step in order to maintain the stability of the system for an explicit integration scheme when high resolution mesh is used. Even by employing an implicit scheme, we still need to decrease the time step in order to maintain the stability of the system in the presence of interactions. In the presence of interactions between objects, the system will easily become unstable. This is due to collisions which increase the stiffness of the system. Collisions change the state of the system and make some regions of the deformable surface store an excessive amount of energy. Moreover, the time step must be sufficiently small in order to make sure that the triangles do not flip their orientation in one step due to an inplane movement.

If the time step decreases, we will need a greater number of iterations to perform the process of integration and collision detection in order to complete a simulation for a fixed duration. Besides these two time–consuming tasks, the time spent in the management of the data structure of the system will also increase significantly. Therefore, the total cost will be much higher when high resolution meshes are used compared to using meshes with low resolution.

8.2   Outline

We propose a two-layer scheme to animate a deformable surface with sharp features and irregular holes stably without using high resolution meshes. This method is employed if the response time is more important than the accuracy of the motion of the deformable surfaces.

We assume that the original deformable surface M_O with sharp features is represented as a set of polygons. Each polygon is a collection of line segments. The line segments of each polygon are organized in counter-clockwise.

In the two-layer scheme, we use two meshes to model the original surface M_O: one for rendering and another for obtaining the dynamics of the deformable surface.

We denote the mesh for rendering and the mesh for dynamics computation by M_R and M_D, respectively. We call M_R the appearance mesh and M_D the ghost mesh. The meshes M_R and M_D capture the geometry structure and the physical properties of the deformable surface, respectively. Thus, the set of polygons defines the contours of the appearance mesh M_R. We embed M_R inside M_D. Therefore, M_R is treated as a sub-region of M_D. The motion of M_D is computed based on the laws of Newtonian mechanics. Consequently, the motion of the sub-regions of M_D would then be conformed to the laws of Newtonian mechanics.

The criteria of M_D should be that the dynamic behavior of its structure should be stable and the computation of it should be fast. For this purpose, we employ a spring-mass system to capture the physical properties of M_D. Thus, we require that the mesh should be structured and the discretization should be uniform so that every part can be deformed uniformly. Moreover, the warp(vertical) and weft (horizontal) directions can be defined clearly. In this study, we employ the rectilinear grid which satisfies the criteria. There are no poor elements with bad aspect ratio in the rectilinear grid. Grid cells have identical dimension and as a result, there is no preference in the deformation direction among different cells. Other properties, such as, anisotropy and inhomogeneity, can be added if necessary.

The organization of the subsequent sections is that Section 8.3 proposes the method to compute the two-layer representation of the original surface. The construction of both meshes is presented. The description is given on how the spring-mass system is embedded into the ghost mesh. Section 8.4 presents two examples in which deformable surfaces with sharp features are animated naturally. The interactions between the sharp features are demonstrated. We present the summary and discussion in Section 8.5.

8.3 Construction of an appearance mesh and a ghost mesh

First, we need to discretize the original surface into grid cells and collect the grid cells overlapping with the original surface. These grid cells form the geometry of the ghost mesh M_D. Second, we embed the spring-mass system into the ghost mesh. Finally, the appearance mesh and the ghost mesh are triangulated. The association relationship is built for particles between the appearance mesh and the ghost mesh .

8.3.1 Collection of cells for a ghost mesh

We compute the AABB[4] for the appearance mesh M_R and denote it by $AABB(M_R)$. The bounding box $AABB(M_R)$ is discretized into grid cells based on the numbers of divisions along the horizontal direction and the vertical direction. The numbers of divisions are provided by a user. Each grid cell is labeled by a pair of grid coordinates (x, y) based on its location along the x-axis and the y-axis.

We need to determine two kinds of cells: i-cell and o-cell. These cells form the geometry of the ghost mesh M_D. Formally, we define these two kinds of cells as follows:

Definition 8.1 : A grid cell is called an o-cell if the cell lies entirely inside the region of the original mesh M_O. An o-cell does not overlap with any polygon lines.

Definition 8.2 : A grid cell is called an i-cell if the cell overlaps with a line segment of M_O.

We determine first the i-cells. We scan the grid cells along each line segment of each polygon by using the digital differential analyzer (DDA) [53]. In every step, we need to record all the grid cells which overlap with the line segment. The intersection

---

[4]The oriented bound box $OBB(M_R)$ of M_R will give a more compact region.

points are recorded also. Consider that the angle of a line segment L is in the range of 0 to 45 degrees and the current grid cell is at coordinates (x, y). When we advance along only the x-axis, we need to record the grid cell $(x + i, y)$. Whenever we advance to a grid cell in both x-axis and y-axis, we need to check the grid cell $(x, y + 1)$ for intersection with the line segment as well. Then, we check the next grid cell $(x + 1, y + 1)$. Other kinds of line segments are just the mirror or the reverse mirror of the line segment L. Hence, the similar strategy is performed for these line segments. In order to avoid numerical errors for the grid coordinates of the endpoints, we should use their exact representation of their coordinates stored in the machine. After processing a polygon, we have all the intersection points between the grid lines and all the line segments of the polygon, and the list of i-cells. During this process, the information of the endpoints of the line segments, like other intersection points, are recorded in the i-cells to which the endpoints belong.

Each intersection point between the grid lines and the line segments are recorded in the form of coordinates with respect to the grid cells. These coordinates are called boundary coordinates. The coordinate system associated with a grid cell is normalized as $([0, 1], [0, 1])$. The origin $(0,0)$ is defined at the lower left vertex of the grid cell. The coordinates $(1,0)$, $(1,1)$ and $(0, 1)$ are defined at the lower right, the upper right and the upper left vertices of the grid cell, respectively. The boundary coordinates (u, v) of an intersection point (on the grid boundary) are just the interpolation parameters based on two vertices of the grid cell. Formally, the boundary coordinates (u, v) of a point $\mathbf{p}$ with respect to a grid cell are defined as:

$$(u, v) \equiv \begin{cases} (u = \frac{p - p_0}{\|p_1 - p_0\|}, v = 0) & \text{If } p \text{ lies on line segment } \overline{p_0 p_1} \\ (u = 1, v = \frac{p - p_1}{\|p_2 - p_1\|}) & \text{If } p \text{ lies on line segment } \overline{p_1 p_2} \\ (u = \frac{p - p_3}{\|p_2 - p_3\|}, v = 1) & \text{If } p \text{ lies on line segment } \overline{p_3 p_2} \\ (u = 0, v = \frac{p - p_0}{\|p_3 - p_0\|}) & \text{If } p \text{ lies on line segment } \overline{p_0 p_3} \text{ (not including } p_0)) \end{cases} \tag{8.1}$$

It can be observed that the boundary coordinates (u, v) of an intersection point satisfy the condition $uv(1 - u)(1 - v) \equiv 0$.

After collecting the i-cells, we employ the well-known in-out test [53] to determine the o-cells. We sort the i-cells in ascending order with respect to their x-coordinates for each scan line. We check the grid cells between (x_0, y) and (x_1, y) and determine whether these cells overlap with the original surface M_O. This is done by employing the in-out test. We can determine whether these grid cells belong to the interior of M_O. After the process, we obtain a list of o-cells. At this stage, we have successfully discretized the given surface M_O into grid cells composed of i-cells and o-cells. The collection of the i-cells and o-cells forms the ghost mesh.

8.3.2 Embedding physical structure inside a ghost mesh

We embed the physical structure into the i-cells and o-cells of the ghost mesh. The assignment of the physical parameters to the cells is based on the structure of the underlying physical models. In our current implementation, we adopt Provot's spring-mass model [114]. The natural lengths are computed for structural, flexion and shearing springs.

8.3.3 Triangulation of meshes

Figure 8.1 shows the triangulation of M_R and the particles. We have three kinds of particles: independent particles, dependent particles and ghost particles. The independent particles and ghost particles form the set of the particles of the ghost mesh. The independent particles and the dependent particles form the set of the particles of the appearance mesh. The positions and velocities of the dependent particles are obtained by performing interpolation between the independent particles and the ghost particles. The dependent particles are obtained when the i-cells and o-cells are computed. What remains is to triangulate the ghost mesh and the appearance mesh. We need to obtain the set of triangles of both meshes for the purposes of collision detection and rendering.

The triangles of M_D can be obtained by triangulating each of i-cells and o-cells into two triangles. In the appearance mesh M_R, we have two kinds of triangulation: o-cell

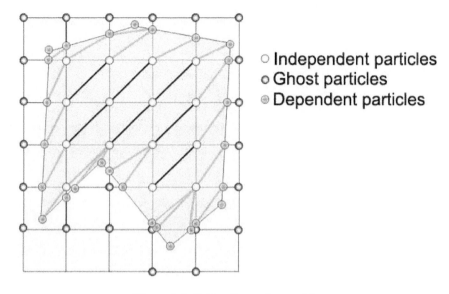

○ Independent particles
◎ Ghost particles
◉ Dependent particles

Figure 8.1: Grid cells overlay on M_R.

triangulation and i-cell triangulation. In o-cell triangulation, we divide each o-cell into two triangles. However, in i-cell triangulation, we need to check for the intersection points and the grid vertices in order to determine the regions of M_R. Then, these regions are triangulated. There are three major steps in i-cell triangulation: mapping interested points to natural coordinate, computing the regions of M_R and triangulating the regions.

We have recorded the information about the intersection points and the endpoints of the line segments for each i-cell when we collected the i-cells. The coordinates of the intersection points are given in the normalized form (u, v), where u is the horizontal coordinate measured from left to right and v is the vertical coordinate measured from bottom to top. The origin is the lower left vertex of the grid cell. Let G be a set composed of the intersection points belonging to the grid cell and the four grid vertices. We map linearly each of the elements of G into a single value. The value is defined as the length measured from the lower left vertex (0,0) to the position of the element along the boundary of the grid cell in counter-clockwise direction. Therefore, the range of the mapping value is $[0, 4)$. We call this mapping value the *natural coordinate* of the element. The mapping function $f_n(\mathbf{p})$ for a point $\mathbf{p}$ with coordinates (u, v) is defined as follows:

$$f_n(\mathbf{p}) \equiv \begin{cases} 4 - v & \text{if } u = 0 \text{ and } v > 0 \\ u + 3v - 2uv & \text{otherwise} \end{cases} \tag{8.2}$$

We say that a point $\mathbf{q}_1$ whose natural coordinate is next to another point $\mathbf{q}_0$ is that if $f_n(\mathbf{q}_1)$ is the smallest value larger than $f_n(\mathbf{q}_0)$ or $f_n(\mathbf{q}_1)$ is the smallest and $f_n(\mathbf{q}_0)$ is the largest.

In order to construct regions of M_R in a grid cell, we pick an intersection point $\mathbf{p}$. Assume that $\mathbf{p}$ belongs to a line segment L of a polygon. Then, there must exist another intersection point or an endpoint $\mathbf{p}'$ belonging to L. Without lose of generality, we assume that $\mathbf{p}$ is ordered before $\mathbf{p}'$ with respect to L. We start from $\mathbf{p}$ and then visit $\mathbf{p}'$ and the other points until we reach $\mathbf{p}$ again. All these points enclose a region which belongs to the original surface M_O. During the process, all the points are marked when they are visited.

If a point $\mathbf{p}_1$ that we visit is an endpoint, the next point we will visit must be an intersection point or an endpoint that belongs to the next line segment of the polygon. If the point $\mathbf{p}_1$ that we visit is the second intersection point of L, then we must visit an element of G whose natural coordinate is next to $\mathbf{p}_1$. We repeat the process to visit the next point. If the first point $\mathbf{p}$ is visited again, the construction of a region for M_R is completed.

After constructing a region for M_R, we construct another new region by visiting another unmarked intersection point as the first point of the new region. The process is repeated until all the intersection points have been visited. Then we check whether there are any endpoints not marked yet. If so, there must exist some polygons which lie totally inside the grid cell. These remaining polygons may or may not form holes of the original surface. We should perform a subtraction between the grid cell and each remaining polygon in order to obtain the regions belonging to the original surface. After that, we triangulate all the regions for M_R.

There are two degeneracies: an endpoint lying on the grid boundary and a line intersecting only a grid cell at one point. If an endpoint lies on the grid boundary, we might have an intersection point which lies near the endpoint due to numerical error. A very slim triangle will be created for M_R. If a line intersects only a grid cell at one point, the regions of M_R may not be formed correctly. In order to handle these two cases, we can perturb the vertices of the grid cell with a small value. The two degeneracies are avoided. After that, the slim triangles are removed.

8.3.4   The bounds on the number of ghost particles

By using the two-layer approach, we need extra memory to store the ghost particles. We prove that the number of ghost particles is not large. Two theorems on the bounds of the number of ghost particles will be proven.

Theorem 8.1 : Let n be the number of dependent particles. If a polygon does not lie entirely inside a grid cell, then the number of ghost particle is at most $2n$.

Proof: Consider that a dependent particle lies on a grid line. If there is only one dependent particle lies on a grid line, then there must be an independent particle as an endpoint of the grid line. If there are more than one dependent particle lying on the grid line, then we need at most two ghost particles to act as the two endpoints of the grid line. In both situations, the number of ghost particles is less than or equal to twice the number of dependent particles.

In the case of a dependent particle lying inside a grid cell, we need two ghost particles in order to make sure that the dependent particle lying inside a grid cell which is formed by ghost particle(s) and independent particle(s). This is justified as follows. Assume that the dependent particle belongs to a line segment L. In order that a dependent particle lies inside a grid cell, there must be an intersection point $\mathbf{q}$ which belongs to L. There must be two particles which already bound $\mathbf{q}$. These two particles lie on the boundary of the grid cell. Thus, we need at almost two extra ghost particles to bound the dependent particle inside the grid cell. □

It can be noticed that if a polygon lies entirely inside a grid cell, then we need at most four ghost particles to bound the polygon.

We define that a set of connected line segments inside a grid cell is that any two line segments can be reached by visiting the line segments which are connected by the endpoints. The involved line segments and endpoints must appear inside the grid cell. Consider that M_R is formed by a polyline and M_R does not entirely lie inside a grid cell. We have the following theorem:

Theorem 8.2 : If the following two conditions are satisfied, then the number of ghost particles is at most $n + k$, where n is the number of intersection points and k is the number of endpoints of the polyline. (1): a grid cell overlaps with at most one line segment if there is no endpoint lying inside the grid cell; (2): a grid cell overlaps with exactly two or more connected line segments if their common points (endpoints of line segments) lie inside the grid cell.

Proof: Consider the case of a dependent particle lying on a grid line. By the assumption, it implies that there are no more than two line segments overlapping the grid line. Therefore, one of the grid points of the grid line must be an independent particle. Thus, we need one ghost particle so that the dependent particle is bounded.

In the case of a dependent particle lying inside a grid cell, then this dependent particle must be an endpoint. In order that there is an endpoint inside a grid cell, there must be two line segments that connect this endpoint. These two line segments may be connected with other line segments and there must exist two line segments that intersect the grid lines of the grid cell at two intersection points. Now, a vertex of the grid cell must be an independent particle; otherwise, four points of the grid cell are ghost particles. Therefore, we need one extra ghost particle to bound the endpoint inside the grid cell. □

8.3.5   Dynamics and collision detection

The forces exerting on the vertices of M_R are distributed to the vertices of M_D according to the barycentric coordinates (treated as weights). The motion equation for the master particles is constructed. Then the new positions and velocities of the master particles are computed. After that, the positions and velocities of the slave particles are updated accordingly.

In our implementation, collision detection is carried out only for the triangles of the ghost mesh. The scheme of the $(\pi, \beta, \mathbf{I})$-surface decomposition is employed for self-collision detection. The BVOX-AABB tree is adopted for inter-collision detection.

8.4   Experiments and results

We applied our proposed method to model cloth pieces. We performed two experiments and the complexity of the deformable surfaces was around twenty thousand triangles. The angle at some of the sharp features is less than 10 degrees. The stability of the proposed method was tested. We report only the construction time for the two-layer meshes. The dynamics computation time and the collision detection time with similar object complexity have been reported in the previous chapters. The experiments were run on a 3.0GHz Pentium 4 PC with 1GB of main memory. A constant time step $\frac{1}{90}$ was used in the experiments.

In the first experiment, we model a piece of 23-star scarf with a 8-star hole in its the center. These 23 fringes with sharp features emit from the center of the scarf. Figure 8.2(a) shows the initial shape of the scarf before its deformation. The grid dimension is 180x180 (grid cells). The ghost mesh has 21,455 triangles, 15,931 vertices and 84,567 springs. It spent 0.08 seconds and 0.13 seconds in computing the i-cells and the construction of the spring-mass system for the ghost mesh, respectively. We also varied the dimensions of the grid from 30x30 to 240x240. The timings of discretization of the given surface and the timings of construction of the spring-mass system changed from 0.05 to 0.14 (sec) and from 0.06 to 0.23 (sec), respectively.

The scarf is placed above a mannequin. In the beginning, it falls onto the mannequin under gravity. The neck of the mannequin passes through the star-shape hole as shown in Figure 8.2(b). The region of the scarf around the hole hangs on the shoulder of the mannequin as shown in Figure 8.2(c). This supports the scarf and prevents the scarf from falling off the mannequin. The rest of the scarf still falls a bit further until it bends inwards. The fringes hit and cling onto the body surface of the mannequin around the waist as shown in Figure 8.2(d). At this moment, a stochastic wind loading is activated and it is blowing onto fringes from the right to the left side as shown in Figure 8.2(e). This external force acts on the fringes and makes them flutter in the air. Figure 8.2(f) is a snapshot of the scarf taken from another viewing direction. Figure 8.3 shows a side view of the fluttering scarf.

In the second experiment, we model a piece of 30-star cloth with a 5-star hole in its the center. Figure 8.4(a) shows the initial shape of the cloth piece before its deformation. The grid dimension is 180x180 (grid cells). The ghost mesh has 24,030 triangles and 18,254 vertices. The similar construction time for the two-layer was obtained. Figure 8.4(b) shows the setup of the scene in which there are 18 green sticks hanging in the air. Each stick has a light blue ball attached at its lower tip. After the scarf is released (Figure 8.4(c)), it falls onto the upper part of the sticks quickly. The inner region of the scarf slides slowly upon the sticks while the fringes still fall towards the area of ground. As the tips of the upper part of the sticks is very sharp, some parts of the scarf are trapped at the tips of these sticks as shown in Figure 8.4(d). Near the end of the animation, these thirty fringes hit and slide upon the area of ground. Figure 8.4(e)(f) shows the final configuration of the fringes.

8.5 Summary and discussion

We have presented a two-layer approach for performing simulation of deformable surfaces with shape features. The performance is mainly depended on the evaluation of the ghost mesh for dynamics and collision detection. The appearance mesh is used for displaying the final shape of the deformable surface.

By employing the proposed method, we do not need to increase the resolution of the mesh in order to maintain the stability of the system. Although we lose the accuracy of the elements at the boundary of the deformable surface, we have reduced significantly the time spent in the evaluation of the motion equation and the process of collision detection.

This method is suitable for handling the developable surfaces [25, 125, 86] with sharp features as this kind of surfaces can be flatten without distortion. For this kind of surfaces, the Gaussian curvature vanishes at every points.

Our proposed method works as if we performed a texture mapping onto a target. The texture is the given surface and the target is the ghost mesh. Therefore, as an extension of the current method, we can render the given surface orthogonally into a viewport. During the process, the dimension of the viewing frustum is the same as the dimension of the AABB of the given surface. We set the alpha value of a pixel to one if the pixel is covered by the given surface; the alpha value of a pixel is zero if the pixel is not covered by the given surface. After that, the AABB is discretized into grid cells. If the grid cells contain at least one pixel with alpha value one, the grid cells form the geometry of the ghost mesh. The particles of the ghost mesh are the vertices of the grid cells. The image of the given surface is texture mapped onto the ghost mesh. Therefore, we need to maintain only one mesh, in this case. However, there is one disadvantage of using this texture mapping scheme. As we do not have the geometry information of the texture, we cannot perform accurate collision detection for the boundary elements.

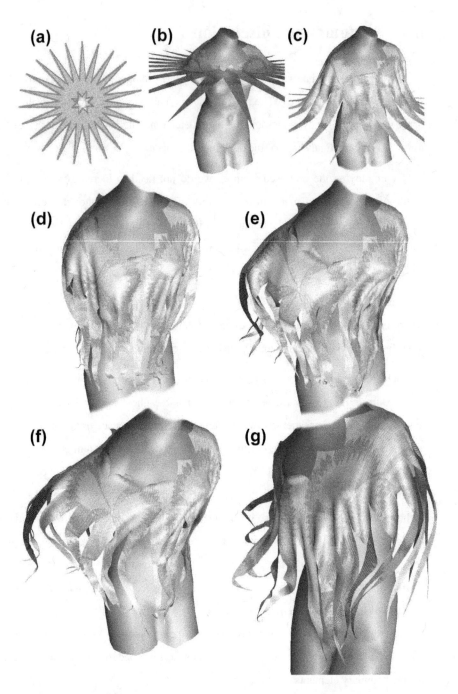

Figure 8.2: The snapshots of the experiment. The upper left image (a) shows the star-shape scarf in 2D space.

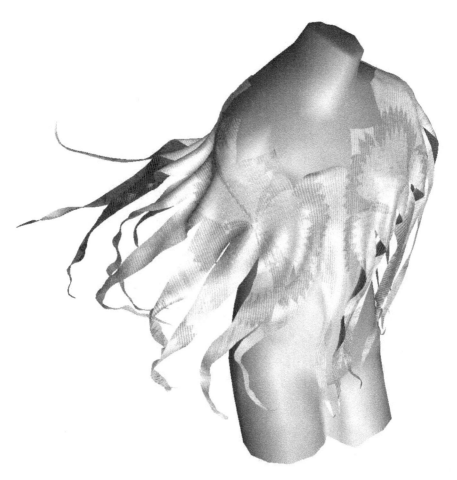

Figure 8.3: A side view of the scarf. The sharp fringes are fluttering naturally under stochastic wind loading.

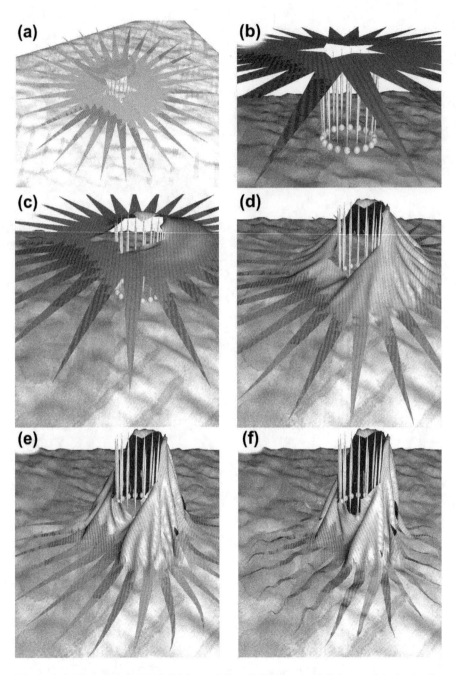

Figure 8.4: Experiment two: Sticks and Scarf. The upper left image (a) shows the shape of scarf in 2D space.

Chapter 9

Multi-Layered Deformable Surfaces

9.1 Introduction and motivation

We address the problem of the multi–layered cloth blending, deformation and dynamic interaction. A multi-layered surface is created by gluing two or more surfaces along lines or over regions. The surfaces which form the multi-layered surface are called subsurfaces of the multi-layered surface. The topology and the anisotropic properties of the subsurfaces are preserved. In garment design, it is common practice to attach different pieces of cloth onto one another in order to make pockets or to embellish garments. From a computational point of view, we need to preserve the anisotropic properties of the cloth surface representation without the necessity to re-mesh it.

Many physical-based techniques have been employed in the past for modeling cloth or deformable surfaces [132, 31, 113, 20, 143, 33]. These methods are applied to either a single deformable surface or several independent deformable surfaces.

Carignan et al. [37] successfully applied two kinds of dynamic constraints [24, 109] in order to join and attach different panels together based on seaming information. However, their method required the particles of the two panels to be matched along the seaming lines. In the garment system developed by Volino et al. [144], they adopted the similar topological merging technique to seam the panels together.

In order to avoid object penetration, collision detection should be performed for computing the accurate contact points. Multi–layered surfaces often lead to non–manifold features. Specific algorithms must be employed in order to perform self–collision detection.

9.2   Outline

We propose a positional constraint method to solve the multi–layered deformable surface problem based on a *master-slave scheme*. This allows the consistent update of the motion of the main layer to propagate into the attachment layers. Two or more deformable surfaces to be attached together in any orientation relative to each other for the purpose of modeling cloth attachments and multi–layered clothing. Different resolutions of the deformable surfaces can be glued together without the need for aligning the particles within the overlapping regions or along the seaming lines. The gluing process is done automatically once the gluing direction and the regions are specified. After the attachment process, the surfaces are treated as a multi-layered surface. This multi-layered surface contains non-manifold features. We employ a technique that prevents self-intersection for the non-manifold features. We demonstrate the stability of this method by performing several experiments with high surface complexity and a large number of colliding feature pairs. Interactive rates can be achieved for multi–layered surfaces with an appropriate discretization level of triangles.

The subsequent sections are organized as follows: Section 9.3 discusses the construction of a multi–layered surface. Section 9.4 describes an interpolation scheme to update the slave layers of a multi–layered surface. Section 9.5 presents a collision detection method for handling non-manifold surface. Section 9.6 presents the experiments and results. We present the summary and discussion in Section 9.7.

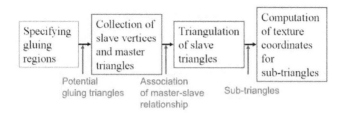

Figure 9.1: The construction pipeline of a multi–layered surface.

9.3 Construction of a multi–layered deformable surface

Our task is to attach two or more of the triangular meshes onto each other in some designated regions or along the seaming lines which can be selected manually or computed automatically. After gluing these meshes together, we treat them as a single deformable surface. The triangles of the meshes inside the gluing region can still deform and they move relative to each other. We assume that the gluing regions are flat at the time we join the meshes. We describe only the method to glue two triangular meshes. The extension to glue more than two meshes is straightforward. We only need to repeat the operations on the other mesh pairs. Figure 9.1 shows the construction pipeline of a multi–layered surface.

We start by gluing a particle (or vertex) with position $\mathbf{p}$ to a deformable triangle $T(\mathbf{p}_0\mathbf{p}_1\mathbf{p}_2)$ by employing a positional constraint method, where $\mathbf{p}_0$, $\mathbf{p}_1$, and $\mathbf{p}_2$ are the vertices of the triangles. We assume that the particle lies inside or on the edge of T with the barycentric coordinates (w_0, w_1, w_2). The particle will move accordingly so that its barycentric coordinates does not change when the triangle deforms. Formally, we have the motion equation for the particle based on its barycentric coordinates and the vertices of the triangle: $\mathbf{p} = w_0\mathbf{p}_0 + w_1\mathbf{p}_1 + w_2\mathbf{p}_2$. In this case, we call this particle a *slave particle* and the triangle a *master triangle*. The vertices and edges of the triangles are called *master vertices* and *master edges*, respectively. The slave particle may be kept at a given (signed) distance d from the triangle while maintaining the same barycentric coordinates of its projected image onto the triangle. Then, we

181

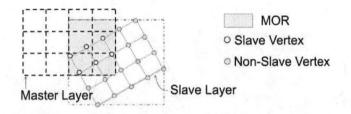

Figure 9.2: Collection of slave vertices and master triangles.

have the expression[1] for the position of the slave particle as follows:

$$\mathbf{p} = w_0\mathbf{p}_0 + w_1\mathbf{p}_1 + w_2\mathbf{p}_2 + d\mathbf{n} \tag{9.1}$$

where $\mathbf{n}$ is the normal of the triangle. If we differentiate Equation 9.1 with respect to time t, we obtain the velocity $\dot{\mathbf{p}}$ of the particle:

$$\dot{\mathbf{p}} = w_0\dot{\mathbf{p}}_0 + w_1\dot{\mathbf{p}}_1 + w_2\dot{\mathbf{p}}_2 + d\dot{\mathbf{n}} \tag{9.2}$$

In order to glue two surfaces S_0 and S_1, we need to know the slave vertices and the master triangles. First, we specify the set of triangles of S_0 that will be glued to the set of triangles in S_1. Let the two sets of triangles of S_0 and S_1, be T_0 and T_1, respectively. We choose S_0 as the master layer and S_1 as the slave layer. After that we determine the master triangle for each vertex of T_1. The distance d is treated as the distance between the two surfaces before deformation. If a vertex of T_1 does not have a master triangle, the vertex is treated the same as the other non–slave vertices.

9.3.1 Collection of slave vertices and master triangles

We propose a method to automatically identify and collect the master triangles and the slave vertices. Without loss of generality, we assume that the regions to be glued are placed parallel to each other. Therefore, both sets T_0 and T_1 have their own supporting plane Q_0 and Q_1, respectively. In this case, Q_0 and Q_1 must be parallel. Figure 9.2 shows an example of gluing two rectangular meshes.

---

[1]For a general expression of the position of the particle, we have $\mathbf{p} = \mathbf{x} + d\mathbf{n}(S, \mathbf{x})$, where S is a mesh, $\mathbf{x}$ is a point of S attached to the particle, $\mathbf{n}(S, \mathbf{x})$ is the normal at $\mathbf{x}$, and d is the (signed) distance.

The gluing direction is perpendicular to the planes Q_0 and Q_1. The potential triangles to be glued lie inside the overlapping region of T_0 and T_1 perpendicular to the gluing direction. In order to improve the overall performance of the gluing process, we collect these potential triangles. If the triangles to be glued only occupy a small portion of T_0 and T_1, the improvement will be significant.

We reduce our problem domain from 3D to 2D by projecting the vertices of the two sets T_0 and T_1 onto the projection plane perpendicular to the gluing direction. We associate this plane with a 2D Cartesian coordinate system. For example, if the gluing direction is along the z–axis, the x– and y–coordinates are kept while the z–coordinate component of the vertices is thrown away. We compute the axis–aligned bounding box (AABB) of the two set of triangles and then compute the minimum overlapping region (MOR). Then, we keep only the triangles of T_0 and T_1 if their bounding boxes overlap with MOR. We denote the remaining triangles in the two sets as T'_0 and T'_1.

In order to void all-pair comparison, we adopt a 2D grid–based approach to collect the slave vertices and the master triangles. The MOR of the gluing regions is subdivided into regular grid cells. The triangles of T'_0 are assigned into the cells which overlap with the AABB of the triangles. If a cell is already occupied, we create a linked list and append the triangles to the list. After assigning all the triangles of T'_0, we check each vertex of T'_1 and compute the cell according to its position. We retrieve the linked list of the cell and determine whether there is a triangle overlapping with the vertex. If there exists such a triangle, we associate the vertex and the triangle with the relationship of slave vertex and master triangle. The barycentric coordinates are computed for the slave vertex with respect to the master triangle.

9.3.2 Triangulation of slave triangles

If a triangle of T'_1 overlaps with T'_0, we call this triangle a slave triangle. A slave triangle is partially covered if it overlaps with T'_0 and it has at most two slave vertices. In the case that a slave triangle is fully covered, the overlapping region between it and

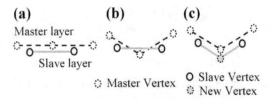

(a)   **(b)**   **(c)**

Master layer

Slave layer

○ Master Vertex   O Slave Vertex
                    ○ New Vertex

Figure 9.3: Amendment for penetration between the master and slave layers. (a) Initial setup; (b) Before triangulation; (c) After triangulation.

T'_0 is itself. Therefore, its three vertices must be slave vertices.

When the master layer deforms, we update the positions of the slave vertices accordingly. During the deformation process, there should not be any penetration between the two layers. However, because of the mismatch of the resolutions of the two layers and the triangles of T'_0 do not align with the triangles of T'_1, the edges of both layers will pass through each other. Figure 9.3 illustrates that improper placement of slave layer will lead to penetration. For example, suppose that the slave layer is glued underneath with the master layer. When the master layer deforms and bends downwards, the slave layer will penetrate the master layer in the middle region. An amendment scheme should be devised.

Penetration occurs because there is a misalignment between the slave triangles and master triangles. More specifically, there exists some slave triangles and each of them do not fully lie inside one master triangle. We tackle this problem by triangulating each slave triangle into sub–triangles so that the edges of the sub–triangles align with the edges of the master triangles. Figure 9.4 shows the mesh of the slave layer after the gluing region of the slave layer is triangulated.

We denote the sets of edges of T'_0 and T'_1 as E'_0 and E'_1. We call the edges of E'_1 the slave edges. A three–step process is adopted to triangulate all the slave triangles: (1) the computation of all the intersection points between E'_0 and E'_1, (2) the computation of the dependent triangles[2] for the vertices of the master layer, and (3) the triangulation of the slave triangles.

---

[2]A dependent triangle is a slave triangle which overlaps with at least one of the triangles of T'_0.

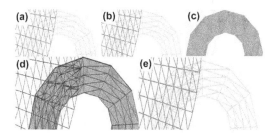

Figure 9.4: Texture and triangulation of slave triangles. (a) before triangulation; (b) triangulation of fully covered triangles; (c) original mesh with texture before triangulation; (d) triangulation of fully covered triangles with texture; (e) triangulation of fully and partially covered triangles.

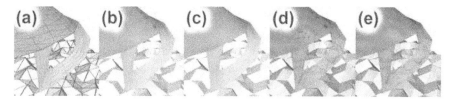

Figure 9.5: Rendering a multi–layered surface. (a) and (b) using original meshes; (c) using sub–triangles; (d) using original meshes with texture; (e) using sub–triangles with texture.

9.3.3 Rendering and computation of texture coordinates for sub–triangles

Figure 9.5 shows the rendering results by using different settings. If we do not render the sub–triangles for the fully attached triangles, penetration between the slave layer and the master layer will be clearly shown. This is illustrated in Figures 9.5(a), (b) and (d). Thus, instead of displaying the fully attached triangles, we display their sub–triangles. In order that we need the texture coordinates of the vertices of the sub–triangles. Assume that a slave triangle has texture coordinates t_0, t_1, and t_2 for its three vertices and the barycentric coordinates of a vertex of a sub–triangle are (w_0, w_1, w_2). By representing in vector form, the texture coordinates of the vertex is computed as: $t_s = w_0 t_0 + w_1 t_1 + w_2 t_2$. If the vertex of the sub–triangle is an intersection point of a master edge and a slave edge, and the texture coordinates of the two endpoints of the

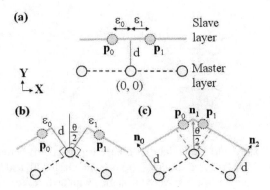

Figure 9.6: Interpolation for a slave vertex. (A side view.) (a) before deformation; (b) using normal of master triangle; (c) using normal of master vertex.

slave edge are $\mathbf{t}_0$ and $\mathbf{t}_1$, then the texture coordinates of the point is $\mathbf{t}_s = w_0 \mathbf{t}_0 + w_1 \mathbf{t}_1$, where (w_0, w_1) is the barycentric coordinates of the intersection point with respect to the slave edge.

9.4 Continuity along edges

If we apply Equation 9.1 to update the slave vertices which are lying near/on the master edges initially, the deformation in the region of the slave layer along the master edges changes rapidly. Figure 9.6 shows an inappropriate method for computing the positions of the slave particles and an amendment method. Assume that two vertices $\mathbf{p}_0$ and $\mathbf{p}_1$ of the slave layer are assigned to different master triangles. At the time of the gluing process, their distance is $\epsilon = \epsilon_0 + \epsilon_1$ and the distance from the master triangle(s) to them is d. We simplify our discussion by considering the case $\epsilon_0 = \epsilon_1$. The distance $d(\mathbf{p}_0, \mathbf{p}_1)$ between the two vertices is given by:

$$
\begin{aligned}
d(\mathbf{p}_0, \mathbf{p}_1) &= \sqrt{[2d\sin\frac{\theta}{2} + (\epsilon_0 + \epsilon_1)\cos\frac{\theta}{2}]^2 + [(\epsilon_0 - \epsilon_1)\sin\frac{\theta}{2}]^2} \\
&= 2d\sin\frac{\theta}{2} + \epsilon\cos\frac{\theta}{2}
\end{aligned}
$$

where $\theta(< \frac{\pi}{2})$ is the bending angle of the two triangles about their common edge. Differentiating $d(\mathbf{p}_0, \mathbf{p}_1)$ with respect to θ, we obtain $d\cos\frac{\theta}{2} - \frac{\epsilon}{2}\sin\frac{\theta}{2}$ which is the rate of the change of the distance with respect to the bending angle. When the bending angle is small, the rate is dominated by the term $d\cos\frac{\theta}{2}$. This term is not related to the initial distance of the two vertices. This is undesirable as the deformation rate of the line segment $\mathbf{p}_0\mathbf{p}_1$ will be too high if d is large comparing to the edge length of the slave layer.[3] If the stiffness of the spring of the slave layer is very high, it will make the motion of the surface abnormal. In order to amend the deficiency of the update scheme, we modify it by using the vertex normal[4] instead of the triangle normal. Let $\mathbf{n}_0$, $\mathbf{n}_1$, and $\mathbf{n}_2$ be the master vertex normal. Then, we have

$$\mathbf{p} = w_0(\mathbf{p}_0 + d\mathbf{n}_0) + w_1(\mathbf{p}_1 + d\mathbf{n}_1) + w_2(\mathbf{p}_2 + d\mathbf{n}_2) \tag{9.3}$$

By using Equation 9.3 to update $\mathbf{p}_0$ and $\mathbf{p}_1$, we have:

$$\begin{aligned}
\mathbf{p}_0 &= \frac{l - \epsilon/2}{l}(0, d) + \frac{\epsilon}{2l}(-l\cos\frac{\theta}{2} - d\sin\frac{\theta}{2}, -l\sin\frac{\theta}{2} + d\cos\frac{\theta}{2}) \\
&= (-\frac{\epsilon}{2}\cos\frac{\theta}{2} - \frac{\epsilon d}{2l}\sin\frac{\theta}{2}, \frac{(l - \epsilon/2)d}{l} - \frac{\epsilon}{2}\sin\frac{\theta}{2} + \frac{\epsilon d}{2l}\cos\frac{\theta}{2})
\end{aligned}$$

and

$$\begin{aligned}
\mathbf{p}_1 &= \frac{l - \epsilon/2}{l}(0, d) + \frac{\epsilon}{2l}(l\cos\frac{\theta}{2} + d\sin\frac{\theta}{2}, -l\sin\frac{\theta}{2} + d\cos\frac{\theta}{2}) \\
&= (\frac{\epsilon}{2}\cos\frac{\theta}{2} + \frac{\epsilon d}{2l}\sin\frac{\theta}{2}, \frac{(l - \epsilon/2)d}{l} - \frac{\epsilon}{2}\sin\frac{\theta}{2} + \frac{\epsilon d}{2l}\cos\frac{\theta}{2})
\end{aligned}$$

where l is the edge length of the two triangles. The distance between the two vertices becomes:

$$d(\mathbf{p}_0, \mathbf{p}_1) = \epsilon(\cos\frac{\theta}{2} + \frac{d}{l}\sin\frac{\theta}{2}) \tag{9.4}$$

From Equation 9.4, the rate of change with respect to the bending angle becomes $\frac{\partial d(\mathbf{p}_0, \mathbf{p}_1)}{\partial \theta} = \frac{\epsilon}{2}(\frac{d}{l}\cos\frac{\theta}{2} - \sin\frac{\theta}{2})$ which depends on the initial distance (ϵ) of the two vertices. Moreover, this rate of change is proportional to their initial distance. Therefore, this update scheme alleviates the problem of a sudden change to the deformation of the slave layer when the master layer deforms.

---

[3] When the resolution tends to infinity, $\epsilon_0 + \epsilon_1$ tends to zero. d will be larger than $\epsilon_0 + \epsilon_1$.

[4] If there is an underlying smooth surface, the vertex normal is the normal of the vertex on the surface.

9.4.1 Derivatives for slave particles

In our system, the net force is composed of internal spring force, viscous damping force between connecting particles, gravity, air resistance force and the fluid damping force. We need to compute two kinds of partial derivatives: (1) the one depending on the particle position: $\frac{\partial f}{\partial x}$, (2) and the term depending on the particle velocity: $\frac{\partial f}{\partial v}$. We describe the method to evaluate these two terms for the spring force and the viscous damping force. According to Hooke's law, the spring force between two particles i and j is modeled by $\mathbf{f}_{s(i,j)} = -k_{ij}(|\mathbf{x}_i - \mathbf{x}_j| - l_{ij}^0)\frac{\mathbf{x}_i - \mathbf{x}_j}{|\mathbf{x}_i - \mathbf{x}_j|}$, where l_{ij}^0 is the natural length of the spring and k_{ij} is the spring stiffness. The viscous damping force with damping coefficient $\mu_{(i,j)}$ is $\mathbf{f}_{d(i,j)} = -\mu_{(i,j)}(\mathbf{v}_i - \mathbf{v}_j)$. Therefore, we have

$$\frac{\partial \mathbf{f}_{s(i,j)}}{\partial \mathbf{x}_i} = -k_{ij}\left[\frac{|\mathbf{x}_i - \mathbf{x}_j| - l_{ij}^0}{|\mathbf{x}_i - \mathbf{x}_j|}\mathbf{I}_3 + l_{ij}^0\frac{(\mathbf{x}_i - \mathbf{x}_j)^T(\mathbf{x}_i - \mathbf{x}_j)}{|\mathbf{x}_i - \mathbf{x}_j|^3}\right]$$

$$\frac{\partial \mathbf{f}_{d(i,j)}}{\partial \mathbf{v}_i} = -\mu_{(i,j)}\mathbf{I}_3$$

Assume that there is a slave particle $\mathbf{y}$ with the barycentric coordinates (w_0, w_1, w_2). Its motion is depended on the master particles $\mathbf{x}_0$, $\mathbf{x}_1$, and $\mathbf{x}_2$. By applying the chain rule with respect to each master particle i, we obtain the derivatives: $\frac{\partial f}{\partial \mathbf{x}_i} = \frac{\partial f}{\partial \mathbf{y}}\frac{\partial \mathbf{y}}{\partial \mathbf{x}_i}$, and $\frac{\partial f}{\partial \mathbf{v}_i} = \frac{\partial f}{\partial \mathbf{u}}\frac{\partial \mathbf{u}}{\partial \mathbf{v}_i}$, where $\mathbf{u} = \dot{\mathbf{y}}$.

We proceed to evaluate $\frac{\partial \mathbf{y}}{\partial \mathbf{x}_i}$ and $\frac{\partial \mathbf{u}}{\partial \mathbf{v}_i}$. Assume that the normals of the particles are $\mathbf{n}_0$, $\mathbf{n}_1$, and $\mathbf{n}_2$. According to the update scheme for $\mathbf{y}$, we have:

$$\mathbf{y} = w_0(\mathbf{x}_0 + d\mathbf{n}_0) + w_1(\mathbf{x}_1 + d\mathbf{n}_1) + w_2(\mathbf{x}_2 + d\mathbf{n}_2)$$

By differentiating $\mathbf{y}$ with respect to $\mathbf{x}_i$, we have:

$$\frac{\partial \mathbf{y}}{\partial \mathbf{x}_i} = w_i + d\sum_{j=0}^{2} w_j \frac{\partial \mathbf{n}_j}{\partial \mathbf{x}_i}, \quad i = 0, 1, 2$$

The evaluation of the term $\frac{\partial \mathbf{n}_j}{\partial \mathbf{x}_i}$ may be expensive. For example, assume that the normal $\mathbf{n}_j$ ($= \frac{\sum \mathbf{n}_k}{|\sum \mathbf{n}_k|} \neq 0$) of a vertex is obtained by averaging the normal $\mathbf{n}_k$ of the

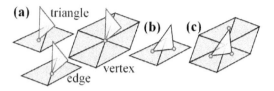

(a) triangle

(b) **(c)**

vertex

edge

Figure 9.7: Collision detection for a non-manifold surface. (a) a vertex glued on features, triangle, edge, vertex; (b) two slave vertices; (c) three slave vertices (fully covered).

triangles attached at the vertex. By expanding the term $\frac{\partial \mathbf{n_j}}{\partial \mathbf{x}_i}$, we obtain:

$$\frac{\partial \mathbf{n_j}}{\partial \mathbf{x}_i} = \frac{|\sum \mathbf{n}_k| \frac{\partial \sum \mathbf{n}_k}{\partial \mathbf{x}_i} - (\sum \mathbf{n}_k) \frac{\partial |\sum \mathbf{n}_k|}{\partial \mathbf{x}_i}}{|\sum \mathbf{n}_k|^2}$$

$$= \frac{\sum \mathbf{n}_k \cdot \sum \mathbf{n}_k \frac{\partial \sum \mathbf{n}_k}{\partial \mathbf{x}_i} - (\sum \mathbf{n}_k) \sum \mathbf{n}_k \cdot \frac{\partial \sum \mathbf{n}_k}{\partial \mathbf{x}_i}}{|\sum \mathbf{n}_k|^3}$$

In the above formula, we need to compute $\frac{\partial \sum \mathbf{n}_k}{\partial \mathbf{x}_i}$ which is time consuming. Instead of computing the exact values, the approximate values are computed. If the motion of the triangle does not change rapidly and the distance d is small compared to the edge length of the master triangles, we have $\frac{\partial \mathbf{y}}{\partial \mathbf{x}_i} \approx w_i$ and $\frac{\partial \mathbf{f}}{\partial \mathbf{x}_i} = \frac{\partial \mathbf{f}}{\partial \mathbf{y}} \frac{\partial \mathbf{y}}{\partial \mathbf{x}_i} \approx \frac{\partial \mathbf{f}}{\partial \mathbf{y}} w_i$. Similarly, we have the velocity of $\mathbf{y}$: $\mathbf{u} = w_0(\mathbf{v}_0 + d\dot{\mathbf{n}}_0) + w_1(\mathbf{v}_1 + d\dot{\mathbf{n}}_1) + w_2(\mathbf{v}_2 + d\dot{\mathbf{n}}_2)$, where $\dot{\mathbf{n}}_i$ is the derivative of $\mathbf{n}_i$ with respect to time for $i = 0, 1$, and 2. We have $\frac{\partial \mathbf{u}}{\partial \mathbf{v}_i} = w_i + d \sum_{j=0}^{2} \frac{\partial \dot{\mathbf{n}}_j}{\partial \mathbf{v}_i}$. When d is small, we have the approximation: $\frac{\partial \mathbf{u}}{\partial \mathbf{v}_i} \approx w_i$ and $\frac{\partial \mathbf{f}}{\partial \mathbf{v}_i} = \frac{\partial \mathbf{f}}{\partial \mathbf{u}} \frac{\partial \mathbf{u}}{\partial \mathbf{v}_i} \approx \frac{\partial \mathbf{f}}{\partial \mathbf{u}} w_i$.

9.5 Collision detection for non-manifold meshes

Since a multi-layered surface may be a non-manifold, a specialized algorithm is employed for collision detection between the slave layer and master layer. Figure 9.7 shows the cases of different of attachments that exist in a multi-layered surfaces. The cases are point–triangle, point–edge, point–point, two-point-two-triangle and three-point-three-triangle. We do not perform collision detection for the slave triangles which are fully attached in the gluing region. If the vertices that are attached onto

Animation	Complexity #triangle / #particles; k (max. spring stiffness)		Time (sec)		
	Deformable Surfaces	Solid	Construction of multi-layer	CD	CGM
1(a)	**5, 640 / 3, 030**	5, 472 / 2, 827	0.006	0.033	0.25
1(b)	**5, 640 / 3, 030**	5, 472 / 2, 827	0.066	0.031	0.29
1(c) low	**5, 640 / 3, 030**	5, 472 / 2, 827	0.082	0.020	0.31
1(c) high	A: 5, 000 / 2, 601; k = 1, 000	5, 472 / 2, 827	0.13	0.0869	3.29
	B: 3, 000 / 1, 581; k = 1, 000				
	C: 12, 000 / 6, 161; k = 1 000				
	D: 21, 760 / 11, 097; k = 1, 000				
	TT: 41, 760 / 21, 440				
2.	C: 18, 000 / 9, 150; k(C) = 1, 500	7, 972 / 4, 079	0.245	0.158	2.53
	9 x R: 576 / 324; k(R) = 1, 000				
	TT: 23, 184 / 12, 066				
3.	C: 21, 600 / 10, 980; k(C) = 2, 000	7, 972 / 4, 079	0.239	0.151	2.66
	9 x R: 144 / 90; k(R) = 1, 000				
	TT: 22, 896 / 11, 790				
4.	A, B, C: 21, 600 / 10, 980	7, 972 / 4, 079	0.466	0.547	7.21
	k(A) = 1, 500; k(B) = 1, 000; k(C) = 500				
	TT: 64, 800 / 32, 940				

Table 9.1: Performance statistics of the first four examples. Average time per time step. CD: Collision detection; CGM: Conjugate gradient method (solving linear system).

the master layer, we do not perform collision detection for the involved feature (vertex, edge, or triangle) pairs . For example, if a slave vertex is glued onto a master triangle, we do not perform vertex–triangle collision test. If two endpoints of an edge are slave vertices, we will ignore the collision tests which involve this edge.

We use the decomposition scheme of $(\pi, \beta, \mathbf{I})$–surfaces to perform subsurface culling for the regions not being glued and then use the intrinsic collision detection unit to compute collision information.

9.6 Experiments and results

We applied our proposed method for modeling cloth pieces which are attached together. First, we performed four simple animations and the complexity of the deformable surfaces ranged from five thousand to sixty-four thousand triangles. There are at most ten pieces of cloth attached together. The performance statistics were collected. Then we performed two complex examples in which there are more than eighteen pieces of cloth are attached together. A stochastic wind loading was implemented. All the experiments were run on a 3.0GHz Pentium 4 PC with 1GB of main memory. Double floating point was used in our implementation [5]. Throughout all the experiments, we used a constant time step size of $\frac{1}{90}$ seconds. The summary of the performance statistics is given in Table 9.1. Most of the time is spent in solving the linear system. Less than 10% of the time is spent in collision detection.

Figure 9.8(1) shows the snapshots from Animation one. There are four rectangular pieces of cloth which have different resolutions. One is placed in the middle (A, light blue) and the vertices of another three (B, C, and D) are fixed along one of their sides. These three pieces are glued with the piece at the middle one by one. There are 1,200 time steps in each of the animation sequences. There is interaction among these four pieces, ground, and an obstacle with a smooth surface. Especially, in (b), the piece of the light blue cloth is pulled fiercely onto the area of ground.

Figure 9.8(2) shows the snapshots from Animation two. The left image is the top view of the garment placed at the initial position. There are 2,400 time steps. An outer garment is placed around the neck of a mannequin model. This outer garment consists of a large surface with a hole at the center and nine rings. The rings are partially attached around the boundary of the large surface. The large surface is selected as the master layer. Initially, the garment is placed horizontally above the mannequin and then they move downwards under the effect of gravity. During the animation, there is a stochastic wind loading which makes the garment flutter. In the end of the animation, the wind is deactivated and the garment drapes stably around the mannequin's body.

Figure 9.8(3) shows the snapshots from Animation three. The left image is the top view of a blouse placed at the initial position. There are 2,000 time steps. A blouse is modeled by a large round surface which has a small hole in the center. The round surface is the master layer. The rings are attached fully to the round surface in its inner

---

[5]If single floating point is used, the performance will be much better, especially for solving the linear system and collision detection.

191

region. All the vertices of the rings are slave vertices and hence only their sub–triangles are rendered on the screen.

Figure 9.8(4) shows the snapshots from Animation four. There are 1,000 time steps. Three blouses are connected at some parts near their boundaries and there is a hole in their middle. The stiffnesses of A, B, and C, are 1500, 1000, and 500 respectively. On average, it took 8-9 seconds to complete one time step and over 90% of time was spent in computing the motion equation (CGM) per frame.

Finally, we carried out another two complex examples to illustrate the stability and scalability of our proposed methods. Figure 9.9 shows the snapshots from these two examples. In these two examples, the deformable rings are partially attached together. The cloth rings fall over the small rigid balls and then slip smoothly over the surface of the balls. The cloth rings fall onto the mannequin model naturally.

In Figure 9.9(a), There are 18 rings partially attached to a large red ring. A green ring appears at the 400th frame and falls onto the large red ring and then onto the mannequin model. The wind loading factor is strong in this example. The complexity (#tri/#particle) of the example is: 360/216 (each small ring), 3,200/1,760 (each large ring), 2,520/1,262 (each ball), and 1,396/711 (mannequin model). There are 2,000 time steps.

In Figure 9.9(b), there are 18 rings in the outer region and another 6 inner rings connecting two red rings together. They fall onto the mannequin model at the end. The complexity (#tri/#particle) of the example is: 360/216 (each small outer ring), 192/120 (each small inner ring), 3,200/1,760 (large outer red ring), 1,080/630 (small inner red ring), 2,520/1,262 (each ball), and 1,396/711 (mannequin model). There are 1,200 time steps.

9.7 Summary and discussion

We have proposed a positional constraint-based method to join two or more deformable surfaces into a single multi–layered surface based a master–slave scheme. This master–salve scheme preserves the topology and anisotropic properties of the surfaces. The slave layer can be considered as a mask. If the region of the master layer is covered by the mask, we can add springs (or other physical properties) to connect the vertices of the master layer according to the topology of the mask. The gluing orientation between a pair of master-slave surfaces is allowed to be arbitrary and the resolutions of the deformable surfaces need not to be the same. Instead of rendering the slave triangles, we render their sub-triangles. We illustrated several examples and showed that our proposed method leads to a dynamically realistic interaction for the attachment of two or more deformable surfaces. The method is stable even when there are strong external forces (e.g. wind loading) applied to the deformable surfaces. The motion of the surfaces shows natural draping with complex collision detection, friction and stiction.

In a dynamic scene with deformable surfaces consisting of 22,896 triangles and 11,790 particles, it took less than 3 hours to produce an animation sequence of 2,000 frames, on a 3GHz Pentium PC and 1GB memory. We observed that most of the time was spent in solving the motion equations. The time spent in generating one frame took only 3 seconds and the time spent in collision detection was, on average, less than 10% of the total time. On similar computers, we can achieve interactive rates if we reduce the complexity of the multi–layered surfaces to about five thousand triangles.

As an immediate future extension of our method, we are working on joined surfaces over the same region. The extension of the decomposition scheme of $(\pi, \beta, \mathbf{I})$-surfaces is researched in order to handle the self-collision detection for non-manifold surfaces efficiently.

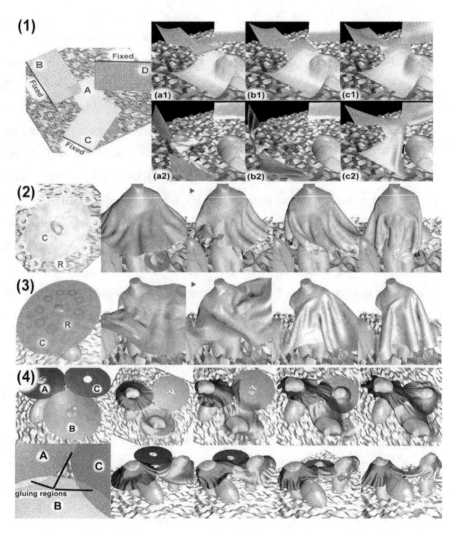

Figure 9.8: Animations 1–4. **Animation one :** Four pieces of cloth with different resolutions. The vertices along the thick lines are fixed. (a) two pieces are glued; (b) three pieces are glued; (c) four pieces are glued. The snapshots were captured at the 300th time step ("1") and the 900th time step ("2"). **Animation two :** An outer garment with nine hanging soft rings. **Animation three :** A blouse with nine rings. **Animation four :** Three connected blouses. Top left image: the initial setup of the scene. Bottom left image: the gluing regions.

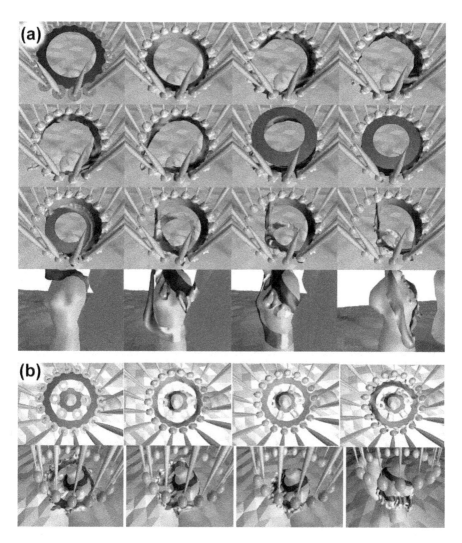

Figure 9.9: Gluing rings. (a) 18 rings partially attached to a large red ring; (b) 18 rings in the outer region and another 6 inner rings connecting two red rings together.

Chapter 10

A Stable Sewing Process

10.1 Introduction and motivation

In computer-aided apparel design, it is common practice to produce virtual cloth-ing by making use of seaming information to join several panels or regions of a panel. This is known as *sewing*. After sewing, the panels are merged into a single sewn sur-face, reserving the internal physical structure of each panel. The seaming information typically consists of: (1) the matching between the sewing nodes of the source and the destination; the sewing nodes of the source and the destination may or may not belong to the same surface; (2) the creation of new faces when the panels are merged; and (3) the sewing forces which bring the panels together. Sewing should be fast and stable. During sewing, unnecessary collisions, in particular, self-collisions, should be prevented. Usually, the panels are warped around a target (if any) after sewing. The completion of sewing is defined as follows:

Definition 10.1 : Sewing is completed if and only if the sewn surface gets to an equi-librium state after the mechanical evolution of the system is done, and the attachment of panels to the target(s) (if any) is satisfied.

Determining whether the product of sewing is satisfied, relies on the judgment from animators. In this chapter, we will focus on the first part: an efficient method of getting the system into an equilibrium state.

In practice, it is difficult to compute the equilibrium state of the system without evolving the system dynamically owing to the complex interactions and the complex dynamics. Employing an analytical approach to shorten the time in sewing is not possible. Rather, numerical methods are required. However, it would be impossible to compute the exact equilibrium state by employing numerical methods. We need another definition for the completion of sewing carried out in computer. We call this a *simulated sewing process* or simply *sewing process*:

Definition 10.2 : A simulated sewing process is completed if and only if the change of potential energy of the sewn surface is lower than a threshold after the mechanical evolution of the system, and the attachment of panels to the target(s) (if any) is satisfied.

This turns out that in order to complete a simulated sewing process, we need to solve an energy minimization problem with changing physical parameters.

10.2 Conventional approaches for sewing

The panels are designed in two-dimension space and then transformed into the three-dimension space. Conventionally, seaming forces are applied to the nodes along the seaming lines of the panels and the panels are put together. As the process is performed dynamically, the panels can deform if they encounter obstacles. If the distances between the matching particles are below a certain threshold, the particles are combined together. The velocities and masses of the particles are adjusted based on the conservation of momentum. The forces that pull the matching particles are computed based on the exact behavior of elastic forces [37, 145] or spring forces [51]. All these methods require that the panels are placed well for the purpose of sewing. Fuhrmann et al. [54] proposed a method for automatical prepositioning of cloth pattern around virtual character if reference points between the planar cloth patterns and the virtual character can be computed. After that, they employed the scheme of [145] to perform sewing.

These methods have three problems. First, there are unnecessary self-collisions that may occur during the sewing process. There is a lack of a control unit to monitor the velocities of particles and forces acting on particles during the sewing process. If the magnitude of the velocities is sufficiently large, inplane self-collisions will easily happen. Second, if there are obstacles lying in the way of two sewing regions. Intersection will easily occur when the merging process is taken place. Third, the obstacles may prevent the matching nodes from getting sufficiently close for merging due to inappropriate handling of collision response or sewing regions that stuck on obstacles. In this case, the sewing process is forced to stop. In order to solve these three problems, it requires further manual manipulation from animators for refinement.

10.3   Outline

The conventional methods employ the exact physical properties of the deformable surfaces to evolve the system dynamically to sew panels together. However, in computer simulation, we can modify all the physical parameters in order to make ease of our work. Starting in this direction, we propose an inverse simulated sewing process. Unlike the conventional methods of the sewing process, our method merges the panels together along the sewing lines in the beginning. The panels are warped around the target(s) after they are merged. This can be done by changing the geometry of the panels or placing the panels at the appropriate positions either manually [107, 144] or automatically [54, 136]. During the sewing process, we monitor and control the physical parameters of the system and evolve the panels dynamically. Gradually, the physical parameters of the system is systematically changed back to the exact values while the system gets to its equilibrium state. As the matching nodes are merged in the beginning, the forces between particles can be spread in the early stage of the sewing process. The internal physical parameters of the system are also converged to their exact values. Our technique has two major advantages. First, it avoid unnecessary self-collisions and second, the sewing process can be stopped any time since the panels are merged in the beginning. Animators can manipulate the sewn surface for further processing. By employing our method, the panels are allowed to be stretched.

10.4 Problem formulation

We consider deformable surfaces consisting of a set of particles. These particles exerting forces upon each other. The motion equation of the particles is given by:

$$\mathbf{M}\ddot{\mathbf{x}} = f(\mathbf{x}, \dot{\mathbf{x}}, \cdots, \mathbf{x}^{(n)}, t) \tag{10.1}$$

where M is the mass matrix of the particles, x is the vector of the positions of the particles, t is time, and $f(\mathbf{x}, \dot{\mathbf{x}}, \cdots, \mathbf{x}^{(n)}, t)$ is the vector of forces. In this study, we restrict the discussion for the following case:

$$\mathbf{M}\ddot{\mathbf{x}} = f(\mathbf{x}, \dot{\mathbf{x}}, t) \tag{10.2}$$

where $\mathbf{f}(\mathbf{x}, \dot{\mathbf{x}}, t)$ depends only on time, and the positions and velocities of the particles. We have three kinds of forces acting on the particles during the sewing process: the internal forces of the particles, friction forces and collision forces.

In our sewing system, we need to evolve quickly the deformable surfaces dynamically in order to compute a state such that they have a minima of potential energy. We have two control functions $\zeta(\mathbf{x}, t)$ (a scalar) and $\phi(x, t)$ (a vector). These two functions modify the motion of the particles into:

$$\mathbf{M}\ddot{\mathbf{x}} = \zeta(\mathbf{x}, t)\mathbf{f}(\mathbf{x}, \dot{\mathbf{x}}, t) + \phi(\mathbf{x}, t) \tag{10.3}$$

The two functions satisfy that there exists $t_0 \geq 0$, such that $\zeta(\mathbf{x}, t) = 1$ and $\phi(\mathbf{x}, t) = \mathbf{0}$ when $t \geq t_0$. We want to compute the optimal functions for $\zeta(\mathbf{x}, t)$ and $\phi(\mathbf{x}, t)$ such that given t_0 and an integration scheme with time step h, the system is brought into an equilibrium state. However, an analytical approach for computing the optimal solution is not possible owing to the unpredictable deformation of the panels for different levels of discretization and complex interactions. We need to evolve the deformable surfaces dynamically and handle interactions appropriately. Therefore, empirical experiments are employed for evaluating some selected functions for $\zeta(\mathbf{x}, t)$ and $\phi(\mathbf{x}, t)$.

10.5 Dynamic sewing problem

We consider a problem that constraining two particles for virtual sewing. Assume that each particle exerts a force upon another and these two forces conform to Newton's third law. The magnitudes of the two forces are the same but the directions of them are opposite. We say that these two particles connecting to each other by a couple of forces. There is a natural distance for two connecting particles with respect to a couple of forces. The natural distance is defined as follows:

Definition 10.3 : The natural distance between particles $\mathbf{x}_i$ and $\mathbf{x}_j$ is $l^0_{(\mathbf{x}_i, \mathbf{x}_j)}$ if and only if the forces exerting on them are nil when their distance is $l^0_{(\mathbf{x}_i, \mathbf{x}_j)}$.

The type of force that we use to connect two particles is an attractive force. A couple of attractive forces between two particles $\mathbf{x}_i$ and $\mathbf{x}_j$ are defined as:

$$f(\mathbf{x}_i, \mathbf{x}_j, l^0_{(\mathbf{x}_i, \mathbf{x}_j)}) = \pm \phi(\mathbf{x}_i, \mathbf{x}_j, l^0_{(\mathbf{x}_i, \mathbf{x}_j)}) \frac{\mathbf{x}_i - \mathbf{x}_j}{\|\mathbf{x}_i - \mathbf{x}_j\|} \tag{10.4}$$

where $\phi(\mathbf{x}_i, \mathbf{x}_j, l^0_{(\mathbf{x}_i, \mathbf{x}_j)})$ is a scalar function satisfying the Lipschitz condition, the value of $sgn(\phi(\mathbf{x}_i, \mathbf{x}_j, l^0_{(\mathbf{x}_i, \mathbf{x}_j)}))$ is the same as the value of $sgn(\|\mathbf{x}_i - \mathbf{x}_j\| - l^0_{(\mathbf{x}_i, \mathbf{x}_j)})$[1], and $\phi(\mathbf{x}_i, \mathbf{x}_j, l^0_{(\mathbf{x}_i, \mathbf{x}_j)}) = 0$ when $\|\mathbf{x}_i - \mathbf{x}_j\| = l^0_{(\mathbf{x}_i, \mathbf{x}_j)}$. When their distance is shorter than the natural distance, they will repel each other; if the distance is larger than the natural distance, they will attract each other.

In our control system, we use two types of springs to model the attractive force: regular spring and bias-spring. A regular spring produces the force whose magnitude is proportional to the strain of the spring. A bias-spring produces the force whose magnitude is larger in compressing than that in stretching. With respect to the spring

---

[1]The value of sgn(s) is 0, 1, and -1 for $s = 0$, $s > 0$ and $s < 0$, respectively.

connecting two particles $\mathbf{x}_i$ and $\mathbf{x}_j$, $l^0_{(\mathbf{x}_i, \mathbf{x}_j)}$ is its natural length. For a regular spring, the force is modeled as: $f(\mathbf{x}_i, \mathbf{x}_j, l^0_{(\mathbf{x}_i, \mathbf{x}_j)}) = k_{(\mathbf{x}_i, \mathbf{x}_j)} \frac{\|\mathbf{x}_i - \mathbf{x}_j\| - l^0_{(\mathbf{x}_i, \mathbf{x}_j)}}{l^0_{(\mathbf{x}_i, \mathbf{x}_j)}}$; for a bias-spring, the force is modeled as $f(\mathbf{x}_i, \mathbf{x}_j, l^0_{(\mathbf{x}_i, \mathbf{x}_j)}) = k_{(\mathbf{x}_i, \mathbf{x}_j)} \frac{\|\mathbf{x}_i - \mathbf{x}_j\| - l^0_{(\mathbf{x}_i, \mathbf{x}_j)}}{\|\mathbf{x}_i - \mathbf{x}_j\|}$. The scalar $k_{(\mathbf{x}_i, \mathbf{x}_j)}$ is the stiffness of the spring. These two types of springs are also used for modeling the spring-mass system for the deformable surfaces.

10.5.1 Constraining two particles for dynamic sewing

We present a non-penetration method for constraining two particles for dynamic sewing in one-dimension space. During the sewing process, the particles should not pass through their rest positions. This is called the *non-passing condition*. Consider that there is a free particle x and another particle fixed at the origin. These two particles are connected by a regular spring with stiffness k_s. The natural distance of these two particles is l and the mass of x is m. Initially, x is displaced from its rest position such that $x > l$. Our task is to bring x back to its rest position or reduce internal potential energy to a mimima as quickly as possible.

If the particle x is released, it will oscillate about its rest position forever. This is because there is no energy lost during the process. Therefore, we need to have some dissipation forces in the system. Viscous damping force is our choice as it not only dissipates energy of the system but also prevents the particle from moving too fast.

The viscous damping force exerting on x is modeled as $-2\beta\dot{x}$. The net force exerting on x becomes: $k(l - x) - 2\beta\dot{x}$, where $k = \frac{k_s}{l}$. By letting $w_0^2 = \frac{k}{m}$ and $y = (x - l)$, we obtain the following damped simple harmonic motion:

$$\ddot{y} + 2\beta\dot{y} + w_0^2 y = 0 \qquad (10.5)$$

where 2β is the damping constant. We want the particle moving back to its rest position. There should be no vibration and the non-passing condition is satisfied. In this case, we could set β such that the motion is critical damping[2] ($\beta = w_0$) or overdamped

---

[2]It should be note that owing to numerical error, we hardly achieve the critical damping condition.

($\beta > w_0$). As the critical damped motion takes shorter time for the particle to come to its rest position comparing to the overdamped motion[96], we set $\beta = w_0$. The motion equation of the particle can be expressed as:

$$y = (A + Bt)e^{-w_0 t} \tag{10.6}$$

Assume that the initial condition is given as: $y = y_0(> 0)$ and $\dot{y} = y_0$. Then the motion equation of the particle becomes:

$$y = [y_0 + (v_0 + y_0 w_0)t]e^{-w_0 t} \tag{10.7}$$

Therefore, in order to satisfy the non-passing condition, i.e. $y_0 + (v_0 + y_0\beta)t \geq 0$ for all $t \geq 0$, we should have $v_0 + y_0\beta \geq 0$. Therefore, the fastest possible way for the particle to come to its rest position is by setting $v_0 + \beta y_0 = 0$. This requires the equilibrium position but this is just what we have to compute. In our simulation, the number of particles is large. By adopting an analytical approach to compute the equilibrium positions for all particles is not possible. In our algorithm, we set $v_0 = 0$.

In the case of two free particles, x_0 and x_1, with masses m_0 and m_1, connecting by a regular spring with stiffness k_s in one-dimension space, the motion equation of the two particles is given by

$$m_0 \ddot{x}_0 = k(x_1 - x_0 - l) + \beta(\dot{x}_1 - \dot{x}_0) \tag{10.8}$$

$$m_1 \ddot{x}_1 = -k(x_1 - x_0 - l) - \beta(\dot{x}_1 - \dot{x}_0) \tag{10.9}$$

where $k = \frac{k_s}{l}$. By letting $y = x_1 - x_0 - l$ and arranging the terms in the equation, we obtain:

$$\ddot{y} = -(\frac{k(m_0 + m_1)}{m_0 m_1}y + \frac{\beta(m_0 + m_1)}{m_0 m_1}\dot{y}) \tag{10.10}$$

Therefore, when $\beta = 2\sqrt{\frac{m_0 m_1}{m_0 + m_1}k}$, the system is critical damped. In particular, when $m_0 = m_1 = m$, we have $\beta = \sqrt{2mk}$.

It is noted that for a given initial condition, the larger the stiffness is, the faster the particle moves to its rest position. However, the increase in stiffness will make the condition number of the system worse. This leads instability to the system. Therefore, we cannot unlimitedly increase the stiffness of the spring.

10.5.2 Constraining multiple connected particles for dynamic sewing

In three-dimension space, we consider a set of particles. Each particle $\mathbf{x}_i$ is connected by a set of particles $\mathbf{x}_j$. Each particle $\mathbf{x}_j$ exerts a force $-f(\mathbf{x}_i, \mathbf{x}_j) - \beta(\dot{\mathbf{x}}_i - \dot{\mathbf{x}}_j)$ on $\mathbf{x}_i$. The particles have the same mass m. (The extension to handle particles with different masses is straightforward.) The motion of $\mathbf{x}_i$ is given by the following equation:

$$m\ddot{\mathbf{x}}_i \;=\; -\sum_j (f_j(\mathbf{x}_i, \mathbf{x}_j) + \beta_{(i,j)}(\dot{\mathbf{x}}_i - \dot{\mathbf{x}}_j)) \tag{10.11}$$

$$\ddot{\mathbf{x}}_i \;=\; -\frac{\sum_j (f_j(\mathbf{x}_i, \mathbf{x}_j) + \beta_{(i,j)}(\dot{\mathbf{x}}_i - \dot{\mathbf{x}}_j))}{m} \tag{10.12}$$

Our task is to compute the value for $\beta_{(i,j)}$ so that the motion of $\mathbf{x}_i$ is either critically damping or overdamped. Consider a particle $\mathbf{x}_j$ exerting force onto $\mathbf{x}_i$. We isolate $\mathbf{x}_i$ and $\mathbf{x}_j$ from the system. Then these two particles should perform critical damping or overdamped. For example if a regular spring with stiffness $k_{(i,j)}$ is adopted, then $\beta_{(i,j)}$ should be larger than or equal to $\sqrt{2mk}$, where $k = \frac{k_{(i,j)}}{l^0_{(\mathbf{x}_i, \mathbf{x}_j)}}$.

As the semi-implicit method is employed for solving the motion equation, the forces acting on a particle will be spread out and affect other particles. The particles will change their positions between time steps. In the presence of interactions, the state of the particles will be greatly affected. Therefore, the viscous damping factor will be higher than the factor that the surrounding particles are fixed. We model this viscous damping factor as $\delta(t)\beta_{(i,j)}$, where $\delta(t)$ is called a *viscous damping multiplier* for the viscous damping factor $\beta_{(i,j)}$. The viscous damping multiplier $\delta(t)$ is obtained from the empirical analysis. We perform experiments and measure potential energy of the system for different values of $\delta(t)$ in order to determine the best choice for it.

The same viscous damping multiplier $\delta(t)$ is used to modify all the viscous damping factors for all the particles.

10.6   Relation between two sewing systems

Two systems are *equivalent in sewing* if and only if they are in an equilibrium state that either the physical parameters are replaced by the parameters of another or the physical connections between particles are altered from one to another without changing the positions of the particles. For example, we consider two systems and their difference is just the forces exerting on the particles. In one system the net force exerting on the particle i is $\sum_j \mathbf{f}_j(\mathbf{x}_i, \mathbf{x}_j)$ and in another system, the net force is $\sum_j \mathbf{f}'_j(\mathbf{x}_i, \mathbf{x}_j)$. If both system are equivalent in sewing, then for all $\mathbf{x}_i$, we have

$$\sum_j \mathbf{f}_j(\mathbf{x}_i, \mathbf{x}_j) = 0 \Leftrightarrow \sum_j \mathbf{f}'_j(\mathbf{x}_i, \mathbf{x}_j) = 0$$

Assume that S_0 and S_1 are two systems. Let the force exerting from $\mathbf{x}_j$ upon $\mathbf{x}_i$ be $\mathbf{f}_j(\mathbf{x}_i, \mathbf{x}_j)$ in S_0 and let the force in S_1 be $c\mathbf{f}_j(\mathbf{x}_i, \mathbf{x}_j)$ exerting from $\mathbf{x}_j$ upon $\mathbf{x}_i$, where c is constant. Then these two systems are equivalence in sewing by definition. Therefore, in order to bring a system faster to equilibrium state, we can increase the stiffness of the springs by multiplying a factor larger than one as long as the system is numerically stable. The factor is (gradually) changed back to one in the end of the sewing process.

Another kind of relation between two sewing systems is called the *implication relation* that if S_0 is in an equilibrium state, then it implies that S_1 is also in an equilibrium state. We can construct S_1 easily if S_0 is given. Let the force exerting from $\mathbf{x}_j$ upon $\mathbf{x}_i$ be $\mathbf{f}_j(\mathbf{x}_i, \mathbf{x}_j)$ in S_0. We model the force as $(\sum_j \mathbf{f}_j(\mathbf{x}_i, \mathbf{x}_j))Q(\mathbf{x}_i, \mathbf{x}_k)$ exerting from $\mathbf{x}_k$ upon $\mathbf{x}_i$ in S_1. The proof is that $\sum_j \mathbf{f}_j(\mathbf{x}_i, \mathbf{x}_j) = 0 \Rightarrow \sum_k ((\sum_j \mathbf{f}_j(\mathbf{x}_i, \mathbf{x}_j))Q(\mathbf{x}_i, \mathbf{x}_k)) = 0$.

10.7 A control system for a sewing process

Assume that the time step is suitable for performing a sewing process. Given that the surfaces are merged along the sewing lines in the beginning of the sewing process. The particles along the sewing lines may still be far away from each other. There is a large amount of potential energy stored in the springs. This makes the system stiff. If the particles are released, the forces exerting on the particles along the sewing lines are very large. If we compute the velocities of the particles without having sufficiently large viscous damping force, the magnitude of the velocities will be very large. This results in a lot of self-collisions. We want to develop a scheme for controlling the sewing process so that unnecessary self-collisions, e.g. in-plane collisions, can be avoided. There are three ways to control the sewing process: (1) spring force control, (2) viscous damping force control and (3) velocity control.

(1) Spring force control: If the magnitude of the forces is too large, the particles will be pulled fiercely that the motion of the surfaces will change drastically. Unnecessary intersections will occur. The presence of the forces with large magnitude is due to two cases. The first case is that the surfaces are too small for warping around the target due to its small size. We must have to stretch them so that they are sufficiently large for warping around the target. They may consist of stiff materials and the magnitude of the forces will be large.

The second case is that the material may not be stiff. However, the distances between the source matching nodes and the destination matching nodes are very large at the time of merging. This makes the magnitude of the forces large. The larger the distance is, the larger the magnitude of the forces will be. This increases the stiffness of the system.

We need to lower the magnitude of the forces exerting on the particles so that (1) the system becomes suitable for numerical integration and (2) the stability of the system is maintained. This also avoids unnecessary self-collisions. Alternatively, we can perform the viscous damping force control to solve the problem of large forces.

(2) Viscous damping force control: The viscous damping forces are depended on the velocities of the particles. By adding a suitable amount of viscous damping forces exerting on the particles, we ameliorate the condition number of the system. If the viscous damping factor is sufficiently large, the particles will move to their rest positions without vibration. In our implementation, we use $\delta(t)\beta_{(i,j)}$ as the viscous damping factor for the spring connecting two particles $\mathbf{x}_i$ and $\mathbf{x}_j$. The function $\delta(t)$ is constant or a function of time. We aim to compute a relative better value for $\delta(t)$ from experiments.

(3) Velocity Control: Although we can control the forces, we may not modify them to suitable values. The speed of the particles may be too large. If the speed of particles is too large, some triangles flip their orientation in one step. This will lead to instability to the system because of "abnormal" collisions. After solving the motion equation, we should modify the velocities of the particles by multiplying them with a small factor in order to lower the speed. The new velocity v_{new} for the particles is tuned as follows:

$$\mathbf{v}_{new} = \eta(\mathbf{x}, t)\mathbf{v} \tag{10.13}$$

where $\eta(\mathbf{x}, t)$ is a function that we use it for velocity control. We call $\eta(\mathbf{x}, t)$ a *velocity tuning function*. Its range is $[0, 1]$. In the beginning of the sewing process, the velocity magnitude of the particles near the sewing lines is very large. Therefore, we expect that $\eta(\mathbf{x}, t)$ is small in the beginning. Gradually, near the end of the sewing process, $\eta(\mathbf{x}, t)$ should converge to 1. When $t \geq t_0$, $\eta(\mathbf{x}, t) = 1$. In this case, the modified velocity $\mathbf{v}_{new}$ is equal to the computed velocity $\mathbf{v}$ obtained from solving the motion equation.

By controlling the velocities of the particles, we avoid instability of the system, especially in the early stage of the sewing process. Viscous damping forces do not appear in the first iteration of the integration method as the velocities are initialized as zero. In an implicit integration scheme, the forces exerting on a particle are spread out and affect the neighboring particles. However, it will take some time for the forces spreading. Therefore, we do not want the speed of the particles to be too high in the early stage of the sewing process. Gradually, we can increase the speed factor as the effect of the sewing forces has been spread out to affect other particles. At this moment, the factor can increase. However, near the end of the sewing process, we need to converge the system parameters to the real ones. Therefore, the factor should gradually decrease and converge to one. We employ the *sine* function as the velocity tuning function since it satisfies the criteria. We define the velocity tuning function as: $\eta(x,t) = (1-\alpha) + \alpha sin\frac{\tau(t)\pi}{2}$, where $\alpha, \tau \in [0,1]$. The velocity tuning function $\eta(x,t)$ is nonlinear. The number τ is defined as: $\tau = \frac{\text{Current Frame Number - 1}}{\text{Total Number of Sewn Frames}}$.

10.8   Computation of natural distances

We propose a method to compute natural distance between two connecting particles if the panels are developable and are represented by triangular meshes. This kind of surfaces can be flattened. A triangle is picked and placed in plane. We pick a neighboring triangle and map the third vertex into plane. We repeat this for other interested triangles. The natural distances are computed in the 2D plane. We initialize the natural lengths of the springs for the sewing nodes (particles) of the panels.

10.9   Experiments and results

First, we investigated the appropriate number of frames for the sewing process. A set of viscous damping multipliers and tuning functions were also evaluated. Then we selected the best combination of sewing frames, viscous damping multipliers and tuning functions. We performed experiments for evaluating the performance of the control sewing system under the new setting. Finally, we applied our sewing system for sewing Chinese dresses. We performed the experiments on a 3.0GHz Pentium 4 PC with 1GB of main memory. Double floating point was used. The spring-mass system proposed by Provot [114] is adopted. (Other kinds of physical systems [67, 83] are also possible.) The type of spring was regular spring. The initial viscous damping factor of

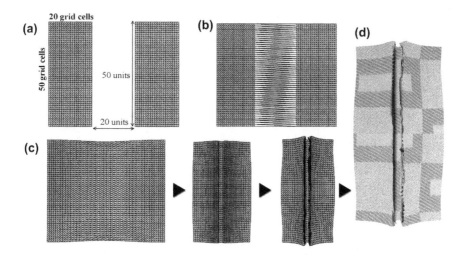

Figure 10.1: A non-control sewing process for two rectangular panels. (a) the initial placements; (b) the merged surface; (c) snapshots from the sewing process; (d) self-penetration due to large speed of particles.

the springs is 2.0 (units). The time step was $\frac{1}{90}$ seconds. Without other specification, the maximum and minimum spring constants are 1000 and 500 (units), the mass of a particle is one unit, and the dynamic and static coefficients are 0.4 and 0.5, respectively.

Figure 10.1(a) shows the initial placement of two rectangular panels. They are coplanar and their distance is 20 units. Each has 20x50 grid cells and 21x51 particles. The dimension of each cell is one by one. Figure 10.1(b) shows the sewn surface after the two panels are merged. Totally, there are 2091 particles after they are merged. Figures 10.1(c) and (d) show the snapshots of the surface while the surface is being pulled to its rest position. However, there are self-collisions (Figure 10.1(d)) due to the large speed of particles. By systematically controlling the sewing process, this problem can be avoided.

We determined: (1) the number of frames that is for sewing; we call this the *number of sewn frames* which is denoted by s^f; (2) the nonlinear tuning function $\eta(\mathbf{x}, t)$ for velocity control; and (3) the viscous damping multiplier $\delta(t)$. Figure 10.2 shows potential energy of the sewn surface under different settings. We checked for $s^f = 100$,

200, and 300. The velocity fraction α is set as 0.5, 0.6, 0.8, and 1.0 for the tuning function $\eta(\mathbf{x}, t) = (1 - \alpha) + \alpha sin\frac{\tau(t)\pi}{2}$. We denote the nonlinear tuning function as **NSV**$d_0 d_1$ and α is represented by the decimal number $d_0.d_1$. The viscous damping multiplier $\delta(t)$ is set as 1, 2, 4, and 6.

The graphs show that the larger the sewn frame is (i.e. longer sewn time), the lower potential energy can be obtained. After the sewn frame, the sewn surface was vibrating. This was due to the exchange of energy between potential energy and kinetic energy. In the cases that s^f is equal to 100, 200, and 300, potential energy is in the order of 10^4, 10^3 and 10^2, respectively. As potential energy is around 10^4 for $s^f = 100$, it is too high to be considered the system as in an equilibrium state compared to the two cases $s^f = 200$ and $s^f = 300$. Therefore, we chose $s^f = 200$ and $s^f = 300$ for further investigation.

Now, we investigated about the nonlinear tuning function for the velocities of particles. The patterns of potential energy are similar in all graphs. The graphs show that the best to the worse performance of α is in the order of 0.5, 0.6, 0.8 and 1.0 almost everywhere. However, the behavior of the sewing process is unstable in the case $\alpha = 0.5$. When $s^f = 100, 300$ and $\alpha = 0.5$, self-collisions happened in the sewn surface. Therefore, we would ignore the case $\alpha = 0.5$. When $\alpha = 0.6, 0.8, 1.0$, there were no self-collisions. The amounts of potential energy are close to each other in the two cases $\alpha = 0.6$ and $\alpha = 0.8$ Therefore, we chose $\alpha = 0.6$ and $\alpha = 0.8$ for further investigation.

We have to choose the viscous damping multiplier $\delta(t)$. In the two cases $s^f = 200$ and $s^f = 300$, the graphs show that if $\delta(t)$ is smaller, potential energy is higher. Now, we consider potential energy of the sewn surface when the large value of the viscous damping multiplier is used, i.e. $\delta = 6$. If s^f (e.g. 200) is small, there is not enough time for the sewn surface to dissipate its potential energy. The best value of δ is 4. In this case, by using **NVS06**, potential energy could be lowered to $10^{2.6}$ in the case $s^f = 200$ and $10^{1.5}$ in the case $s^f = 300$.

The performance for the following settings would be evaluated further. We chose $s^f = 200$, $s^f = 300$, $\alpha = 0.6$ and $\alpha = 0.8$ and $\delta = 4$. Two basic tests were performed: varying distances and varying angles between two panels. We varied the distance D between two panels from 10 to 100 units and varied the angle θ from 10 to 70 degrees. Figure 10.3 and Figure 10.4 show the snapshots from the experiments and the graphs of potential energy of the sewn surface for different settings.

Figures 10.3(b) and (c) show that the larger the distance D is, the larger amount of potential energy will be remained in the end of the sewing process. After the sewing process, the sewn surface vibrated and the lowest amount of potential energy was obtained for the sewing process using a larger sewn frame ($s^f = 300$ compared to $s^f = 200$). The performance patterns are similar in all cases.

During the sewing process, potential energy is dissipated. Although a greater amount of energy is dissipated in the case $s^f = 200$ than that in the case $s^f = 300$ in the early stage of the sewing process (frame 0 to frame 200), the lowest amount of potential energy is obtained in the case $s^f = 300$. With the same distance of the two panels, **NVS06** is better than **NVS08**. However, their difference is quite small. We illustrate this by using the absolute relative log energy.

We define the *absolute relative log energy* of method $\mathcal{N}_0$ against method $\mathcal{N}_1$ in the i-th frame as:

$$E_i^{log}(\mathcal{N}_0, \mathcal{N}_1) = \left| \frac{\log E_i^{\mathcal{N}_0} - \log E_i^{\mathcal{N}_1}}{\log E_i^{\mathcal{N}_1}} \right| \tag{10.14}$$

where E_i denotes potential energy of the sewn surface at i-th frame. Table 10.1 shows the absolute relative log energy (per frame) of **NVS08** against **NVS06** in the cases of different distances. In the case $s^f = 200$, the average absolute relative log energy ranges from 0.053 to 0.06. The standard deviation is in the range of 0.022 to 0.034. In the case $s^f = 300$, the average absolute relative log energy ranges from 0.076 to 0.087. The standard deviation is in the range of 0.038 to 0.052. In both cases, the average is less than 7%. The standard deviation is less than the average by around 50%.

In the experiments of different angles, the same conclusion can be drawn. **NVS06**

	Relative Log Energy of NVS08 to NVS06: Different Distances							
	s^f= 200				s^f= 300			
	D = 10	D = 30	D = 50	D = 100	D = 10	D = 30	D = 50	D = 100
Average	0.060	0.054	0.053	0.054	0.087	0.077	0.076	0.076
STD	0.034	0.027	0.025	0.022	0.052	0.041	0.040	0.038

Table 10.1: Absolute relative log energy of **NVS08** against **NVS06** in the cases with different distances.

is better than **NVS08** in the cases that the angle between the two panels are the same. Figures 10.3(b) and (c) show that the larger the angle θ between the two panels is, the greater amount of potential energy of the sewn surface will remain in the end of the sewing process. After that, the sewn surface vibrated and the lowest amount of potential energy was obtained for the sewing process using longer sewn time ($s^f = 300$ comparing to $s^f = 200$). Table 10.2 shows the absolute relative log energy (per frame) of **NVS08** against **NVS06** in the experiments of different angles. In the case $s^f = 200$, the average absolute relative log energy ranges from 0.038 to 0.052. The standard deviation is in the range of 0.008 to 0.024. In the case $s^f = 300$, the average absolute relative log energy ranges from 0.045 to 0.068. The standard deviation is in the range of 0.011 to 0.035. In both cases, the average is less than 10%. The standard deviation is less than the average by 40% at least.

	Relative Log Energy of NVS08 to NVS06: Different Angles							
	s^f= 200				s^f= 300			
	θ = 10	θ = 30	θ = 50	θ = 70	θ = 10	θ = 30	θ = 50	θ = 70
Average	0.052	0.045	0.041	0.038	0.068	0.055	0.050	0.045
STD	0.024	0.015	0.011	0.008	0.035	0.021	0.015	0.011

Table 10.2: Absolute relative log energy of **NVS08** against **NVS06** in the cases with different angles.

Therefore, in the experiments of varying distances and varying angles, we conclude that the performance of **NVS08** is almost the same as **NVS06** in the case $\delta = 4$ and $s^f = 300$. We had repeated the same experiments by using bias-spring. We recorded that potential energy of the sewn surface could be much lower, in the order of 10^{-5} in some cases.

	Before sewing	After sewing	Friction	Spring stiffness
	#particles / #triangles	#particles / #triangles	static / dynamic	min / max
Short and tight skirt	2 panels Each: 4, 246 / 9, 000 Stretched by 25%	9, 160 / 18, 000	0.5/0.4	500 / 1, 000
Long skirt	2 panels Each: 14, 661 / 28, 800	29, 080 / 57, 600	0.5/0.4	500 / 1, 000
Long skirt with long sleeves	2 panels for torso 9, 246 / 1, 8000 Stretched by 25% 4 panels for sleeves Each: 2, 626 / 5, 000	28, 316 / 56, 000	0.5/0.4	500 / 1, 000
Blouse and trousers	2 panels for blouse Each: 6, 161 / 12, 000 4 panels for trousers Each: 2, 626 / 5, 000 Stretched by 66.67%	Blouse 12, 168 / 24, 000 Trousers 10, 099 / 20, 000	2.0/2.0	Blouse front part: 500 / 1, 000 Blouse back part: 800 / 1, 500 Trousers: 500 / 1, 000

Table 10.3: Information about the four sewing examples on Chinese dresses.

We had tried smaller value (< 0.5) of the velocity fraction α for the nonlinear tuning function but self-collisions occurred. We had also tried a linear function $(1 - \alpha) + \alpha\tau$ for modifying the velocities of the particles. However, it would lead to self-collisions too. If the nonlinear tuning function for velocities of particles was not applied, self-collisions would happen within several frames. We noticed that it did not work well if the number of sewn frames was lower than fifty.

We applied the control system to perform sewing process for modeling four kinds of Chinese dresses and trousers. The number of sewn frames s^f was set as 300 and δ was set as 4. **NVS08** was employed since the rate of change of potential energy of **NVS08** is smaller than the rate of change in **NVS06**. In the experiment, the bias-springs were used in the spring-mass system of the deformable surfaces. The time step was $\frac{1}{90}$ seconds. After the sewn frame, stochastic wind loading and gravity were activated. Table 10.3 lists the number of particles and spring stiffness for modeling the virtual garments.

In Example one, there is a short Chinese dress formed by two panels, one placed in the back of a mannequin and one placed in front of it. It takes 200 frames for the sewn surface to converge to its equilibrium position. Figure 10.5 shows the snapshots. Figure 10.6 and Figure 10.7 show the side view and the front view of the tight dress dressed on the mannequin. In Example two, there are two panels which are long enough to cover the torso and the legs of the mannequin. Figure 10.8 shows the snapshot. Figure 10.9 and Figure 10.10 show the back view and the front view of the dress dressed on the mannequin. In Example three, a Chinese dress with long sleeves are modeled. We have 6 panels; 2 panels (each 18,000 tri. 9,246 particles) for forming garment around the torso and the other 4 panels (each 5,000 tri., 2,626 v) for forming two sleeves. After the sewing process, the dress is composed of 56,000 tri. and 28,316 particles. Figure 10.11 shows the snapshots. Figure 10.12 and Figure 10.13 show the side view and the front view of the Chinese dress dressed on the mannequin. In Example four, there are a blouse and a pair of trousers. The trousers are stretched by 66.67% initially. The dynamics and static friction coefficients are set to a high value 2.0. The support for the trousers is mainly due to the friction force when the trousers interact with the legs. Owing to the high friction between the blouse and the mannequin, wrinkles are formed on the chest naturally. Figure 10.14 and Figure 10.15 show the snapshots. Figure 10.16 and Figure 10.17 show the back view and the front view of a blouse and trousers dressed on the mannequin.

After the sewn frame, we applied stochastic wind blowing on the sewn garments and checked their stability and realism of garments. The dresses were animated realistically. There were no anchors. The virtual garments were supported solely due to the reaction force exerting from the mannequin.

10.10   Summary and discussion

We have proposed a control system which stably performs the sewing process for deformable surfaces. By systematically controlling the internal physical properties of the deformable surfaces, we performed the sewing process for several independent panels together stably and efficiently. By employing the robust and efficient collision response unit and collision detection unit developed in the previous chapters, we demonstrated realistic simulation for the sewn Chinese dresses and trousers under wind loading and gravity.

We can stop the sewing process any time as the panels are merged together in the beginning. Animators can add new panels to the sewn surface at any time. We do not have the two problems that will happen in a conventional sewing process: (1) unable to perform sewing due to small sewing forces and (2) intersections happen when the particles are merged.

If the sewing process can be performed in real time, it will be a powerful editing tool. There are three ways for improving the performance of the proposed method. For example, we could apply low cost methods in the early stage of the sewing process:

- Instead of using an exact collision detection method, we can use the low cost intersection test, for example, large bounding volume test. We need not to call the intrinsic collision detection. When there is collision, the involved part is back-tracked and frozen. After a certain duration, we switch to employ the exact collision detection method in order to obtain the final shape of the sewn surface.

- We can also use some low cost integration method, for example, the forward Euler. We shift the integration method by using implicit methods and change the physical properties back to the exact values after a certain duration.

- If the panels are too complex, we use their simplified models for performing the sewing process. Gradually, we change the panels back to their original complexity.

If there are external drivers affecting the motion of the sewn surface during the sewing process, these greatly affect the final shape of the sewn surface. We have tried to perform the sewing process when gravity is enabled. We increased the strength of gravity in the beginning and then gradually decreased it to its real value. If the strength of gravity was too large and gravity was suddenly reset to its real value, the particles would be pulled up fiercely. This was due to the large amount of potential energy stored in the springs. Once the strength of gravity is reduced, the potential energy is converted to forces in the opposite direction of gravity. Further research is required for minimizing the sewing process under the effect of external force drivers.

215

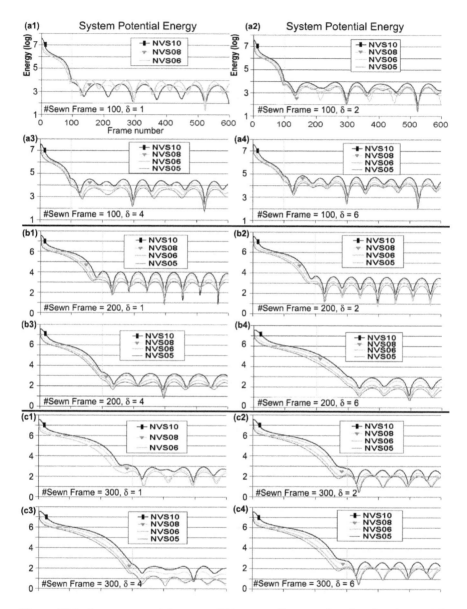

Figure 10.2: System potential energy. Using a nonlinear tuning function for particle velocity in a sewing process. The numbers of sewn frames are 100, 200, and 300. The multiplier $\delta(t)$ for the viscous damping factor is set as 1, 2, 4, and 6. By applying **NSV05** in the cases of #sewn frame = 100 and 300, self-collisions occur when $\delta = 1$.

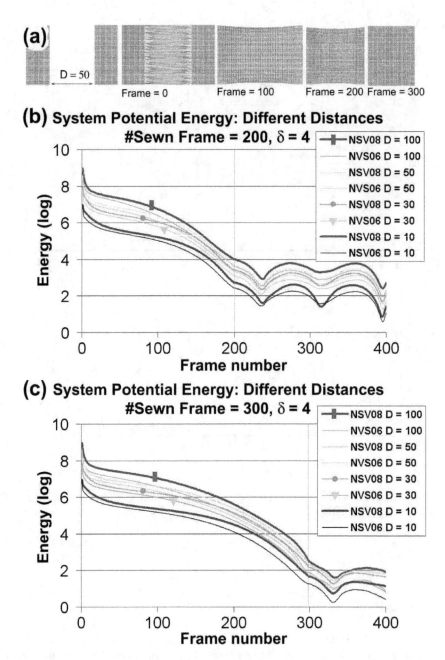

Figure 10.3: System potential energy for applying the nonlinear tuning functions **NSV06** and **NSV08** in the sewing process with different initial distances (D) between two panels. The numbers of sewn frames are 200 and 300. The multiplier $\delta(t)$ for the viscous damping factor is set to 4.

(a)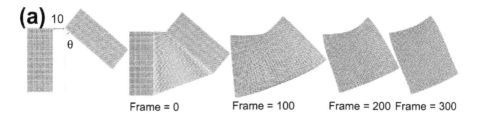

Frame = 0   Frame = 100   Frame = 200 Frame = 300

(b) **System Potential Energy: Different Angles**
#Sewn Frame = 200, δ = 4

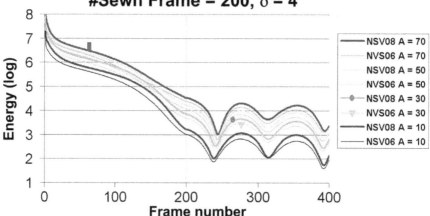

(c) **System Potential Energy: Different Angles**
#Sewn Frame = 300, δ = 4

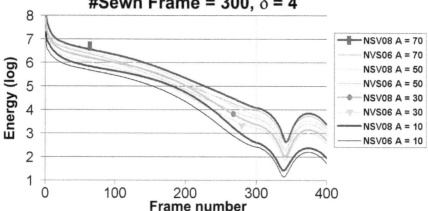

Figure 10.4: System potential energy for applying the nonlinear tuning functions **NSV06** and **NSV08** in the sewing process with different initial angles (D) between two panels. The numbers of sewn frames are 200 and 300. The multiplier $\delta(t)$ for the viscous damping factor is set to 4.

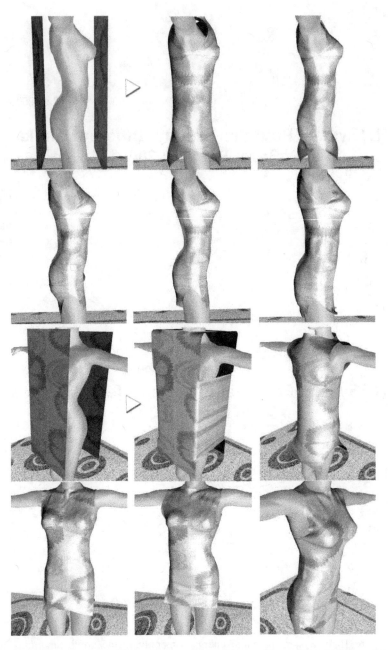

Figure 10.5: Example one: Snapshots of a tight Chinese dress. The tight dress nicely fits onto the mannequin. Wrinkles with small amplitude are formed near the neck.

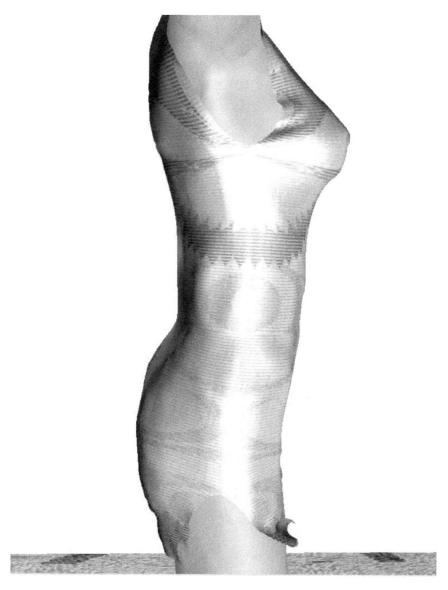

Figure 10.6: Example one: The side view of the short Chinese dress after the sewing process. The tight dress nicely fits onto the mannequin.

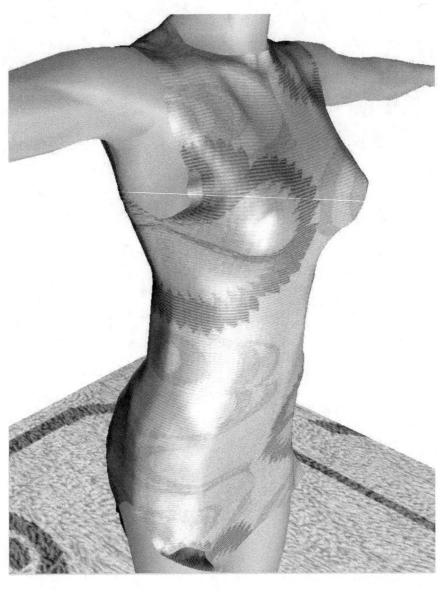

Figure 10.7: Example one: The front view of the short Chinese dress after the sewing process. The tight dress nicely fits onto the mannequin.

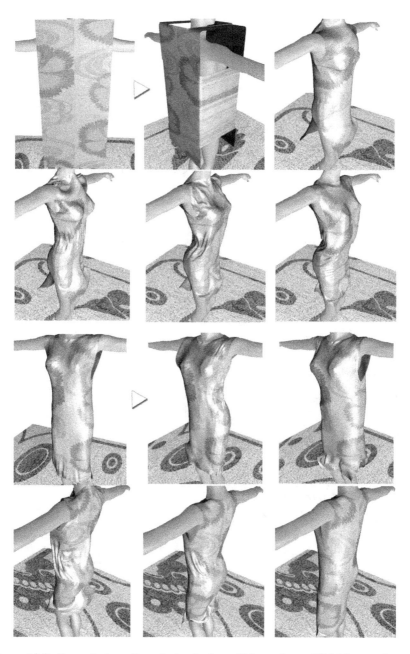

Figure 10.8: Example two: Snapshots of a long Chinese dress. Wrinkles are formed when the dress interacts with the mannequin.

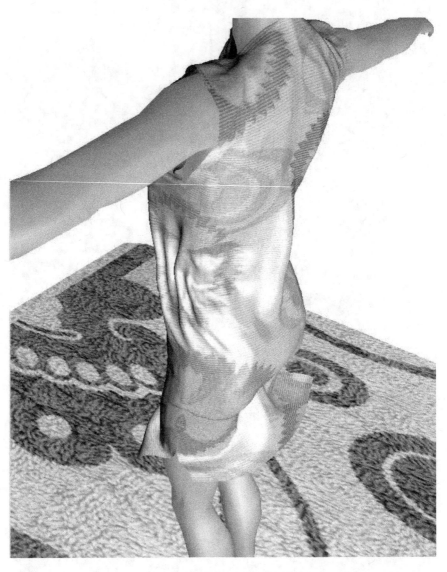

Figure 10.9: Example two: The back view of the Chinese dress after the sewing process. The dress is being pulled downwards due to gravity. Realistic wrinkles appear.

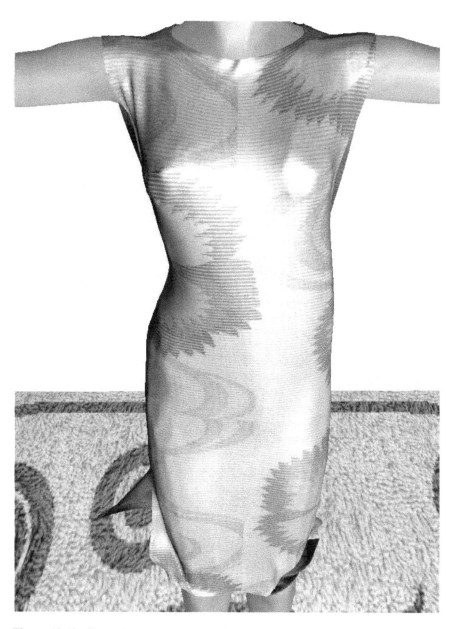

Figure 10.10: Example two: The front view of the Chinese dress after the sewing process. During wind blowing, the bottom-part of the dress flutters naturally. The system handle the self-collisions appropriately and there is no intersection.

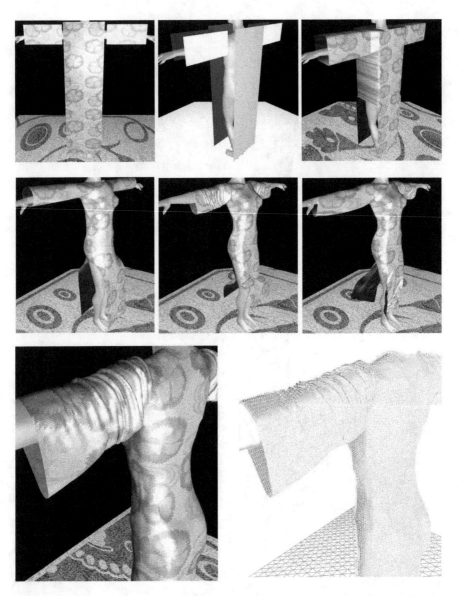

Figure 10.11: Example three: Snapshots of Chinese dress with long sleeves. During wind blowing, the bottom-part of the dress flutters naturally. When the sleeves interact with the arms of the mannequin, wrinkles appear and disappear realistically. The lower left image shows the wireframe of the dress.

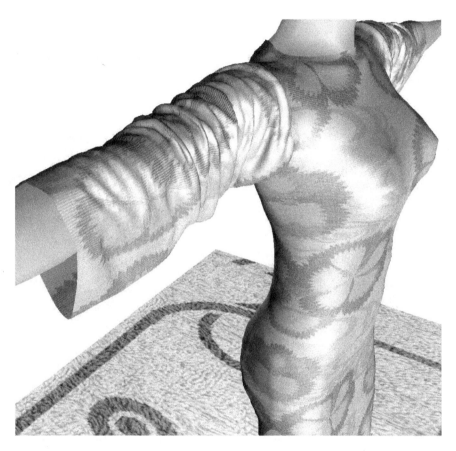

Figure 10.12: Example three: The side view of the Chinese dress with long sleeves the sewing process. The dress fits onto the mannequin smoothly. Natural wrinkles are formed on the sleeves.

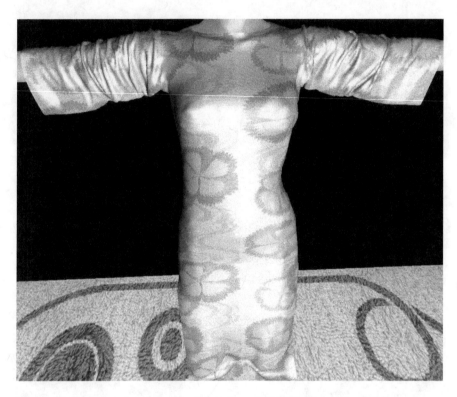

Figure 10.13: Example three: The front view of the Chinese dress with long sleeves after the sewing process. The realistic wrinkles of the sleeves are formed.

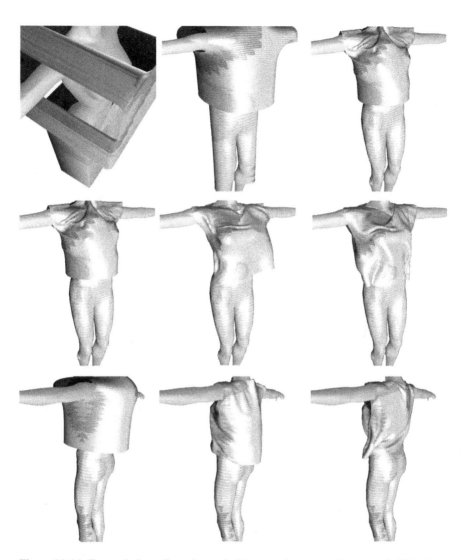

Figure 10.14: Example four: Snapshots of a blouse and trousers. During wind blowing, the interactions between the blouse, trousers and the mannequin are natural.

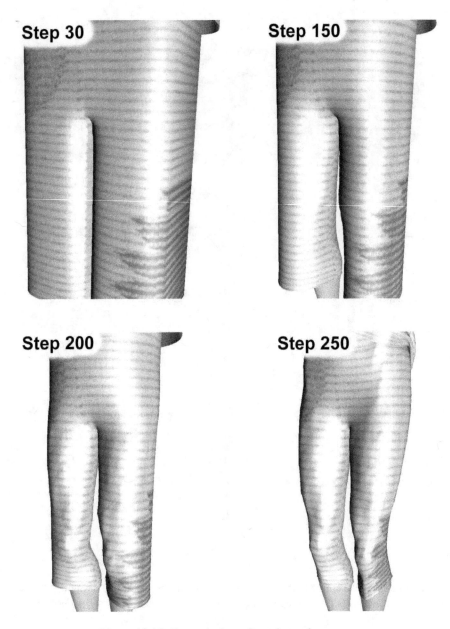

Figure 10.15: Example four: Snapshots of trousers.

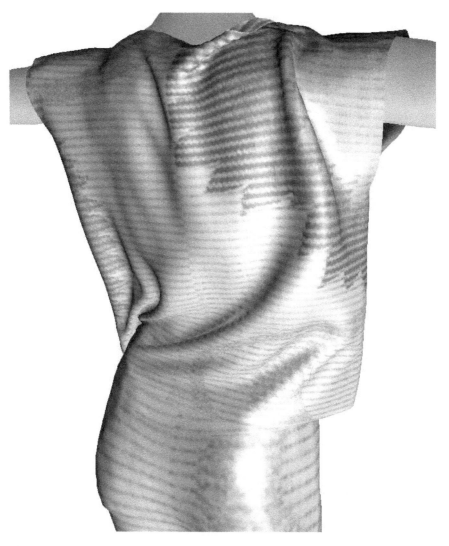

Figure 10.16: Example four: The back view of a blouse and trousers after the sewing process. Wrinkles are formed naturally at both places: waist and neck. A large area of wrinkle appears from the right shoulder and goes smoothly to the left side of the waist.

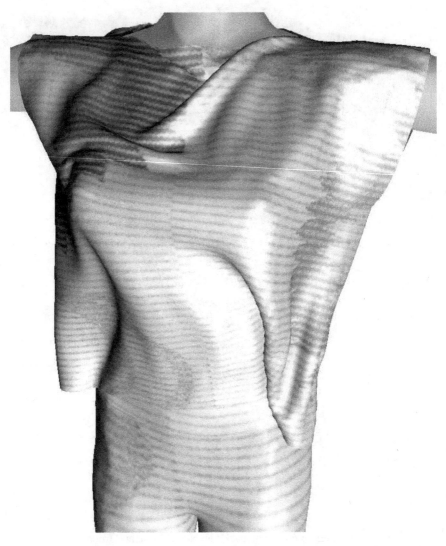

Figure 10.17: Example four: The front view of the garments after the sewing process.

Chapter 11

A Piecewise Stable Sewing Process

11.1 Introduction and motivation

Chapter 10 presents a non-linear tuning function $\eta(\mathbf{x}, t)$ for adjusting the velocities of the particles in order to avoid unnecessary inplane self-collisions. The method quickly brings the sewn surface into an equilibrium state after the panels are merged. We observed that there are two ways for improving the non-linear tuning method.

First, we should prevent potential energy from increasing. During the sewing process, a portion of kinetic energy that is converted to potential energy. At this moment, we could reset the velocities of the particles for the next frame so that kinetic energy will be vanished and there will be no more kinetic energy that is converted to potential energy.

Second, an adaptive viscous damping coefficient should be used according to the state of the sewn surface. If the viscous damping coefficient is too large, it will slow down the speed of the particles too much; if it is too small, self-collisions will happen and the particles will vibrate or oscillate. When the particles are near their equilibrium positions, we can treat that as if the particles connecting to the particles were fixed. Thus, a smaller viscous damping multiplier can be used.

11.2 A new approach for stable sewing

According to these two observations, we propose a piecewise stable sewing process. Assume that the total number of sewn frames is s^f. We divide the sewing process into k stages. The stages are indexed from 1 to k. Each stage i occupies a number of frames s_i^f. In each stage, we control the physical parameters based on the state of the system in order to improve the performance of the sewing process.

11.3 Experiments and results

We need to compute two parameters τ_i and δ_i. They are used for modifying the physical parameters of the sewn surface. The frame fraction τ_i and the viscous damping multiplier $\delta_i(\tau_i)$ in the i-th stage are given by:

$$\tau_i = \frac{\text{current frame index in the } i\text{-th stage minus one}}{s_i^f} \tag{11.1}$$

and

$$\delta_i(\tau_i) = \delta_{min} + (1 - \tau_i)(\delta_{max} - \delta_{min}) \tag{11.2}$$

The value of τ_i changes from 0 to $\frac{s_i^f - 1}{s_i^f}$ with the step size $\frac{1}{s_i^f}$ and the value of $\delta_i(\tau_i)$ changes from δ_{max} to $\delta_{min} + \frac{\delta_{max} - \delta_{min}}{s_i^f}$ with the step size $\frac{\delta_{max} - \delta_{min}}{s_i^f}$.

We compare the performance of six methods. Table 11.1 describes each of them.

Methods	Description	#Sewn frames	δ_{min}	Reset velocity when potential energy increases ?
RegularNR	one sewing interval	$s_1^f = 300$	4	no
P1x300FNR	three sewing intervals	$s_1^f = s_2^f = s_3^f = 100$	4	no
P3x100V1.0R	three sewing intervals	$s_1^f = s_2^f = s_3^f = 100$	1.0	yes
P3x100V0.25R	three sewing intervals	$s_1^f = s_2^f = s_3^f = 100$	0.25	yes
P100+200FV1.0R	two sewing intervals	$s_1^f = 100$; $s_2^f = 200$	1.0	yes
P100+200FV0.25R	two sewing intervals	$s_1^f = 100$; $s_2^f = 200$	0.25	yes

Table 11.1: Description of six sewing methods.

In **RegularNR** and **P1x300FNR**, we do not reset the velocities of the particles to zero except in the end of the sewing process. In **P3x100V1.0R**, **P3X100V0.25R**,

P100+200FV1.0R and **P100+200FV0.25R**, we reset the velocities of the particles to zero in the end of the sewing process or when potential energy is increasing.

In the experiments, we used the non-linear velocity tuning function **NVS06**. We set s^f and δ_{max} as 300 and 4, respectively. Regular springs were used without other specification. The mass of the particles was one unit. We performed empirical experiments to collect the best values for s_i^f and δ_{min} in three test cases. After that we performed another two complex examples to compare the performance of the methods in details. Potential energy of the sewn surface was recorded from frame to frame and it is taken by logarithm to the base ten on the graphs.

In the three test cases, we have two panels in two-dimension space. The dimension of each of the panels is 20x50. The two panels are divided into 20x50 grid cells evenly. The sewn surface consists of 2,091 particles, 400 triangles, and 12,238 springs.

In the first test case, the two panels are placed in parallel with a distance of 40 units. The spring stiffnesses (max/min) are 1,000/500. Therefore, the magnitude of the sewing forces between two matching particles (nodes) is up to 40,000 units. The time step was 0.02 seconds. Figure 11.1(a) shows the snapshots and the graphs of potential energy of the sewn surface in different methods. The snapshots were taken from **P100+200FV0.25R**. The right graph is a zoom-in for a particular portion of the left graph. The best two methods are **P100+200FV0.25R** and **P100+200FV1.0R**. Then, it is followed by **P3x100V0.25R** and **P3x100V1.0R**. The worst two methods are **P3x100NR** and **RegularNR**. In **P100+200FV0.25R**, potential energy is lowered from $10^{-2.2}$ at frame 200 to 10^{-4} at frame 300. The figure shows that at frame 200 and onwards, potential energy of sewn surface is lowered than 10^{-2}. The dimension of the sewn surface is shrunk to 40.00x50.00. The error of the dimension of the sewn surface compared to the dimension of the theoretical result of the sewn surface is less than 0.0125% x 0.01%.

In the second test case, the two panels are placed in parallel with a distance of 10 units and then the panel on the right is rotated about its upper left corner by 50 degrees counter-clockwise. The spring stiffnesses (max/min) are 1,000/500. Therefore, the magnitude of the sewing forces between each pair of matching particles (nodes) varies from around 10, 000 to 80, 677 (or $10000\sqrt{51 + 10sin\frac{5\pi}{18} - 50cos\frac{5\pi}{18}}$) units. The time step was 0.02 seconds. Figure 11.1(b) shows the snapshots and the graphs of potential energy of the methods. The right graph is a zoom-in for a particular portion of the left graph. The snapshots were taken from **P100+200FV0.25R**. The best two methods are **P100+200FV0.25R** and **P100+200FV1.0R**. Then, it is followed by **P3x100V0.25R** and **P3x100V1.0R**. The worst two methods are **P3x100NR** and **RegularNR**. In **P100+200FV0.25R**, potential energy is lowered from $10^{-1.2}$ at frame 200 to 10^{-3} at frame 300.

In the third test case, we evaluated only the performance of **P100+200FV0.25V** for different spring stiffnesses. One panel is displaced to the right side of another in parallel by 20 units. The spring stiffnesses (max/min) are changed from 500/250 to 3,000/2,000. The time step was $\frac{1}{90}$ seconds. Figure 11.2 shows the graph of potential energy of the system for different stiffnesses. The graph shows that the larger the stiffnesses of the springs, the faster potential energy is dissipated. In the case of the spring stiffnesses 3,000/2,000, potential energy of the system changes from 10^8 to 10^2, to $10^{-2.2}$ and finally to 10^{-4} at frame 0, 100, 200, and 300, respectively. However, in the case of the spring stiffnesses 500/250, potential energy of the system changes from 10^8 to 10^4, to $10^{1.6}$ and finally to $10^{0.6}$ at frame 0, 100, 200, and 300, respectively. The dissipation rate in the case the spring stiffnesses 3,000/2,000 is around 10^2 faster per 100 frames than potential energy in the case the spring stiffnesses 500/250.

After we had experimented the methods with three simple test cases, we tested the methods in two complex examples. In the examples, we had two panels. One panel is displaced along the normal direction by 100 units relatively to another panel. The dimension of each of the panels is 100x100 units. One panel is stretched by 25%. They are divided into 50x50 grid cells evenly. Spring stiffnesses are 1000 and 500. The sewn surface consists of 5,038 particles, 10,000 triangles, and 30,524 springs. The snapshots were taken from **P100+200FV0.25R**. The graph for potential energy of the sewn surface is plotted. A portion of the upper graph is enlarged in the lower graph.

In the first example, there is a sphere placed in the middle of the two panels. The sphere consists of 3202 vertices and 6400 triangles. Figure 11.3 shows the snapshots and the graph of potential energy of the sewn surface. The best two methods are **P100+200FV0.25R** and **P100+200FV1.0R**. Then, it is followed by **P3x100V0.25R**, **P3x100V1.0R** and **P3x100NR**. The worst is **RegularNR**. In this example, potential energy of the sewn surface is close in all the methods. From frame 200 to frame 300, potential energy is in the range of $[10^{6.167}, 10^{6.25}]$ for all methods. At frame 200, **P100+200FV0.25R** already dissipates energy of the sewn surface to the lowest level: $10^{6.167}$ units.

In the second example, the configuration is the same as the one in the first example except that there is no sphere in the middle of the two panels. Figure 11.4 shows the snapshots and the graph of potential energy of the sewn surface. The best is **P100+200FV0.25R** and then it is followed by **P100+200FV1.0R**, **P3x100V0.25R**, **P3x100V1.0R** and **P3x100NR**. The worst is **RegularNR**.

After the sewn frame, the control mechanism was deactivated. It can be seen from the graphs that beyond frame 300, potential energy of the system went up and vibrated. This is due to kinetic energy converted to potential energy and numerical errors.

We had tried δ_{min} in the range of $[0, 0.25]$ but there was no significant improvement. To the contrary, it would make the performance worse in some cases. When potential energy started increasing, we had also tried not to perform the reset operation on the velocities of the particles but to modify the velocities of the particles by a fraction. These methods did not perform consistently and they did not perform better than **P100+200FV0.25R**.

11.4 Summary and discussion

We have shown that by controlling the viscous damping multiplier and controlling the velocity of the sewn surface will dissipate potential energy faster compared to fixing the viscous damping multiplier. When potential energy gets lower, a smaller viscous multiplier can be used. However, we could not decrease the viscous multiplier too much as we need it to dissipate energy and to prevent vibration. The methods that have the mechanism of resetting velocities of particles perform better than those methods that do not have the mechanism.

By dividing the sewing process into stages and then using different methods for computing the viscous damping multiplier is equivalent to constructing a function which can be used for adapting to the state of the sewn surface throughout the sewing process. This adaptation of the function to the state of the sewn surface dissipates potential energy of the sewn surface faster than the method using a fixed viscous damping multiplier. Based on this observation, we propose the following directions for further improvement on the proposed control piecewise sewing process:

- If the sewing process is divided into infinite number stages, the function of the viscous damping multiplier can be built continuously as long as there are no interactions.

- An automatic system for generating the function of the viscous damping multiplier can be run off-line based on the specific physical structure of the sewn surface. We require that the method should be general enough so that there are as few assumptions about the targets and obstacles as possible. After that we can use the same set of data to perform the sewing process for a sewn surface with the similar physical structure in real time.

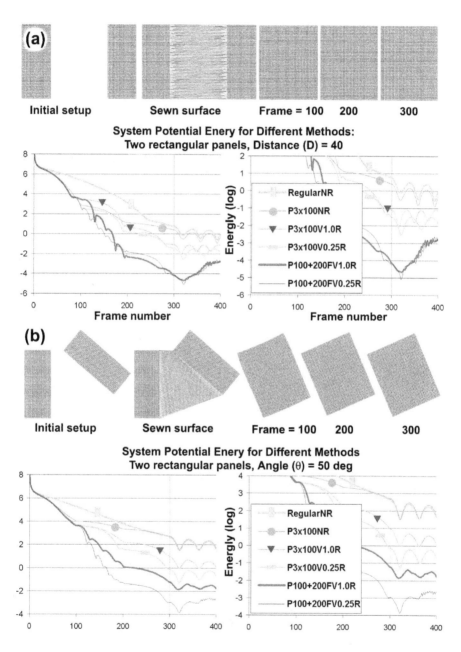

Figure 11.1: Comparison among six sewing methods for (a) different distances and (b) different angles.

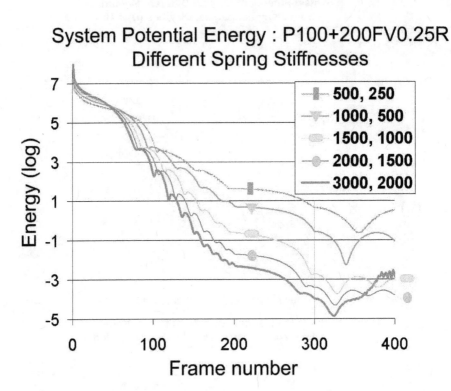

Figure 11.2: Potential energy of the sewn surface for different spring stiffnesses. **P100+200FV0.25R** was employed.

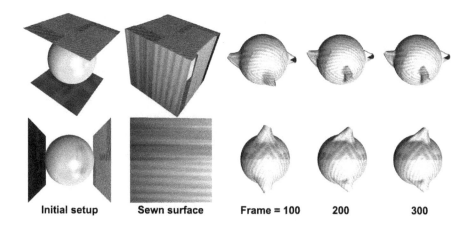

Initial setup   Sewn surface   Frame = 100   200   300

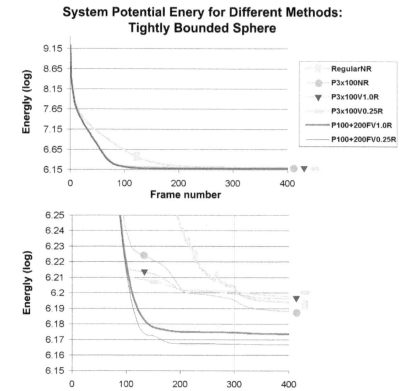

Figure 11.3: Example one for piecewise sewing process: Two rectangular panels and a sphere. Snapshots and results.

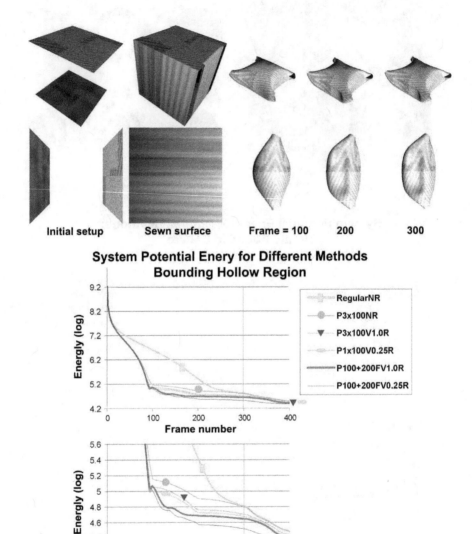

Figure 11.4: Example two for piecewise sewing process: Two rectangular panels. Snapshots and results.

Chapter 12

Conclusions

We have devised techniques for animating deformable surfaces, in particular, virtual clothing, robustly and efficiently. Our collision techniques report accurate collision information for dynamics computation. We classify these techniques into four categories: (1) culling non-colliding pairs for collision detection, (2) intrinsic collision detection, (3) collision response, and (4) the editing and simulation of three kinds of special deformable surfaces.

12.1   Summaries of the proposed techniques

We summarize the techniques in each category as follows:

1. **Culling non-colliding pairs for collision detection**

   - **An image-based method for interference test:** We developed an image-based method to perform interference test for deformable surfaces. A surface is decomposed into (π, β)-surfaces dynamically. These (π, β)-surfaces are rendered into the frame buffer and a frame buffer scanning process is employed to collect the potential colliding pairs. We balance the work load between the main processor and the Graphics Processing Unit. This method successfully reduces the number of potential colliding pairs.

- **A $(\pi, \beta, \mathbf{I})$-surface decomposition scheme:** We devised the scheme of $(\pi, \beta, \mathbf{I})$-surface decomposition for self-collision detection in the time domain. We have shown that this method can detect the first contact point for a closed two-manifold. This method allows large out of plane deformation. For a developable surface with convex shape in 2D space, small in-plane deformation is allowed.

  - **An adaptive backward voxel-based (BVOX) hierarchical structure:** We developed an adaptive BVOX-AABB hierarchical structure which adapts to the shape of the deformable surfaces. It suits to handle highly deformable surfaces for collision detection.

2. **Intrinsic collision detection:** We proposed an architecture for implementing the unit of the intrinsic collision detection in the bottom-layer of a collision detector. We have implemented this architecture for performing the intrinsic collision detection successfully in the time domain. By exploiting the coherent and temporal properties of the motion of the potential colliding pairs, we have improved the overall performance of the collision detection process. The method is an exact method which reports collision information accurately, including, collision time, collision normal, and collision points. Numerical errors which have been a major problem in collision detection are managed robustly by using this architecture.

   We have shown that under certain condition, the absolute relative error between a root of a cubic equation and the corresponding root of the truncated equation is small.

3. **Collision response:**

   - **Penetration-free motion space:** We proposed a penetration-free motion space for preventing penetration. The penetration-free motion space is computed for each particle of the colliding features. By constraining the velocities and the forces of these particles inside the motion space, penetration will be prevented. The colliding feature pairs will not pass through each other in the current frame. By employing this method, we have shown that the motion of the deformable surfaces interacting with nonsmooth objects is produced realistically.

- **Handling friction and stiction:** In order to handle friction and stiction, we proposed to adopt a static analysis in order to determine the forces exerting on the particles. The forces exerting on the particles are modified according to the Coulomb's model of friction. We have successfully applied the technique in handling friction and stiction when the deformable surfaces interact with nonsmooth objects.

4. **The editing and simulation of three kinds of special deformable surfaces**
   We proposed three methods to perform simulation for three kinds of special deformable surfaces. These methods can be treated as editing tools for compositing and manipulating these deformable surfaces. The three methods are detailed as follows:

   - **A two-layer scheme:** We developed a two-layer scheme for stably animating deformable surfaces with sharp features (and probably with holes). In the scheme, we use two meshes, an appearance mesh and a ghost mesh, to represent a single deformable surface. By employing this scheme, we avoid using high resolution meshes. We have shown that this method work stably even when there are collisions.

   - **A master-slave scheme:** We devised a master-slave scheme for gluing several surfaces together either along lines or over regions. The scheme preserves the anisotropic properties of the composite surface. The composite surface may not be a manifold surface. A scheme has been proposed for collision detection for this kind of composite surface.

   - **A control system for sewing:** We proposed a system for systematically controlling the sewing (or merging) process for deformable surfaces. The result of the sewing process is a composite surface, namely sewn surface, which is composed of several deformable surfaces. By controlling the internal physical parameters and internal structure of the deformable surfaces, we quickly bring the surfaces into or near the equilibrium state without producing unnecessary self-collisions. We have demonstrated the success of applying the sewing process in creating realistic Chinese dresses. This method can be used for editing surfaces which conform to the laws of Newtonian mechanics.

These techniques, in the four categories, range from the basic operations in the collision detection pipeline for deformable surfaces and the mechanism of handling their interactions to the methods of handling composite surfaces and editing tools. Successfully, we have integrated and applied them to perform simulation for virtual clothing.

In our current implementation, we employ the velocity-based method for collision detection. We only invoke the collision detection one time per frame. Overall, the time spent in collision detection is less than 15% of the total time when the scheme of $(\pi, \beta, \mathbf{I})$-surface decomposition is employed. Most of the time (over 80%) is spent in solving the motion equation.

We found that our proposed collision detection method has one major limitation. In particular, if there are several deformable surfaces entangling together, we may miss collisions. This is due to the ordering of the collision detection for the pairs. Although this can be solved by calling the collision detection handler iteratively, this approach will greatly degrade the performance of the system. Thus, we have devised the piecewise continuous collision detection to ameliorate the problem. In future, we expect more powerful methods will be devised for collision detection for deformable surfaces.

12.2   Extensions of the proposed techniques

There are some immediate extensions of the proposed methods in three areas as follows.

(1) Collision Detection:

- **Velocity buffer:**   The image-based method described in this thesis can be extended to take into consideration the relative motion of the triangles and establish an intermediate checkpoint based on the relative velocities of the vertices of the triangles. The velocities of the vertices are stored in a velocity buffer. The content of the velocity buffer indicates the motion direction of each pixel within the current frame. We want to "visualize" collision events when we perform collision detection. After collecting all the "colliding" pixel pairs, we perform intrinsic collision detection for their corresponding triangles.

- **Hybrid collision detector:**   When the surfaces are low complexity, it will be more efficient to collect the PCPs in the object space directly. This task can be done faster in CPU than it is done in GPU. A scheme of determining whether which tasks should be done in which units required further investigation. An effective arrangement of tasks between CPU and GPU will greatly improve the overall performance.

- **Identifying of non-colliding subsurfaces:**   In the simulation of multiple deformable surfaces, there are subsurfaces which are very close to each other but they will not collide. Consider that there are three deformable surfaces. One deformable surface separates the other two surfaces. These two surfaces do not have a chance to collide even though they are very close to each other. However, this kind of phenomenon may not be known at the preprocessing stage. It will be worthwhile developing techniques to identify these surfaces at run-time efficiently.

(2) Multiple collisions: We group the deformable objects involved in the multiple collisions and embed them inside an auxiliary closed deformable object (or auxiliary object in short). The idea that is to deform the objects inside this auxiliary object, which is similar to the mechanism done for free-form deformation. We need to make sure that the collision status does not change during the deformation. The dynamics of the auxiliary object is based on the laws of mechanics.

(3) Post-refinement:

- **Seam lines:** Seam lines play an important role in a garment. The structure of the seam lines affects the motion of the regions around the seam lines. They also affect the appearance of a garment. They are primitive elements compositing a garment. By modeling the seam lines, we enhance the realism of garments.

- **Wrinkles:** The dimensions of elements of a surface limit the deformation. Within an element, like a triangle, there are no wrinkles. In order to subsidize this limitation, techniques should be designed for enhancing the appearance of each element. This can be done by perturbing the normal per pixel using hardware. Some work has been done in this area [36]. We want to devise a system for automatically computing the wrinkle patterns for specific clothing materials. The wrinkle patterns can be stored in a database for future manipulation.

12.3   Other problems related to simulation of clothing

There are some problems that are not addressed in this thesis. These problems include:

- **Interaction under hard-constraints:** Given a body that is controlled by a user. The body may deform. The trajectory of the body is not known beforehand. We need to compute the motion of a deformable surface interacting with it. Although some techniques have been developed, they are not capable of handling them in complex situations robustly.

- **Rendering of cloth:** The photorealistic rendering of cloth materials has been studied [45, 153]. However, these works assume cloth is motionless. When cloth is deformed, the underlying geometry structure of the threads will change accordingly. We are not sure whether the existing techniques will render cloth realistically during its deformation. The techniques are slow and they hardly achieve at interactive rates.

- **Exploitation of Graphics Processing Unit (GPU):** Currently, it is a trend to exploit the capability of GPU to share the workload of CPU. In order to strive for a balance of workload between them, many techniques have been devised for this purpose. The goal behind this is that real-time performance should be achieved. In presence, we can perform real-time simulation for some deformable surfaces only with low complexity. Further research should be carried out for animating complex deformable surfaces, like garments, in real-time.

- **Point-based interaction:** In the real world, objects are composed of a huge number of particles. In order to model real objects more accurately, it will be natural for us to adopt point cloud as a mean for modeling deformable surfaces. The huge number of particles hinders our progress in this direction at the moment. However, as the power of the computational machines (for example quantum computers) increases, we can afford to perform more sophisticated tasks in relatively short time. Point-based interaction will become available. With respect to the current computation power, we can develop techniques to model a specific region of cloth by using point cloud, when high accuracy is required. Some work has been done on using point-cloud for rendering [41, 15] and point-based collision detection [78].

Appendix A

A Theoretical Analysis on Collision Orientation

Definition A.1 : A function $\mathbf{f}$ is *Lipschitz* of rank L over a subset X of $\mathcal{R}^n$ if there exists a finite number L in X such that for all points $\mathbf{p}_1, \mathbf{p}_2 \in X$ we have $\|\mathbf{f}(\mathbf{p}_2) - \mathbf{f}(\mathbf{p}_1)\| \leq L\|\mathbf{p}_2 - \mathbf{p}_1\|$.

The Lipschitz value L is a generalization of the derivative of $\mathbf{f}(\mathbf{p})$. A function $\mathbf{f}(\mathbf{p})$ satisfying the Lipschitz has finite partial derivatives.

Definition A.2 : A surface is said to be a *parametric surface* if it can be represented by a parametric function with the form $\mathbf{S}(u, v, t)$, where u and v are parametric variables that span each of the surfaces, and t is time.

In the following discussion, we assume that $\mathbf{S}_P(u_p, v_p, t)$ and $\mathbf{S}_Q(u_q, v_q, t)$ are parametric Lipschitz surfaces, where u_p, v_p, u_q and v_q are parametric variables.

Definition A.3 : Two surfaces have a *0–collision* (or *intersection*) at time t_c if:

$$\mathbf{S}_P(u_p, v_p, t_c) = \mathbf{S}_Q(u_q, v_q, t_c) \tag{A.1}$$

Because of numerical errors intrinsically carried along in the computation, in practice, we rarely have 0–collisions. Therefore, we need another kind of collision which is suitable for a practical situation.

251

Definition A.4 : Two surfaces $S_P(u_p, v_p, t)$ and $S_Q(u_q, v_q, t)$ are said to have a γ–*collision* (or *proximity collision*) [146, 147] at time t_c if their shortest distance is smaller than a given positive number γ:

$$\|S_P(u_p, v_p, t_c) - S_Q(u_q, v_q, t_c)\| < \gamma. \tag{A.2}$$

The number γ is chosen to be larger than the machine precision.

Definition A.5 : Two surfaces $S_P(u_p, v_p, t)$ and $S_Q(u_q, v_q, t)$ have exactly one γ-collision at time t_c if and only if there exist $\mathbf{p} \in S_P(u_p, v_p, t_c)$ and $\mathbf{q} \in S_Q(u_q, v_q, t_c)$ such that (1) $\|\mathbf{p} - \mathbf{q}\| < \gamma$; and (2) $\forall \mathbf{p}' \in S_P(u_p, v_p, t_c)$ and $\forall \mathbf{q}' \in S_Q(u_q, v_q, t_c)$, we have $\|\mathbf{p}' - \mathbf{q}'\| \geq \gamma$ if $(\mathbf{p}', \mathbf{q}') \neq (\mathbf{p}, \mathbf{q})$.

Theorem A.1 : Assume that S_P and S_Q have exactly one γ-collision and their shortest distance is non-zero. Then there exists a plane with normal $\mathbf{n}_{PQ}$ separating two sufficiently small regions which enclose the two contact points.

Proof:

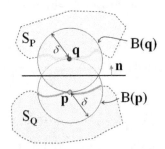

Figure A.1: Separating plane.

Let the collision time be t_c. Assume that the two contact points are $\mathbf{p} = S_p(u_p, v_p, t_c)$ and $\mathbf{q} = S_q(u_q, v_q, t_c)$. Let the distance between $\mathbf{p}$ and $\mathbf{q}$ be δ. Formally, we have:

$$\|\mathbf{p} - \mathbf{q}\| = \delta > 0 \tag{A.3}$$

Define two closed balls $B(\mathbf{p})$ and $B(\mathbf{q})$ which center at $\mathbf{p}$ and $\mathbf{q}$, respectively. The radius of each of the closed balls is δ. Let W be a plane with normal $\mathbf{n}_{PQ} = \frac{\mathbf{q}-\mathbf{p}}{\|\mathbf{q}-\mathbf{p}\|}$

passing through the point $\mathbf{r} = \frac{\mathbf{p+q}}{2}$. Figure A.1 illustrates the position of the plane. We will show that $\mathbf{S}_P \cap B(\mathbf{p})$ and $\mathbf{S}_Q \cap B(\mathbf{q})$ lie on the opposite sides of W.

As the two surfaces have the shortest distance only at points $\mathbf{p}$ and $\mathbf{q}$, there are no other points inside $B(\mathbf{p})$ and $B(\mathbf{q})$. Therefore, $\mathbf{S}_P \cap B(\mathbf{p})$ and $\mathbf{S}_Q \cap B(\mathbf{q})$ do not intersect with W. Consequently, $(\mathbf{S}_Q \cap B(\mathbf{q}) - \mathbf{r}) \cdot \mathbf{n}_{PQ} > 0$ and $(\mathbf{S}_P \cap B(\mathbf{p}) - \mathbf{r}) \cdot \mathbf{n}_{PQ} < 0.$ □

Corollary A.1 : Assume that two surfaces have exactly one γ-collision and their distance is non-zero. Consider a sufficiently small region bounding the two contact points. There exists a vector $\mathbf{n}$ such that for any two points $\mathbf{p}$ and $\mathbf{q}$, one from each surface inside the region, satisfying the following condition:

$$(\mathbf{q} - \mathbf{p}) \cdot \mathbf{n} \geq 0. \tag{A.4}$$

Theorem A.2 : Assume that two surfaces have exactly one 0-collision. Let B be a sufficiently small bounding volume. There exists a vector $\mathbf{n}$ such that for any two points $\mathbf{p}$ and $\mathbf{q}$ selected from each surface inside the volume, we have $(\mathbf{q} - \mathbf{p}) \cdot \mathbf{n} \geq 0$.

Proof: Let B be a sufficiently small closed ball so that it bounds the two regions containing $\mathbf{p}$ and $\mathbf{q}$. Consider that inside B with non-zero radius, the medial surface of these two regions separates these two surfaces except at the contact points. Then there exists a direction so that if the medial surface is projected onto either one of the two regions along the direction, it is an one-to-one mapping. Consequently, we have $(\mathbf{q} - \mathbf{p}) \cdot \mathbf{n} \geq 0$ for all points $\mathbf{p}$ and $\mathbf{q}$ inside B.

Assume that there is no such direction. Then in any viewing direction, there is a line intersecting the medial surface at two points in any direction inside an arbitrarily small ball B. Because of the arbitrary direction and B, the medial surface must lie inside B. If this is the case, the corresponding surface must be contained inside B and the surface must be a point. This is a contradiction. □

Definition A.6 : Assume that two surfaces S_P and S_Q have exactly one collision. Given that p and q belong to S_P and S_Q, respectively, and the two points are sufficiently close to the respective contact point. Then, there exists a vector n such that $(q - p) \cdot n \geq 0$. The vector n is said to be consistent with the *collision orientation* of the two surfaces.

Appendix B

Deformable Triangles, Collision Detection and Properties

Denote $\mathbf{x}_i(t)$ as $\mathbf{x}_i + t\mathbf{w}_i$ and $\vec{\mathbf{x}}_{ij}(t)$ as $(\mathbf{x}_j + t\mathbf{w}_j) - (\mathbf{x}_i + t\mathbf{w}_i)$. We define $\mathbf{n}(t)$ and $D(t)$ as follows:

$$\mathbf{n}(t) \;\equiv\; \vec{\mathbf{x}}_{k2}(t) \times \vec{\mathbf{x}}_{34}(t) \tag{B.1}$$

$$D(t) \;\equiv\; \mathbf{n}(t) \cdot \vec{\mathbf{x}}_{l1}(t) \tag{B.2}$$

where $\mathbf{x}_i$ and $\mathbf{w}_i$ are the position and velocity of a vertex i in the interval **I**. Two triangles collide in two ways: point–triangle and edge–edge. In the point–triangle case, we denote the point as $\mathbf{x}_1(t)$ and the triangle as $(\mathbf{x}_2(t), \mathbf{x}_3(t), \mathbf{x}_4(t))$. This is done by setting $k = l = 3$. The vector $\mathbf{n}(t)$ is the normal of the supporting plane of the triangle and the number $\frac{D(t)}{\|\mathbf{n}(t)\|}$ is the perpendicular distance from the point $\mathbf{x}_1$ to the supporting plane of the triangle. In the edge–edge case, we denote the first edge as $\overline{\mathbf{x}_1(t)\mathbf{x}_2(t)}$ and the second edge as $\overline{\mathbf{x}_3(t)\mathbf{x}_4(t)}$. This is done by setting $k = 1$ and $l = 3$. If the two edges are not parallel, then $\mathbf{n}(t)$ is perpendicular to the supporting lines of the two edges and $\frac{D(t)}{\|\mathbf{n}(t)\|}$ is the distance between these two lines.

We are interested only in the normalized interval $\mathbf{I} = [0, 1]$ for time t. The coplanar equation of four points $\mathbf{x}_i$, $i = 1, 2, 3$ and 4, is given by:

$$
\begin{aligned}
& t^3(\vec{\mathbf{w}}_{k2} \times \vec{\mathbf{w}}_{34} \cdot \vec{\mathbf{w}}_{l1}) \\
+\ & t^2((\vec{\mathbf{x}}_{k2} \times \vec{\mathbf{w}}_{34} + \vec{\mathbf{w}}_{k2} \times \vec{\mathbf{x}}_{34}) \cdot \vec{\mathbf{w}}_{l1} + \vec{\mathbf{w}}_{k2} \times \vec{\mathbf{w}}_{34} \cdot \vec{\mathbf{x}}_{l1}) \\
+\ & t((\vec{\mathbf{x}}_{k2} \times \vec{\mathbf{w}}_{34} + \vec{\mathbf{w}}_{k2} \times \vec{\mathbf{x}}_{34}) \cdot \vec{\mathbf{x}}_{l1} + \vec{\mathbf{x}}_{k2} \times \vec{\mathbf{x}}_{34} \cdot \vec{\mathbf{w}}_{l1}) \\
+\ & \vec{\mathbf{x}}_{k2} \times \vec{\mathbf{x}}_{34} \cdot \vec{\mathbf{x}}_{l1} \qquad\qquad\qquad\qquad\qquad\qquad\qquad = 0
\end{aligned}
\tag{B.3}
$$

We further define:

$$
\begin{aligned}
a_3 &\equiv \vec{\mathbf{w}}_{k2} \times \vec{\mathbf{w}}_{34} \cdot \vec{\mathbf{w}}_{l1} \\
a_2 &\equiv (\vec{\mathbf{x}}_{k2} \times \vec{\mathbf{w}}_{34} + \vec{\mathbf{w}}_{k2} \times \vec{\mathbf{x}}_{34}) \cdot \vec{\mathbf{w}}_{l1} + \vec{\mathbf{w}}_{k2} \times \vec{\mathbf{w}}_{34} \cdot \vec{\mathbf{x}}_{l1} \\
a_1 &\equiv (\vec{\mathbf{x}}_{k2} \times \vec{\mathbf{w}}_{34} + \vec{\mathbf{w}}_{k2} \times \vec{\mathbf{x}}_{34}) \cdot \vec{\mathbf{x}}_{l1} + \vec{\mathbf{x}}_{k2} \times \vec{\mathbf{x}}_{34} \cdot \vec{\mathbf{w}}_{l1} \\
a_0 &\equiv \vec{\mathbf{x}}_{k2} \times \vec{\mathbf{x}}_{34} \cdot \vec{\mathbf{x}}_{l1}
\end{aligned}
$$

By substituting a_i into the coplanar equation B.3, we have:

$$
a_3 t^3 + a_2 t^2 + a_1 t + a_0 = 0
\tag{B.4}
$$

Assume that the maximum distance between two points is L. The magnitude of the velocity is w and $\eta L \geq w$. The positive number η is treated as the maximum deformation ratio of an edge. Then, we have

$$
a_0 \in [-L^3, L^3]
\tag{B.5}
$$

$$
a_1 \in [-3\eta L^3, 3\eta L^3]
\tag{B.6}
$$

$$
a_2 \in [-3\eta^2 L^3, 3\eta^2 L^3]
\tag{B.7}
$$

$$
a_3 \in [-\eta^3 L^3, \eta^3 L^3]
\tag{B.8}
$$

If a_3 is zero, the coplanar equation becomes a quadratic equation. In the following discussion, we will assume a_3 is non-zero.

B.1 Contact and separation

Lemma B.1 : Assume that two features are initially in contact. If they start to move apart from each other in the beginning, it is possible for them to collide or pass through each other.

Proof: This can be proved by performing empirical tests. The features are placed at a distance ϵ (either zero or non-zero). After that $\mathbf{w}_i$ are randomly computed with a preset maximum magnitude. We perform the intrinsic tests in the cases that the departure condition is satisfied. It turns out that the features will collide with each other in some cases. $\square$

B.2 Sufficient conditions for non-penetration

Theorem B.1 : **Point–triangle:** The signed distance from the point to the supporting plane of the triangle is ε. If $(\mathbf{w}_1 - \mathbf{w}_i) \cdot \mathbf{n}(0) \geq 0$, $\forall i \in \{2,3,4\}$, and $\varepsilon > 0$, then the point does not pass through the triangle.

Proof: Without loss of generality, we assume that the triangle lies on the x-y plane and $\mathbf{n}(0) = (0,0,l)$, $l > 0$. We show that the triangle will not enter the interior of the axis-aligned bounding box of the triangle. Let $x_{1_z}(0) = \varepsilon$ and $x_{i_z}(0) = 0$. So that $x_{1_z}(t) - x_{i_z}(t) = (x_{1_z} + tw_{1_z}) - (x_{i_z} + tw_{i_z}) = (x_{1_z} - x_{i_z}) + t(w_1 - w_{i_z})$ for $t > 0$. Since $\forall i \in \{2,3,4\}$ $(\mathbf{w}_1 - \mathbf{w}_i) \cdot \mathbf{n}(0) \geq 0 \Rightarrow (w_1 - w_i) \cdot (0,0,l) \geq 0 \Rightarrow (w_{1_z} - w_{i_z}) \geq 0 \Rightarrow t(w_{1_z} - w_{i_z}) \geq 0 \Rightarrow x_{1_z}(t) - x_{i_z}(t) > 0$. The result follows. $\square$

Similarly, if $(\mathbf{w}_1 - \mathbf{w}_i) \cdot \mathbf{n}(0) \leq 0$, $\forall i \in \{2,3,4\}$, and $\varepsilon < 0$, the point does not pass through the triangle.

Theorem B.2 : **Edge–edge:** The perpendicular distance from edge e_1 to edge e_0 is ε. If $\varepsilon > 0$ and $(\mathbf{w}_i - \mathbf{w}_j) \cdot \mathbf{n}(0) \geq 0$, $i = 1, 2$ and $j = 3, 4$, then the two edges do not pass through each other.

Proof: Without loss of generality, we assume the vertices x_3 and x_4 lie on the x-y plane. So that $\mathbf{n}(0) = (0,0,l)$, $l > 0$. and $x_{1_z}(0) = x_{2_z}(0) = \varepsilon$. Let $x_{3_z} = x_{4_z} = 0$.

Assume that a point p(t) lies on edge e_0. We have $\mathbf{p}(t) = \mathbf{x}_1(t) + u_p(\mathbf{x}_2(t) - \mathbf{x}_1(t))$

257

and $\mathbf{q}(t) = \mathbf{x}_3(t) + u_q(\mathbf{x}_4(t) - \mathbf{x}_3(t))$, where $u_p, u_q \in [0,1]$. We will show that $p(s)_z - q(t)_z > 0 \ \forall s, t \in [0,1]$.

From the condition, we have $min\{w_{1_z}, w_{2_z}\} \geq max\{w_{3_z}, w_{4_z}\}$. As $\mathbf{p}(t)$ is a point lying on the edge e_0, its velocity along the z-axis is at least $min\{w_{1_z}, w_{2_z}\}$ and $q_z(t)$ is at most $max\{w_{3_z}, w_{4_z}\}$. Thus, $p(s)_z - q(t)_z > 0$. $\square$

Similarly, if $\varepsilon < 0$ and $(\mathbf{w}_i - \mathbf{w}_j) \cdot \mathbf{n}(0) \leq 0$, the two edges do not pass through each other.

B.3 Triangle orientation

In this section, we show the minimum vertex speed that is required for flipping the orientation of a deformable triangle. Let $\mathbf{n}_{before}$ and $\mathbf{n}_{after}$ be the two normals of a triangle before and after the deformation, respectively. We want to know the minimum speed of a vertex so that we will have $\mathbf{n}_{before} \cdot \mathbf{n}_{after} \leq 0$. We are going to answer this question.

Let the three edges of a triangle be a, b and c. We assume that c is the longest edge with length L.

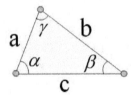

Figure B.1: A deformable triangle.

Lemma B.2 : Let $f(\eta) = \frac{\eta}{1+\eta^2 - 2\eta cos\theta}$. If $0 < \eta \leq 1$ and $\eta - 2cos\theta \leq 0$ for $0 < \theta \leq \theta_{max} \leq \frac{\pi}{2}$, then $0 < f(\eta) \leq 1$.

Proof: It can be written that $1 + \eta^2 - 2\eta cos\theta = (1 - \eta)^2 + 2\eta(1 - cos\theta)$. As $0 < 1 - \eta \leq 1$ and $1 - cos\theta > 0$, we have $1 + \eta^2 - 2\eta cos\theta > 0$. Then we obtain

$$\eta^2 - (1 + \eta^2 - 2\eta cos\theta) = -(1 - 2\eta cos\theta) \leq 0 \Rightarrow 0 < f(\eta) \leq 1. \square$$

Lemma B.3 : If c is the longest edge of a triangle and the angle between the longest edge and one of the other two edges is θ. Then we have $\eta - 2cos\theta \leq 0$, where η is the ratio of the length of that edge to the length of the longest edge.

Proof: The length of the longest edge is L. Let $a = \eta L$. We have $b^2 = (\eta L sin\theta)^2 + (L - \eta L cos\theta)^2 \leq L^2 \Rightarrow \eta^2 L^2 - 2L^2 \eta cos\theta \leq 0 \Rightarrow \eta - 2cos\theta \leq 0$.

$\square$

Theorem B.3 : The necessary condition that a deformable triangle flips its face orientation is that the maximum speed w_{max} of a vertex is at least $\frac{\eta L sin\theta}{2}$, where η is the ratio of a shorter edge to L ($0 < \eta \leq 1$), and θ is the angle between the two shorter edges.

Proof: In order to flip the orientation of a deformable triangle, the minimum speed is obtained when a vertex passes the facing edge. This can be achieved in that one vertex moves perpendicularly to the facing edge in the plane of the triangle. According to this, the minimum speed is equal to the half the shortest distance from a vertex to the facing edge. Without loss of generality, we assume that the positions of the three vertices are $x_3 = (0,0,0)$, $x_2 = (L,0,0)$, and $x_4 = (\eta L cos\theta, \eta L sin\theta, 0)$, where $x_3 x_4 = \eta L$. The angle between $x_3 x_2$ and $x_3 x_4$ is θ. Let h_i ($i = 2, 3, 4$) be the distance from vertex x_i to its facing edge.

We have $h_2 = L sin\theta_3 \geq \eta L sin\theta_3 = h_4$. Based on the area of the triangle, we have $\frac{bh_3}{2} = \frac{Lh_4}{2} \Rightarrow h_3 = \frac{Lh_4}{\sqrt{(\eta L sin\theta)^2 + (L - \eta L cos\theta)^2}} \Leftrightarrow h_3 = \frac{\eta L sin\theta_3}{\sqrt{1 + \eta^2 - 2\eta cos\theta_3}}$. According to Lemma B.2 and Lemma B.3, we have $h_3 \leq L sin\theta_3$.

We want to know which one of h_2 and h_3 is the smallest. Consider the ratio: $\frac{h_4}{h_3} = \sqrt{1 + \eta^2 - 2\eta cos\theta_3}$. According to Lemma B.2, $h_4 \leq h_3$. So that we have $h_4 \leq h_3 \leq h_2$. The necessary condition for the triangle flipping its face orientation is that the maximum speed w_{max} of a vertex is at least $\frac{h_4}{2} = \frac{\eta L sin\theta_3}{2}$. $\square$

By applying this theorem, we may be able to skip the low curvature test when the

$(\pi, \beta, \mathbf{I})$-surface is constructed.

B.4   Other properties of deformable triangles

Lemma B.4 : If $c \geq a, b$, then $\gamma \geq \alpha, \beta$.

Proof: Based on the area of the triangle, we have $ac\,sin\alpha = bc\,sin\beta = ab\,sin\gamma \Rightarrow$ $c\,sin\alpha = b\,sin\gamma, c\,sin\beta = a\,sin\gamma \Rightarrow sin\gamma \geq sin\beta, sin\alpha$. As $\beta + \alpha + \gamma = \pi$ and $\beta, \alpha, \gamma > 0$, the result follows. $\square$

This lemma states that the larger an edge is, the larger its facing angle will be.

Lemma B.5 : Assume that the ratio η of the length of the other two edges to the length of the longest edge lies in the interval $[\eta_{min}, \eta_{max}]$. Given that $0 < \eta_{min} \leq \eta_{max} \leq 1$ and $0.5 < \eta_{max}, \eta_{min} + \eta_{max} > 1$. Then, $arccos\min\{1, \frac{1}{2\eta_{min}}\} \leq \alpha, \beta \leq arccos\min\{1, \frac{1}{2\eta_{max}}\}$.

Proof: Let $a = \eta L$. We have:

$b = \sqrt{((\eta L sin\alpha))^2 + (L - \eta L cos\alpha)^2} = L\sqrt{1 + \eta^2 - 2\eta cos\alpha}$. As $b \leq L \Rightarrow b^2 \leq L^2 \Rightarrow \eta^2 L^2 - 2L^2 \eta cos\alpha \leq 0 \Rightarrow \frac{\eta}{2} \leq cos\alpha \Rightarrow \alpha \leq arccos\frac{\eta}{2}$, we have

$$\alpha \leq arccos\frac{\eta_{max}}{2}, \forall \eta \in [\eta_{min}, \eta_{max}] \tag{B.9}$$

Also $\eta_{min} \leq \sqrt{1 + \eta^2 - 2\eta cos\alpha} \leq \eta_{max} \Leftrightarrow \frac{1+\eta^2-\eta_{max}^2}{2\eta} \leq cos\theta_3 \leq \frac{1+\eta^2-\eta_{min}^2}{2\eta} \Leftrightarrow arccos\min\{1, \frac{1+\eta^2-\eta_{max}^2}{2\eta}\} \geq \alpha \geq arccos\min\{1, \frac{1+\eta^2-\eta_{min}^2}{2\eta}\}$. Therefore, we have:

$$arccos\min\{1, \frac{1}{2\eta_{max}}\} \geq \alpha \geq arccos\min\{1, \frac{1}{2\eta_{min}}\}, \forall \eta \in [\eta_{min}, \eta_{max}] \tag{B.10}$$

By the symmetric property, we also have the same conclusion for β. $\square$

This lemma gives the bound of the angles α and β.

Lemma B.6 : Assume that two vertices of an edge are $\mathbf{x}_1$ and $\mathbf{x}_2$, and their linear velocities are $\mathbf{w}_1$ and $\mathbf{w}_2$ satisfying the condition $\|\mathbf{w}_1 - \mathbf{w}_2\| < \|\mathbf{x}_1 - \mathbf{x}_2\|$. If the two vertices move in the interval $[0, 1]$, the shortest and the longest length of the edge is either $\|\mathbf{x}_1 - \mathbf{x}_2\|$, $\|(\mathbf{x}_1 + \mathbf{w}_1) - (\mathbf{x}_2 + \mathbf{w}_2)\|$, or $\sqrt{\frac{(\mathbf{x}_1 - \mathbf{x}_2)^2(\mathbf{w}_1 - \mathbf{w}_2)^2 - ((\mathbf{x}_1 - \mathbf{x}_2)\cdot(\mathbf{w}_1 - \mathbf{w}_2))^2}{(\mathbf{w}_1 - \mathbf{w}_2)^2}}$.

Proof: The square $D^2(t)$ of the distance of the two vertices (length of the edge) is given by:

$$D(t)^2 \;=\; \|(\mathbf{x}_1 + t\mathbf{w}_1) - (\mathbf{x}_2 + t\mathbf{w}_2)\|^2 \tag{B.11}$$

We differentiate $D^2(t)$ with respect to time t:

$$\frac{dD^2(t)}{dt} \;=\; 2(\|\mathbf{w}_1 - \mathbf{w}_2\|^2 t + (\mathbf{x}_1 - \mathbf{x}_2)\cdot(\mathbf{w}_1 - \mathbf{w}_2)) \tag{B.12}$$

If $(\mathbf{x}_1 - \mathbf{x}_2)\cdot(\mathbf{w}_1 - \mathbf{w}_2) \geq 0$, then the length is increasing when t is increasing; if $(\mathbf{x}_1 - \mathbf{x}_2)\cdot(\mathbf{w}_1 - \mathbf{w}_2) \leq -\|\mathbf{w}_1 - \mathbf{w}_2\|^2$, the length is decreasing when t is increasing; otherwise, the shortest length is $\|(\mathbf{x}_1 - \mathbf{x}_2) + (\mathbf{w}_1 - \mathbf{w}_2)t_0\|$, where $t_0 = -\frac{(\mathbf{x}_1 - \mathbf{x}_2)\cdot(\mathbf{w}_1 - \mathbf{w}_2)}{\|\mathbf{w}_1 - \mathbf{w}_2\|^2}$. In summary, the shortest length D_s and the longest length D_l are equal to:

$$D_s \;=\; \begin{cases} \|\mathbf{x}_1 - \mathbf{x}_2\|, & \text{if } (\mathbf{x}_1 - \mathbf{x}_2)\cdot(\mathbf{w}_1 - \mathbf{w}_2) \geq 0 \\[4pt] \|(\mathbf{x}_1 + \mathbf{w}_1) - (\mathbf{x}_2 + \mathbf{w}_2)\|, & \text{if } (\mathbf{x}_1 - \mathbf{x}_2)\cdot(\mathbf{w}_1 - \mathbf{w}_2) \leq -\|\mathbf{w}_1 - \mathbf{w}_2\|^2 \\[4pt] \sqrt{\frac{(\mathbf{x}_1 - \mathbf{x}_2)^2(\mathbf{w}_1 - \mathbf{w}_2)^2 - ((\mathbf{x}_1 - \mathbf{x}_2)\cdot(\mathbf{w}_1 - \mathbf{w}_2))^2}{(\mathbf{w}_1 - \mathbf{w}_2)^2}}, & \text{otherwise} \end{cases}$$

$$D_l \;=\; \begin{cases} \|(\mathbf{x}_1 + \mathbf{w}_1) - (\mathbf{x}_2 + \mathbf{w}_2)\|, & \text{if } (\mathbf{x}_1 - \mathbf{x}_2)\cdot(\mathbf{w}_1 - \mathbf{w}_2) \geq 0 \\[4pt] \|\mathbf{x}_1 - \mathbf{x}_2\|, & \text{if } ((\mathbf{x}_1 - \mathbf{x}_2)\cdot(\mathbf{w}_1 - \mathbf{w}_2) \leq -\|\mathbf{w}_1 - \mathbf{w}_2\|^2 \\[4pt] \max\{\|\mathbf{x}_1 - \mathbf{x}_2\|, \|(\mathbf{x}_1 + \mathbf{w}_1) - (\mathbf{x}_2 + \mathbf{w}_2)\|\}, & \text{otherwise} \end{cases}$$

□

As an edge deforms, its length changes. Consider that the edge has a collision at the time that its length is the shortest near the middle of the interval. This will produce the phenomenon of ghost particle pulling. In order to avoid this problem, we should make sure that there is not much variation in the length of an edge.

Appendix C

Probability of Roots of Linear, Quadratic and Cubic Equations on Interval $(0, 1]$

Given a polynomial equation:

$$a_n t^n + a_{n-1} t^{n-1} + \cdots + a_1 t + a_0 = 0 \qquad \text{(C.1)}$$

where the coefficients a_i are uniformly distributed in the interval $[-b_i, b_i]$ and b_i are positive. We want to know the probability that there is at least one root of Equation C.1 in the interval $(0, 1]$ given that $a_0, a_n \neq 0$. In this chapter, we will compute the probability for linear and quadratic equations. In the case of a cubic equation, we will adopt a Monte Carlo simulation to obtain the probability under a specific condition.

Definition C.1 : A Heaviside function H(x) is defined by

$$H(x) = \begin{cases} 1 & x \geq 0 \\ 0 & x < 0 \end{cases}$$

In the following discussion, we assume that in the real number space, $\int_a^x f(x)dx = F(x) - F(a)$ and $b \geq a$.

Lemma C.1 : $\int_a^b H(x - c)f(x)dx = H(b - c)[F(b) - F(\max\{a, b\})]$. The proof is omitted. $\square$

Lemma C.2 : $\int_a^b H(c-x)f(x)dx = H(c-a)[F(min\{b,c\}) - F(a)]$ The proof is omitted. $\square$

Lemma C.3 : If $c_0 \geq c_1 \geq 0$, then

$$\int_a^b H(c_0+x)H(-c_1-x)f(x)dx \tag{C.2}$$
$$= H(b+c_0)H(-c_1+a)[F(min\{b,-c_1\}) - F(max\{a,-c_0\})].$$

Proof : The interval of integration is $[a,b] \cap [-c_0,-c_1] = [a_m, b_m]$, where $a_m = max\{a,-c_0\}$ and $b_m = min\{b,-c_1\}$, and $b_m \geq a_m$; otherwise the interval of integration is $[a,b] \cap [-c_0,-c_1] = \emptyset$. By integrating $f(x)$ over the interval, we obtain the result. $\square$

Lemma C.4 : Assume that $\mathbf{I} = \bigcup_{i=1}^{i=n}[x_{2i-1}, x_{2i}]$, where $a = x_1 \leq x_2 \leq \cdots \leq x_{2n-1} \leq x_{2n} = b$. We have:

$$\int_{x \in \mathbf{I}} f(x)dx = \sum_{i=1}^{i=n} \int_a^b H(x_{2i}-x)H(x-x_{2i-1})f(x)dx. \tag{C.3}$$

Proof : We have:

$$H(x_{2i}-x)H(x-x_{2i-1}) = \begin{cases} 1 & x \in [x_{2i-1}, x_{2i}] \\ 0 & \text{otherwise} \end{cases} \tag{C.4}$$

The result follows. $\square$

Lemma C.5 : Assume that x is positive. The probability that $a_i \geq x$ or $a_i > x$ is given by:

$$pr\{a_i \geq x\} = H(b_i - x)\frac{b_i - x}{2b_i} \tag{C.5}$$

Proof : The probability density function of a_i is given by $\frac{1}{2b_i}$. Now assume that $x \geq b_i$. Then

$$pr\{a_i \geq x\} = \int_x^{b_i} \frac{1}{2b_i}da_i = \frac{b_i - x}{2b_i} \tag{C.6}$$

264

If $x > b_i$, it is impossible to have $a_i \geq x$. In this case, $pr\{a_i \geq x\} = 0$. $\square$

Similarly, we have the following lemma:

Lemma C.6 : Assume that x is positive. The probability that $a_i \leq -x$ or $a_i < -x$ is given by:

$$pr\{a_i \leq -x\} = H(b_i - x)\frac{b_i - x}{2b_i} \tag{C.7}$$

Proof : The proof is omitted. $\square$

C.1 Linear equation

Given a linear equation:

$$a_1 t + a_0 = 0 \tag{C.8}$$

The root of the equation is $\alpha = -\frac{a_0}{a_1}$. Consequently, we have $0 < -\frac{a_0}{a_1} \leq 1$. Let $b = \min\{b_0, b_1\}$ and assume that $a_0 > 0$. Therefore, $a_1 \leq -a_0$. We have the following:

$$
\begin{aligned}
pr\{0 < a_0 \leq b_0; \alpha \in (0, 1]\} &= pr\{0 < a_0 \leq b_0; a_1 \leq -a_0 < 0\} \\
&= \int_0^b \frac{1}{2b_0} pr\{-b \leq a_1 \leq -x\} dx + H(b_1 - b_0) \int_{b_0}^{b_1} \frac{1}{2b_1} \frac{b_0}{2b_0} dx \\
&= \int_0^b \frac{1}{2b_0} \frac{(b_1 - x) - (b_1 - b)}{2b_1} dx + H(b_1 - b_0) \frac{b_1 - b_0}{4b_1} \\
&= \frac{b^2}{8b_0 b_1} + H(b_1 - b_0) \frac{b_1 - b_0}{4b_1}
\end{aligned}
$$

By symmetry, the probability p that at least one root in the interval $(0, 1]$ is given by:

$$
\begin{aligned}
p &= pr\{0 < a_0 \leq b_0; \alpha \in (0, 1]\} + pr\{-b_0 \leq a_0 < 0; \alpha \in (0, 1]\} \\
&= 2pr\{0 < a_0 \leq b_0; \alpha \in (0, 1]\} \\
&= \frac{b^2}{4b_0 b_1} + H(b_1 - b_0) \frac{b_1 - b_0}{2b_1}
\end{aligned}
$$

C.2 Quadratic equation

Given a quadratic equation

$$a_2 t^2 + a_1 t + a_0 = 0 \qquad (C.9)$$

The two roots of Equation C.9 are:

$$\alpha \equiv \frac{-a_1 + \sqrt{a_1^2 - 4a_0 a_2}}{2a_2}$$

$$\beta \equiv \frac{-a_1 - \sqrt{a_1^2 - 4a_0 a_2}}{2a_2}$$

We define

$$p_1 \equiv pr\{a_0 > 0, a_2 > 0, a_1 \leq 0; 0 < \alpha \leq 1 \text{ or } 0 < \beta \leq 1\}$$

$$p_2 \equiv pr\{a_0 > 0, a_2 < 0, a_1 \geq 0; 0 < \alpha \leq 1 \text{ or } 0 < \beta \leq 1\}$$

$$p_3 \equiv pr\{a_0 > 0, a_2 < 0, a_1 \leq 0; 0 < \alpha \leq 1 \text{ or } 0 < \beta \leq 1\}$$

By symmetry, the probability p that at least one root in the interval $(0, 1]$ is given by:

$$p = 2(p_1 + p_2 + p_3) \qquad (C.10)$$

We compute p_1, p_2 and p_3 as follows.

Case one: $a_0 > 0, a_2 > 0, a_1 \leq 0$

If $a_1 \leq 0$, we have $a_1 \in [-b_1, 0]$. If $0 \leq \alpha \leq 1$, we have $a_1 \in [-2a_2, 0] \cap [-(a_0 + a_2), 0]$. If $0 \leq \beta \leq 1$, then $a_1 \in [-2a_2, 0] \cup ((-\infty, -2a_2] \cap [-\infty, -(a_0 + a_2)])$. As $a_1^2 - 4a_0 a_2 \geq 0$, we have $a_1 \in (-\infty, -2\sqrt{a_0 a_2}]$.

We summarize the possible intervals for a_1 as follows:

$$a_1 \in \{[-b_1, 0] \cap (-\infty, -2\sqrt{a_0 a_2}])$$
$$\cap \{([-2a_2, 0] \cap [-(a_0 + a_2), 0])$$

266

$$\bigcup([\,-2a_2, 0\,]\bigcup((\,-\infty, -2a_2\,]\bigcap[\,-\infty, -(a_0+a_2)\,]))\}\}$$

$$\in \begin{cases} [\,-b_1, -(a_0+a_2)\,] & \text{if } a_0 \geq a_2 \text{ and } -b_1 \leq -(a_0+a_2) \\ [\,-b_1, -2\sqrt{a_0 a_2}\,] & \text{if } a_0 < a_2 \text{ and } -b_1 \leq -2\sqrt{a_0 a_2} \\ \emptyset & \text{otherwise} \end{cases}$$

$$p_1 = \frac{1}{8 b_0 b_1 b_2}\left\{ \int_0^{b_0}\int_0^{b_2} H(a_0-a_2)H(b_1-(a_0+a_2))[\,b_1-(a_0+a_2)\,]\,da_2 da_0 \right.$$
$$\left. + \int_0^{b_0}\int_0^{b_2} H(a_2-a_0)H(b_1-2\sqrt{a_0 a_2})[\,b_1-2\sqrt{a_0 a_2}\,]\,da_2 da_0 \right\}$$

Let

$$A_1 \equiv \int_0^{b_0}\int_0^{b_2} H(a_0-a_2)H(b_1-(a_0+a_2))[\,b_1-(a_0+a_2)\,]\,da_2 da_0$$

$$B_1 \equiv \int_0^{b_0}\int_0^{b_2} H(a_2-a_0)H(b_1-2\sqrt{a_0 a_2})[\,b_1-2\sqrt{a_0 a_2}\,]\,da_2 da_0$$

$$A_1 = \int_0^{b_0} H(b_1-a_0)\left[a_2 b_1 - a_0 a_2 - \frac{a_2^2}{2} \right]_0^{\min\{a_0, b_1-a_0, b_2\}} da_0$$

$$= \int_0^{b_0} H(b_1-a_0)\left\{ H(b_1-2a_0)H(b_2-a_0)\left[a_2 b_1 - a_0 a_2 - \frac{a_2^2}{2} \right]_0^{a_0} \quad ; a_0 \leq b_1 - a_0, b_2 \right.$$

$$+ H(2a_0-b_1)H(b_2-b_1+a_0)\left[a_2 b_1 - a_0 a_2 - \frac{a_2^2}{2} \right]_0^{b_1-a_0} \quad ; b_1 - a_0 \leq a_0, b_2$$

$$\left. + H(a_0-b_2)H(b_1-b_2-a_0)\left[a_2 b_1 - a_0 a_2 - \frac{a_2^2}{2} \right]_0^{b_2} \right\} da_0 \quad ; b_2 \leq a_0, b_1 - a_0$$

$$= \int_0^{b_0} H(b_1-a_0)\left\{ H(b_1-2a_0)H(b_2-a_0)\left[a_0 b_1 - \frac{3a_0^2}{2} \right] \right.$$

$$+ H(2a_0-b_1)H(b_2-b_1+a_0)\left[\frac{b_1^2 + a_0^2 - 2a_0 b_1}{2} \right]$$

$$\left. + H(a_0-b_2)H(b_1-b_2-a_0)\left[b_1 b_2 - a_0 b_2 - \frac{b_2^2}{2} \right] \right\} da_0$$

$$= \left[\frac{a_0^2 b_1 - a_0^3}{2} \right]_0^{\min\{b_0, \frac{b_1}{2}, b_2\}}$$

$$+ H(b_0 - \frac{b_1}{2})H(b_0 - (b_1 - b_2))\left[\frac{3a_0 b_1^2 + a_0^3 - 3a_0^2 b_1}{6} \right]_{\max\{\frac{b_1}{2}, b_1 - b_2\}}^{\min\{b_0, b_1\}}$$

$$+ H(b_0 - b_2)H(b_1 - 2b_2)\left[\frac{2a_0 b_1 b_2 - a_0^2 b_2 - a_0 b_2^2}{2} \right]_{b_2}^{\min\{b_0, b_1, b_1 - b_2\}}$$

267

$$B_1 = \int_0^{b_0}\int_0^{b_2} H(a_2 - a_0)H(\frac{b_1^2}{4a_0} - a_2)[\, b_1 - 2\sqrt{a_0 a_2}\,]\,da_2 da_0$$

$$= \int_0^{b_0} H(b_2 - a_0)H(\frac{b_1^2}{4a_0} - a_0)\left[a_2 b_1 - \frac{4\sqrt{a_0}a_2^{\frac{3}{2}}}{3}\right]_{max\{a_0,0\}}^{min\{b_2,\frac{b_1^2}{4a_0}\}} da_0$$

$$= \int_0^{b_0} H(b_2 - a_0)H(\frac{b_1^2}{4a_0} - a_0)H(\frac{b_1^2}{4a_0} - b_2)\left[a_2 b_1 - \frac{4\sqrt{a_0}a_2^{\frac{3}{2}}}{3}\right]_{a_0}^{b_2} da_0$$

$$+ \int_0^{b_0} H(b_2 - a_0)H(\frac{b_1^2}{4a_0} - a_0)H(b_2 - \frac{b_1^2}{4a_0})\left[a_2 b_1 - \frac{4\sqrt{a_0}a_2^{\frac{3}{2}}}{3}\right]_{a_0}^{\frac{b_1^2}{4a_0}} da_0$$

$$= \int_0^{b_0} H(b_2 - a_0)H(\frac{b_1^2}{4a_0} - a_0)H(\frac{b_1^2}{4a_0} - b_2)\left[b_1 b_2 - \frac{4\sqrt{a_0}b_2^{\frac{3}{2}}}{3} - a_0 b_1 + \frac{4a_0^2}{3}\right] da_0$$

$$+ \int_0^{b_0} H(b_2 - a_0)H(\frac{b_1^2}{4a_0} - a_0)H(b_2 - \frac{b_1^2}{4a_0})\left[\frac{b_1^3}{4a_0} - \frac{4\sqrt{a_0}}{3}(\frac{b_1^2}{4a_0})^{\frac{3}{2}} - a_0 b_1 + \frac{4a_0^2}{3}\right]$$

$$= \int_0^{b_0} H(b_2 - a_0)H(b_1 - 2a_0)H(\frac{b_1^2}{4b_2} - a_0)\left[b_1 b_2 - \frac{4\sqrt{a_0}b_2^{\frac{3}{2}}}{3} - a_0 b_1 + \frac{4a_0^2}{3}\right] da_0$$

$$+ \int_0^{b_0} H(b_2 - a_0)H(b_1 - 2a_0)H(a_0 - \frac{b_1^2}{4b_2})\left[\frac{b_1^3}{12a_0} - a_0 b_1 + \frac{4a_0^2}{3}\right]$$

$$= \left[a_0 b_1 b_2 - \frac{8(a_0 b_2)^{\frac{3}{2}}}{9} - \frac{a_0^2 b_1}{2} + \frac{4a_0^3}{9}\right]_0^{min\{b_0,b_2,\frac{b_1}{2},\frac{b_1^2}{4b_2}\}}$$

$$+ H(b_0 - \frac{b_1^2}{4b_2})H(b_2 - \frac{b_1^2}{4b_2})H(\frac{b_1}{2} - \frac{b_1^2}{4b_2})\left[\frac{b_1^3 \ln a_0}{12} - \frac{a_0^2 b_1}{2} + \frac{4a_0^3}{9}\right]_{\frac{b_1^2}{4b_2}}^{min\{b_0,\frac{b_1}{2},b_2\}}$$

$$= \left[a_0 b_1 b_2 - \frac{8(a_0 b_2)^{\frac{3}{2}}}{9} - \frac{a_0^2 b_1}{2} + \frac{4a_0^3}{9}\right]_0^{min\{b_0,b_2,\frac{b_1^2}{4b_2}\}}$$

$$+ H(4b_0 b_2 - b_1^2)H(2b_2 - b_1)\left[\frac{b_1^3 \ln a_0}{12} - \frac{a_0^2 b_1}{2} + \frac{4a_0^3}{9}\right]_{\frac{b_1^2}{4b_2}}^{min\{b_0,\frac{b_1}{2},b_2\}}$$

$$p_1 = \frac{1}{8b_0 b_1 b_2}[A_1 + B_1]$$

$$= \frac{1}{8b_0 b_1 b_2}\left\{\left[\frac{a_0^2(b_1 - a_0)}{2}\right]_0^{min\{b_0,\frac{b_1}{2},b_2\}} + \left[a_0 b_1 b_2 - \frac{8(a_0 b_2)^{\frac{3}{2}}}{9} - \frac{a_0^2 b_1}{2} + \frac{4a_0^3}{9}\right]_0^{min\{b_0,b_2\}}\right.$$

$$+H(b_0 - \frac{b_1}{2})H(b_0 - (b_1 - b_2))\left[\frac{a_0(a_0^2 + 3b_1(b_1 - a_0))}{6}\right]_{max\{\frac{b_1}{2},b_1-b_2\}}^{min\{b_0,b_1\}}$$

$$+H(b_0 - b_2)H(b_1 - 2b_2)\left[\frac{a_0b_2(2b_1 - a_0 - b_2)}{2}\right]_{b_2}^{min\{b_0,b_1,b_1-b_2\}}$$

$$+H(4b_0b_2 - b_1^2)H(2b_2 - b_1)\left[\frac{b_1^3 \ln a_0}{12} - \frac{a_0^2 b_1}{2} + \frac{4a_0^3}{9}\right]_{\frac{b_1^2}{4b_2}}^{min\{b_0,\frac{b_1}{2},b_2\}}\Bigg\} \tag{C.11}$$

Case two: $a_0 > 0, a_2 < 0, a_1 \geq 0$

In this case, $\alpha < 0$. If $0 \geq \beta \geq 1$, then $-(2a_2 + a_1) \geq \sqrt{a_1^2 - 4a_0a_2}$ and $-(2a_2 + a_1) \geq 0 \Rightarrow a_1 \in [-2a_2, 0] \cap [-(a_0 + a_2), 0] \Rightarrow a_1 \in [-(a_0 + a_2), 0].$

We have:

$$p_2 = \frac{1}{8b_0b_1b_2}\left\{\int_0^b \int_{-b_2}^0 H(b_1 + (a_0 + a_2))H(-a_0 - a_2)(-a_2 - a_0)da_2da_0\right.$$

$$\left. + \int_0^b \int_{-b_2}^0 H(-a_0 - a_2 - b_1)b_1 da_2da_0\right\}$$

$$A_2 \equiv \int_0^b \int_{-b_2}^0 H(b_1 + (a_0 + a_2))H(-a_0 - a_2)(-a_2 - a_0)da_2da_0$$

$$B_2 \equiv \int_0^b \int_{-b_2}^0 H(-a_0 - a_2 - b_1)b_1 da_2da_0 \tag{C.12}$$

$$A_2 = \int_0^{b_0} H(0 + b_1 + a_0)H(-a_0 + b_2)\left[-\frac{a_2^2}{2} - a_0a_2\right]_{max\{-b_2,-(a_0+b_1)\}}^{min\{0,-a_0\}} da_0$$

$$= \int_{b_2-b_1}^{b_0} H(a_0)H(b_0 - (b_2 - b_1))H(b_2 - a_0)\left(\frac{a_0^2 + b_2^2 - 2a_0b_2}{2}\right)da_0$$

$$+ \int_0^{b_2-b_1} H(a_0)H(b_0 - a_0)H(b_2 - a_0)\left(\frac{b_1^2}{2}\right)da_0$$

$$= H(b_0 - (b2 - b_1))\left[\frac{a_0^3 + 3a_0b_2^2 - 3a_0^2b_2}{6}\right]_{max\{b_2-b_1,0\}}^{min\{b_0,b_2\}} + H(b_2 - b_1)\left[\frac{a_0b_1^2}{2}\right]_0^{min\{b_0,b_2,b_2-b_1\}}$$

$$B_2 = b_1\int_0^{b_0}\int_{-b_2}^0 H((-a_0 - b_1) - a_2)da_2da_0$$

$$= b_1 \int_0^{b_0} [a_2]_{-b_2}^{min\{0,-a_0-b_1\}} \, da_0$$

$$= b_1 \int_0^{b_0} H((b_2 - b_1) - a_0) \, [b_2 - b_1 - a_0] \, da_0$$

$$= b_1 H(b_2 - b_1) \left[\frac{2a_0 b_2 - 2a_0 b_1 - a_0^2}{2} \right]_0^{min\{b_0, b_2 - b_1\}}$$

$$
\begin{aligned}
p_2 &= \frac{1}{8b_0 b_1 b_2} \{A_2 + B_2\} \\
&= \frac{1}{8b_0 b_1 b_2} \left\{ H(b_0 - (b_2 - b_1)) \left[\frac{a_0(a_0^2 + 3b_2(b_2 - a_0))}{6} \right]_{max\{b_2 - b_1, 0\}}^{min\{b_0, b_2\}} \right. \\
&\quad \left. + b_1^2 H(b_2 - b_1) \left[\frac{a_0}{2} \right]_0^{min\{b_0, b_2, b_2 - b_1\}} + b_1 H(b_2 - b_1) \left[\frac{a_0(2(b_2 - b_1) - a_0)}{2} \right]_0^{min\{b_0, b_2} \right.
\end{aligned}
$$

Case three: $a_0 > 0, a_2 < 0, a_1 \leq 0$

We have:

$$a_1^2 - 4a_0 a_2 \geq 0 \tag{C.14}$$

In this case, $\alpha < 0$. If $0 \leq \beta \leq 1$, we have $-(a_1 + 2a_2) \geq 0$ and $(a_1 + 2a_2)^2 \geq a_1^2 - 4a_0 a_2$. Consequently, $a_1 \in (-\infty, -(a_0 + a_2)] \cap [-b_1, 0]$.

$$
\begin{aligned}
p_3 &= \frac{1}{8b_0 b_1 b_2} \left\{ \int_0^{b_0} \int_{-b_2}^0 H(a_0 + a_2) H(b_1 - (a_0 + a_2)) \, [b_1 - (a_0 + a_2)] \, da_2 da_0 \right. \\
&\quad \left. + \int_0^{b_0} \int_{-b_2}^0 H(-(a_0 + a_2)) \, [b_1] \, da_2 da_0 \right\}
\end{aligned}
$$

Let

$$
\begin{aligned}
A_3 &\equiv \int_0^{b_0} \int_{-b_2}^0 H(a_0 + a_2) H(b_1 - (a_0 + a_2)) \, [b_1 - (a_0 + a_2)] \, da_2 da_0 \\
B_3 &\equiv \int_0^{b_0} \int_{-b_2}^0 H(-(a_0 + a_2)) \, [b_1] \, da_2 da_0 \tag{C.15}
\end{aligned}
$$

$$A_3 = \int_0^{b_0} \int_{-b_2}^0 H(a_0 + a_2) H((b_1 - a_0) - a_2) \left[b_1 - (a_0 + a_2) \right] da_2 da_0$$

$$= \int_0^{b_0} H(b_1 - a_0 + b_2) \left[a_2 b_1 - a_0 a_2 - \frac{a_2^2}{2} \right]_{max\{-a_0, -b_2\}}^{min\{b_1 - a_0, 0\}} da_0 \; ; \; a_2 \in [-a_0, b_1 - a_0] \cap [-b_2, ($$

$$= \int_{b_1}^{b_0} H(b_0 - b_1) H(b_1 + b_2 - a_0) \left[a_2 b_1 - a_0 a_2 - \frac{a_2^2}{2} \right]_{max\{-a_0, -b_2\}}^{b_1 - a_0} da_0 \; ; \; b_1 - a_0 \leq 0$$

$$+ \int_0^{b_1} H(b_0 - a_0) H(b_1 + b_2 - a_0) \left[a_2 b_1 - a_0 a_2 - \frac{a_2^2}{2} \right]_{max\{-a_0, -b_2\}}^{0} da_0 \; ; \; b_1 - a_0 > 0$$

Let

$$A_{31} \equiv \int_{b_1}^{b_0} H(b_0 - b_1) H(b_1 + b_2 - a_0) \left[a_2 b_1 - a_0 a_2 - \frac{a_2^2}{2} \right]_{max\{-a_0, -b_2\}}^{b_1 - a_0} da_0$$

$$A_{32} \equiv \int_0^{b_1} H(b_0 - a_0) H(b_1 + b_2 - a_0) \left[a_2 b_1 - a_0 a_2 - \frac{a_2^2}{2} \right]_{max\{-a_0, -b_2\}}^{0} da_0$$

$$A_{31} = H(b_0 - b_1) \left\{ \int_{b_1}^{b_0} H(b_1 + b_2 - a_0) H(b_2 - a_0) \left[a_2 b_1 - a_0 a_2 - \frac{a_2^2}{2} \right]_{-a_0}^{b_1 - a_0} da_0 \; ; \; -a_0 \geq - \right.$$

$$+ \int_{b_1}^{b_0} H(b_1 + b_2 - a_0) H(-b_2 + a_0) \left[a_2 b_1 - a_0 a_2 - \frac{a_2^2}{2} \right]_{-b_2}^{b_1 - a_0} da_0 \right\} \; ; \; -b_2 \geq -a_0$$

$$= H(b_0 - b_1) \left\{ \int_{b_1}^{b_0} H(b_2 - a_0) \frac{b_1^2}{2} da_0 \right.$$

$$+ \int_{b_1}^{b_0} H(b_1 + b_2 - a_0) H(-b_2 + a_0) \left[\frac{b_1^2 + b_2^2 + a_0^2}{2} - a_0 b_1 + b_1 b_2 - a_0 b_2 \right] da_0 \right\}$$

$$= H(b_0 - b_1) \left\{ H(b_2 - b_1) \frac{b_1^2}{2} [a_0]_{max\{0, b_1\}}^{min\{b_0, b_2\}} \right.$$

$$\left. + H(b_0 - b_2) \left[\frac{3 a_0 b_1^2 + 3 a_0 b_2^2 + a_0^3 - 3 a_0^2 b_1 + 6 a_0 b_1 b_2 - 3 a_0^2 b_2}{6} \right]_{max\{b_1, b_2\}}^{min\{b_0, b_1 + b_2\}} \right\}$$

$$A_{32} = \int_0^{b_1} H(b_0 - a_0) H(b_1 + b_2 - a_0) \left[a_2 b_1 - a_0 a_2 - \frac{a_2^2}{2} \right]_{max\{-a_0, -b_2\}}^{0} da_0$$

$$= \int_0^{b_2} H(b_1 - a_0) H(b_0 - a_0) H(b_1 + b_2 - a_0) \left[a_0 b_1 - \frac{a_0^2}{2} \right] da_0 \; ; \; -a_0 \geq -b_0$$

$$+ \int_{b_2}^{b_1} H(b_1 - b_2)H(b_0 - a_0)H(b_1 + b_2 - a_0) \left[b_1 b_2 - a_0 b_2 + \frac{b_2^2}{2} \right] da_0 \; ; \; -a_0 \leq -b$$

$$= \left[\frac{3a_0^2 b_1 - a_0^3}{6} \right]_0^{min\{b_0, b_1, b_2\}} + H(b_1 - b_2)H(b_0 - b_2) \left[\frac{2a_0 b_1 b_2 + a_0 b_2^2 - a_0^2 b_2}{2} \right]_{b_2}^{min\{b_0,}$$

$$B_3 = b_1 \int_0^{b_0} H(-a_0 + b_2) \left[a_2 \right]_{-b_2}^{min\{-a_0, 0\}} da_0$$

$$= b_1 \int_0^{b_0} H(b_2 - a_0) \left[b_2 - a_0 \right] da_0$$

$$= b_1 \left[\frac{2a_0 b_2 - a_0^2}{2} \right]_0^{min\{b_0, b_2\}}$$

$$p_3 = \frac{1}{8b_0 b_1 b_2} \left(A_{31} + A_{32} + B_3 \right)$$

$$= \frac{1}{8b_0 b_1 b_2} \left\{ H(b_0 - b_1) \left\{ H(b_2 - b_1) \frac{b_1^2}{2} \left[a_0 \right]_{max\{0, b_1\}}^{min\{b_0, b_2\}} \right.\right.$$

$$+ H(b_0 - b_2) \left[\frac{a_0 (a_0^2 + 3(b_1 + b_2)(b_1 + b_2 - a_0))}{6} \right]_{max\{b_1, b_2\}}^{min\{b_0, b_1 + b_2\}} \Bigg\}$$

$$+ \left[\frac{a_0^2 (3b_1 - a_0)}{6} \right]_0^{min\{b_0, b_1, b_2\}} + H(b_1 - b_2)H(b_0 - b_2) \left[\frac{a_0 (2b_1 b_2 + b_2^2 - a_0 b_2)}{2} \right]_{b_2}^{min}$$

$$+ b_1 \left[\frac{a_0 (2b_2 - a_0)}{2} \right]_0^{min\{b_0, b_2\}} \Bigg\}$$

(

C.2.1 Discussion

We performed a Monte Carlo simulation to verify the result. The random generator is Mersenne Twister (MT19937) [94]. The error is less than 2%. In the simulation, the values of a_i were restricted in the following intervals:

$$a_0 \in [-L^3, L^3] \setminus \{0\} \tag{C.17}$$

$$a_1 \in [-3\eta L^3, 3\eta L^3] \tag{C.18}$$

$$a_2 \in [-3\eta^2 L^3, 3\eta^2 L^3] \tag{C.19}$$

$$a_3 \in [-\eta^3 L^3, \eta^3 L^3] \setminus \{0\} \tag{C.20}$$

The value L was set as 1.0 and η was varied from 0.05 to 1.0 with step size 0.05. In each test, 100,000 sets of quadratic equations were generated. The probability was computed for the experiments. After that we compared it with the theoretical result.

C.3   Cubic equation

We performed a Monte Carlo simulation to obtain the probability given that:

$$a_0 \in [-L^3, L^3] \setminus \{0\} \tag{C.21}$$

$$a_1 \in [-3\eta L^3, 3\eta L^3] \tag{C.22}$$

$$a_2 \in [-3\eta^2 L^3, 3\eta^2 L^3] \tag{C.23}$$

$$a_3 \in [-\eta^3 L^3, \eta^3 L^3] \setminus \{0\} \tag{C.24}$$

where $\eta \in (0, 2.0]$ and $L \in (0, \infty)$. We applied Mersenne Twister (MT19937) [94] as the random generator to produce a_i for $L = 1$ and then computed the roots. After that, we checked whether there was a root in the interval $(0, 1]$. We performed 30, 000 times for each η. We sampled η from 0.001 to 2.0. Figure C.1 plots the graph for the probability.

When η increases, the probability increases. The number η could be considered as a deformation rate of the edge or speed of a vertex. When η is around 0.2, the probability that a real root in the interval $(0, 1]$ is lower than 20%.

The result obtained in this section is just for reference. In real simulation example, the distribution of a_i may not be uniformly distributed. For example, consider that the interaction between a particle and a triangle. If the particle is sliding on the support plane of the triangle, all a_i will almost be constant. After all, if there is no prior knowledge, the result provides with us a reference for deciding whether we should perform a front-end check (e.g. coefficient check) before solving the cubic equation.

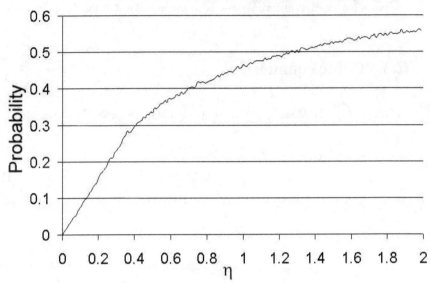

Figure C.1: Cubic equation: probability of existence of roots on $(0, 1]$.

Appendix D

Timings for Basic Operations in Collision Detection

We compare the timings of the following six basic operations:

1. **Coef_Check:** Coefficient check

2. **Quadratic_Exact:** Solving a quadratic equation using exact method

3. **Cubic_Exact:** Solving a cubic equation using exact method

4. **Cubic_Appro:** Solving a cubic equation using the truncated equation

5. **Cubic_Exact_Coef:** Solving a cubic equation with coefficient check but without using truncated equation

6. **Cubic_Appro_Coef:** Solving a cubic equation with coefficient check; solving the truncated equation if necessary.

The experiments were run on a computer with 3.0GHz Pentium 4 CPU, 1GB of main memory. We randomly generated the coefficients a_i in the following intervals:

$$a_0 \in [-L^3, L^3] \setminus \{0\} \tag{D.1}$$

$$a_1 \in [-3\eta L^3, 3\eta L^3] \tag{D.2}$$

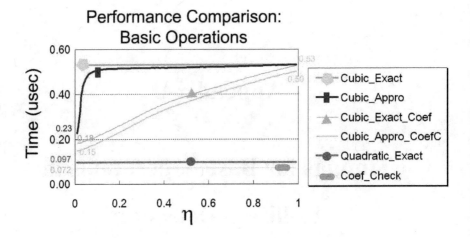

Figure D.1: Timings of six basic operations in collision detection in the time domain.

$$a_2 \in [-3\eta^2 L^3, 3\eta^2 L^3] \tag{D.3}$$

$$a_3 \in [-\eta^3 L^3, \eta^3 L^3] \setminus \{0\} \tag{D.4}$$

In the experiments, L is set as 1. The number η can be treated as the speed of the vertices or the deformation ratio of an edge and the value of η changes from 0.005 to 1.0. If $\eta = \eta_0$, this implies that the deformation of an edge can reach $100h\eta_0\%$. Usually, η is less than 0.005 for a small time step h, e.g. $h = 0.01$ seconds. In this case, the deformation of an edge can reach 50% but this is not likely to happen, in practice, for clothing simulation.

In each experiment, the number η is set to a specific value and there are 10, 000 sets of tests for each specific η. Each test is executed for 1, 000 times. In total, there are 10,000 x 1,000 tests. We collected the timing information and then computed the average time per test. The timings include time spent on function calls.

Graph D.1 shows the timing information of the six basic operations for different values of η. The timings for performing **Cubic_Exact** and **Quadratic_Exact** are 0.53 usec and 0.097 usec, respectively, for one operation. One operation of **Coef_Check** requires 0.072 usec (not including function calls).

Cubic_Appro takes less time to solve a cubic equation compared to **Cubic_Exact**. In particular, if the deformation ratio η is in the range from 0.005 to 0.05, the timing changes linearly from 0.23 usec to 0.5 usec. As for a smaller deformation ratio, the probability is higher that the truncated equation is solved in **Cubic_Appro**. If the deformation ratio is larger than 0.1, the timing is around 0.52 usec. In this case, the probability is high for solving a cubic equation in **Cubic_Appro**.

Coef_Exact_Check and **Coef_Appro_Check** perform the front-end coefficient check before solving a cubic equation. It can be observed that the front-end coefficient check greatly improves the performance. If the deformation ratio changes from 0.005 to 1.0, the timings change linearly from 0.18 usec to 0.53 usec and from 0.15 usec to 0.50 usec, respectively, in **Coef_Exact_Check** and **Coef_Appro_Check**. If the deformation ratio is less than 0.05, **Coef_Appro_Check** is at least two times faster than **Cubic_Exact**.

278

Appendix E

Absolute Relative Error Bounds between Roots of Linear, Quadratic and Cubic Equations

In this chapter, we present the absolute relative error bounds between two roots of linear, quadratic and cubic equations. We shall prove that under certain condition, the absolute relative error between two roots of two different equations is bounded by a number formed by the coefficients of the equations.

E.1 Absolute relative error bounds between two roots of linear and quadratic equations

Given a quadratic equation:

$$a_2 t^2 + a_1 t + a_0 = 0 \tag{E.1}$$

We define a_i as follows:

$$
\begin{aligned}
a_2 &\equiv 1 \\
a_1 &\equiv -(\alpha + \beta) \\
a_0 &\equiv \alpha\beta
\end{aligned}
\tag{E.2}
$$

279

where α and β are the two roots of Equation E.1. We also have the following restrictions:

1. $|a_0| \leq |a_1| + |a_2|$

2. $|a_2| \ll |a_1|$

From (1), the magnitude of both roots cannot be larger than 2; from (2), one of the root must be much larger than one. Let this larger root be α and the smaller root be β.

After truncating the highest term of Equation E.1, we obtain a linear equation:

$$a_1 t + a_0 = 0 \qquad (E.3)$$

Theorem E.1 : If $\beta \in (0,1]$ is a real root of Equation E.1, and β' is the root of Equation E.3, then $|\frac{\beta - \beta'}{\beta}| = O(\frac{1}{|a_1|})$ in the worst case and $|\frac{\beta - \beta'}{\beta}| = O(\frac{1}{|a_1|^2})$ in the best case.

Let the root of Equation E.3 be β'. Then we have:

$$
\begin{aligned}
\beta' &= -\frac{a_0}{a_1} \\
&= \frac{\alpha \beta}{\alpha + \beta}
\end{aligned}
\qquad (E.4)
$$

From Equation E.4, as α tends to infinity, β' tends to β. Therefore the linear equation always approximates β. This is desirable as we want to compute β by using the linear equation instead of the quadratic equation. By using Equation E.4, we do not obtain the exact value of β. However, we can derive the absolute relative error e between β and β'.

$$
\begin{aligned}
e &= \left| \frac{\beta' - \beta}{\beta} \right| \\
&= \left| \frac{\frac{\alpha \beta}{\alpha + \beta} - \beta}{\beta} \right| \\
&= \left| \frac{\beta}{\alpha + \beta} \right| \\
&= O\left(\left| \frac{a_0/a_1}{a_1} \right| \right) \\
&= O\left(\left| \frac{a_0}{a_1^2} \right| \right)
\end{aligned}
\qquad (E.5)
$$

The result follows. $\square$

E.2 Absolute relative error bounds between two roots of quadratic and cubic equations

Given a cubic equation:

$$a_3 t^3 + a_2 t^2 + a_1 t + a_0 = 0 \tag{E.6}$$

We define a_i as follows:

$$
\begin{aligned}
a_3 &\equiv 1 \\
a_2 &\equiv -(\alpha + \beta + \gamma) \\
a_1 &\equiv \alpha\beta + \alpha\gamma + \beta\gamma \\
a_0 &\equiv -\alpha\beta\gamma
\end{aligned} \tag{E.7}
$$

where α, β, and γ are the three roots of Equation E.6. The truncated equation of Equation E.6 is obtained by discarding the third order term:

$$a_2 t^2 + a_1 t + a_0 = 0 \tag{E.8}$$

Assume that the following conditions are satisfied:

1. $|a_0| \le |a_1| + |a_2| + |a_3|$

2. $|a_3| \ll max\{|a_1|, |a_2|\}$

We have the following theorem:

Theorem E.2 : If $t \in (0, 1]$ is a root of equation (E.6), then we have the absolute relative error $\left|\frac{t'-t}{t}\right| = O(f(a_1, a_2))$, where t' is the corresponding root in the truncated equation (E.8). In the worse case, $f(a_1, a_2) = \sqrt{\frac{1}{max\{|a_1|,|a_2|\}}}$; in the best case, $f(a_1, a_2) = \frac{1}{(max\{|a_1|,|a_2|\})^2}$; if there is only one root inside $(0, 1]$, then $f(a_1, a_2)$ can be selected as $\frac{1}{max\{|a_1|,|a_2|\}}$.

Before proving the theorem, we first prove two lemmas.

Lemma E.1 : (1) There exist two roots such that (1) the magnitude of one root is smaller than or equal to $2^{\frac{2}{3}} + 2^{\frac{1}{3}} + 1$ and (2) the magnitude of another root is much larger than 1.

Proof: Assume that the magnitude of all roots are larger than $2^{\frac{2}{3}} + 2^{\frac{1}{3}} + 1 \approx 3.8473$, then we have $|a_0| > |a_1| + |a_2| + |a_3|$ which contradicts the first condition.

From the definition, we have that:

1. $|a_1|$ is at most $3 \max\{|\alpha\beta|, |\beta\gamma|, |\alpha\gamma|\}$, and

2. $|a_2|$ is at most $3 \max\{|\alpha|, |\beta|, |\gamma|\}$.

If there is no root that its magnitude is much larger than 1, then both of $|a_1|$ and $|a_2|$ will not be much larger than 1. This contradicts the second condition. $\square$

Lemma E.2 : If $|x| < 1$, then $\sqrt{1 - x^2} = 1 - \frac{x^2}{2} - \frac{x^4}{8} + o(x^6)$.

Proof: This can be proved by expanding $\sqrt{1 - x^2}$ in Taylor series. The detail is omitted. $\square$

In the following, we are going to prove Theorem E.2. If there is no other specification, we assume that: (1) $\alpha \geq \beta \geq \gamma > 0$; (2) $\gamma \in (0, 1]$; and (3) $\alpha \gg 1$.

We define A, B and D as follows:

$$
\begin{aligned}
D &\equiv (\alpha\beta + \alpha\gamma + \beta\gamma)^2 - 4\alpha\beta\gamma(\alpha + \beta + \gamma) \\
&= \alpha^2(\beta - \gamma)^2 + \beta^2\gamma^2 - 2\alpha\beta\gamma(\beta + \gamma) \\
A &\equiv \alpha^2(\beta - \gamma)^2 \\
B &\equiv -2\alpha\beta\gamma(\beta + \gamma) + \beta^2\gamma^2
\end{aligned}
\tag{E.9}
$$

The two roots, t_1 and t_2, of the truncated equation are given by:

$$
\begin{aligned}
t_1 &= \frac{(\alpha\beta + \alpha\gamma + \beta\gamma) + \sqrt{D}}{2(\alpha + \beta + \gamma)} \\
t_2 &= \frac{(\alpha\beta + \alpha\gamma + \beta\gamma) - \sqrt{D}}{2(\alpha + \beta + \gamma)}
\end{aligned}
\tag{E.10}
$$

We derive the absolute relative error bounds for β and γ in five cases: (1) D = 0, (2) D > 0, (3) D < 0 and two special cases. Denote the higher order terms as $o(.)$.

E.2.1 Case one: $D = 0$

In this case, D becomes:

$$D = \alpha^2(\beta - \gamma)^2 - 2\alpha\beta\gamma(\beta + \gamma) + \beta^2\gamma^2 = 0 \qquad \text{(E.11)}$$

If $\beta = \gamma$, then $\beta = \gamma = 0$. In this case, we obtain the trivial roots $t_1 = t_2 = 0$. Assume that $\beta \neq \gamma$. We solve the equation (E.11) for α and obtain

$$\alpha = \frac{\beta\gamma(\beta + \gamma) \pm \sqrt{\beta^2\gamma^2(\beta + \gamma)^2 - \beta^2\gamma^2(\beta - \gamma)^2}}{(\beta - \gamma)^2} \qquad \text{(E.12)}$$

$$= \frac{\beta\gamma(\beta + \gamma) \pm |\beta\gamma|\sqrt{\beta\gamma}}{(\beta - \gamma)^2} \qquad \text{(E.13)}$$

As $|\alpha| \gg 1$, we have $\beta \approx \gamma$. We set $\alpha = \frac{\beta\gamma(\beta+\gamma)+|\beta\gamma|\sqrt{\beta\gamma}}{(\beta-\gamma)^2}$.

Now, $t_1 = t_2 = \frac{(\alpha\beta+\alpha\gamma+\beta\gamma)}{2(\alpha+\beta+\gamma)}$. The absolute relative error e_1 between t_1 and β is computed as follows:

$$e_1 = \left| \frac{t_1 - \beta}{\beta} \right| \qquad \text{(E.14)}$$

$$= \left| \frac{\frac{(\alpha\beta+\alpha\gamma+\beta\gamma)}{2(\alpha+\beta+\gamma)} - \beta}{\beta} \right| \qquad \text{(E.15)}$$

$$= \left| \frac{(\beta - \gamma)(\beta + \gamma\sqrt{\beta\gamma})}{\beta^3 + \gamma^3 + 2\beta\gamma\sqrt{\beta\gamma}} \right| \qquad \text{(E.16)}$$

$$= O\left(\left| \frac{\beta - \gamma}{\beta} \right| \right) \qquad \text{(E.17)}$$

$$= O\left(\left| \frac{\sqrt{\beta^2 + \gamma^2 - 2\beta\gamma}}{\frac{\alpha\beta+\alpha\gamma+\beta\gamma}{\alpha+\beta+\gamma}} \right| \right) \qquad \text{(E.18)}$$

$$= O\left(\left| \frac{\sqrt{\frac{(\alpha\beta+\alpha\gamma+\beta\gamma)^2}{(\alpha+\beta+\gamma)^2} - \frac{4\alpha\beta\gamma}{\alpha+\beta+\gamma} - \frac{2(\beta^2\gamma+\beta\gamma^2)}{\alpha}}}{\frac{\alpha\beta+\alpha\gamma+\beta\gamma}{\alpha+\beta+\gamma}} \right| \right) \qquad \text{(E.19)}$$

$$= O\left(\left| \frac{\sqrt{\frac{(\alpha\beta+\alpha\gamma+\beta\gamma)^2}{(\alpha+\beta+\gamma)^2} - \frac{4\alpha\beta\gamma}{\alpha+\beta+\gamma} - \frac{2\alpha\beta\gamma(\alpha\beta+\alpha\gamma+\beta\gamma)}{(\alpha+\beta+\gamma)^3}}}{\frac{\alpha\beta+\alpha\gamma+\beta\gamma}{\alpha+\beta+\gamma}} \right| \right) \qquad \text{(E.20)}$$

$$= O\left(\left| \frac{\sqrt{\frac{a_1^2}{a_2^2} - \frac{4a_0}{a_2} - \frac{2a_0 a_1}{a_2^3}}}{\frac{a_1}{a_2}} \right| \right) \qquad \text{(E.21)}$$

283

$$= O\left(\left|\sqrt{\frac{2a_0 a_1}{a_2^3}\frac{a_1^2}{a_1^2}}\right|\right) \qquad \text{since } \left|\frac{a_0 a_1}{a_2^3}\right| \gg \left|\frac{a_1^2}{a_2^2} - \frac{4a_0}{a_2}\right| \tag{E.22}$$

$$= O\left(\sqrt{\left|\frac{a_0}{a_1 a_2}\right|}\right) \tag{E.23}$$

$$= O\left(\sqrt{\frac{|\beta|}{\max\{|a_1|, |a_2|\}}}\right) \tag{E.24}$$

$$= O\left(\sqrt{\frac{1}{\max\{|a_1|, |a_2|\}}}\right) \tag{E.25}$$

E.2.2   Case two: D > 0

In this case, we have $A + B > 0$. We assume that $\alpha \gg \beta > 2\gamma$. Then we have $|A| \gg |B|$.

$$t_1 = \frac{(\alpha\beta + \alpha\gamma + \beta\gamma) + \alpha(\beta - \gamma) + o(.))}{2(\alpha + \beta + \gamma)} \tag{E.26}$$

We compute the absolute relative error e_1 as follows.

$$e_1 = \left|\frac{t_1 - \beta}{\beta}\right| \tag{E.27}$$

$$= \left|\frac{\frac{(\alpha\beta + \alpha\gamma + \beta\gamma) + \alpha(\beta - \gamma) + o(.))}{2(\alpha + \beta + \gamma)} - \beta}{\beta}\right| \tag{E.28}$$

$$= O\left(\left|\frac{\beta}{\alpha}\right|\right) \tag{E.29}$$

$$= O\left(\left|\frac{a_1}{a_2^2}\right|\right) \tag{E.30}$$

Notice that, if $\beta \in (0, 1]$, we have $|a_2| = \Omega(|a_1|)$. Therefore, $e_1 = O(\frac{1}{\max\{|a_1|, |a_2|\}})$.

By expanding $\sqrt{D}$ using Taylor series, we have:

$$t_2 = \frac{(\alpha\beta + \alpha\gamma + \beta\gamma) - \sqrt{A + B}}{2(\alpha + \beta + \gamma)} \tag{E.31}$$

$$= \frac{(\alpha\beta + \alpha\gamma + \beta\gamma) - \alpha(\beta - \gamma)(1 - \frac{1}{2}\frac{2\alpha\beta\gamma(\beta + \gamma) - \beta^2\gamma^2}{\alpha^2(\beta - \gamma)^2} + o(.)))}{2(\alpha + \beta + \gamma)} \tag{E.32}$$

The absolute relative error e_2 between t_2 and γ is computed as follows:

$$e_2 = \left| \frac{t_2 - \gamma}{\gamma} \right| \tag{E.33}$$

$$= \left| \frac{1}{4} \frac{\gamma^2(\beta^2 - 4\alpha\gamma)}{\alpha\gamma(2\alpha + 2\beta + \gamma)(\beta - \gamma)} \right| \tag{E.34}$$

$$= O\left(\left| \frac{\gamma^2}{\alpha\beta} \right| \right) \tag{E.35}$$

$$= O\left(\left| \frac{\gamma}{\alpha} \right| \right) \tag{E.36}$$

$$= O\left(\left| \frac{a_0}{a_1 a_2} \right| \right) \tag{E.37}$$

$$= O\left(\frac{1}{\max\{|a_1|, |a_2|\}} \right) \tag{E.38}$$

E.2.3 Case three: D < 0

From $D < 0$, we have:

$$\alpha^2(\beta - \gamma)^2 - 2\alpha\beta\gamma(\beta + \gamma) + \beta^2\gamma^2 < 0 \tag{E.39}$$

Solving for α, we obtain:

$$\alpha \in \left(\frac{\beta\gamma(\beta+\gamma) - \sqrt{\beta^2\gamma^2(\beta+\gamma)^2 - \beta^2\gamma^2(\beta-\gamma)^2}}{(\beta-\gamma)^2}, \frac{\beta\gamma(\beta+\gamma) + \sqrt{\beta^2\gamma^2(\beta+\gamma)^2 - \beta^2\gamma^2(\beta-\gamma)^2}}{(\beta-\gamma)^2} \right).$$

In this case, we will discard $\sqrt{D}$ when we compute t_1 and t_2. Thus, we have:

$$t_1 = t_2 = \frac{\alpha\beta + \alpha\gamma + \beta\gamma}{2(\alpha + \beta + \gamma)} \tag{E.40}$$

Notice that:

$$\beta\gamma(\beta + \gamma) > \sqrt{\beta^2\gamma^2(\beta+\gamma)^2 - \beta^2\gamma^2(\beta-\gamma)^2} = \left(\frac{\beta\gamma(\beta\gamma) - \beta\gamma\sqrt{\beta\gamma}}{(\beta-\gamma)^2}, \frac{\beta\gamma(\beta\gamma) + \beta\gamma\sqrt{\beta\gamma}}{(\beta-\gamma)^2} \right).$$

As $\alpha \gg 1$, then we have $\beta\gamma(\beta + \gamma) \gg (\beta - \gamma)^2$. Therefore, $\beta \approx \gamma$.

$$e_1 = O\left(\left| \frac{\frac{\alpha\beta + \alpha\gamma + \beta\gamma}{2(\alpha+\beta+\gamma)} - \beta}{\beta} \right| \right) \tag{E.41}$$

$$= O\left(\left| \frac{\alpha(\beta - \gamma) + \beta\gamma + 2\beta^2}{2\beta(\alpha + \beta + \gamma)} \right| \right) \tag{E.42}$$

285

We substitute $\alpha = \frac{\beta\gamma(\beta\gamma)+\beta\gamma\sqrt{\beta\gamma}}{(\beta-\gamma)^2}$ into equation (E.42) and according to Section E.2.1, we have

$$e_1 \;=\; O\left(\sqrt{\left|\frac{a_0}{a_1 a_2}\right|}\right) \tag{E.43}$$

$$\;=\; O\left(\sqrt{\frac{1}{\max\{|a_1|, |a_2|\}}}\right) \tag{E.44}$$

E.2.4 Case four: $\alpha = -\beta$

The best bound is obtained in this case. The truncated equation becomes:

$$\gamma t^2 + \alpha^2 t - \alpha^2 \gamma = 0 \tag{E.45}$$

We discard the second root $t_2 = \frac{-\alpha^2 - \alpha^2\sqrt{1+(\frac{2\gamma}{\alpha})^2}}{2\gamma}$ as $|t_2| \gg 1$. The first root is $t_1 = \frac{-\alpha^2 + \alpha^2\sqrt{1+(\frac{2\gamma}{\alpha})^2}}{2\gamma}$. Thus, we compute only the absolute relative error bound for the first root.

By using the Taylor series of $\sqrt{1 + (\frac{2\gamma}{\alpha})^2}$, we have:

$$e_1 \;=\; \left|\frac{t_1 - \gamma}{\gamma}\right| \tag{E.46}$$

$$\;=\; \left|\frac{\frac{-\alpha^2 + \alpha^2(1+\frac{1}{2}(\frac{2\gamma}{\alpha})^2 + \frac{1}{8}(\frac{2\gamma}{\alpha})^4 + o(.))}{2\gamma} - \gamma}{\gamma}\right| \tag{E.47}$$

$$\;=\; O\left(\left(\frac{\gamma}{\alpha}\right)^2\right) \tag{E.48}$$

$$\;=\; O\left(\frac{a_0^2}{a_1^4}\right) \tag{E.49}$$

$$\;=\; O\left(\frac{1}{(\max\{|a_1|, |a_2|\})^2}\right) \tag{E.50}$$

E.2.5 Case five: complex roots

Complex roots appear in a conjugate pair. Let $\alpha = \alpha_0 + i\alpha_1$ and $\beta = \alpha_0 - i\alpha_1$, where α_0 and α_1 are real number, and $\alpha_1 \neq 0$. Then, the truncated equation becomes:

$$(2\alpha_0 + \gamma)t^2 - ((\alpha_0^2 + \alpha_1^2) + 2\alpha_0\gamma)t + \gamma(\alpha_0^2 + \alpha_1^2) = 0 \tag{E.51}$$

In this case, $|(\alpha_0^2 + \alpha_1^2) + 2\alpha_0\gamma| \gg |2\alpha_0 + \gamma|$. Instead of solving the quadratic equation, we solve the following linear equation:

$$-((\alpha_0^2 + \alpha_1^2) + 2\alpha_0\gamma)t + \gamma(\alpha_0^2 + \alpha_1^2) = 0 \tag{E.52}$$

Notice that $a_1 = -((\alpha_0^2 + \alpha_1^2) + 2\alpha_0\gamma)$ and $a_0 = \gamma(\alpha_0^2 + \alpha_1^2)$. The absolute relative error for the root is given by:

$$e = \left| \frac{\frac{\gamma(\alpha_0^2+\alpha_1^2)}{(\alpha_0^2+\alpha_1^2)+2\alpha_0\gamma} - \gamma}{\gamma} \right| \tag{E.53}$$

$$= O\left(\left| \frac{2\alpha_0\gamma}{(\alpha_0^2 + \alpha_1^2) + 2\alpha_0\gamma} \right| \right) \tag{E.54}$$

Therefore, if $|a_1| \gg |a_0|$, we have $e = O(|\frac{1}{a_1}|)$; otherwise $e = O(\frac{1}{\sqrt{|a_1|}})$.

E.2.6 Discussion

Let γ be a root of the cubic equation E.6 and γ' be the corresponding root of the truncated quadratic equation E.8. Assume that $a_3 = 1$. When β changes from γ to α, the absolute relative error between γ and γ' changes from $O(\frac{1}{\sqrt{\max\{|a_1|,|a_2|\}}})$ to $O(\frac{1}{\max\{|a_1|,|a_2|\}})$. As both the cubic and quadratic equations are continuous, the general the absolute relative error bound between the two small roots will be in the range of $O(\frac{1}{\sqrt{\max\{|a_1|,|a_2|\}}})$ and $O(\frac{1}{\max\{|a_1|,|a_2|\}})$, in the worse and best case, respectively. In the case of $\alpha = -\beta \gg 1$, the error bound can be improved to $O(\frac{1}{(\max\{|a_1|,|a_2|\})^2})$. $\square$

Corollary E.1 : If γ is the smallest positive root of the cubic Equation E.6 and γ' is the corresponding root of the truncated Equation E.8, then $\gamma\gamma' > 0$.

Appendix F

A Thresholding Scheme for Stable Collision Detection

Real numbers are represented in finite precision in computer. A common representation is IEEE Standard 754 floating point [2]. The number of effective digits is 7 and 16 in single precision and double precision, respectively. We denote x as the exact value (exact representation of the number) and $\tilde{x}$ as the computed value (the value stored in computer).

Owing to numerical errors [7], the computed value is not the same as its exact value. This is a major intrinsic problem which coevals with the computation of the floating point in computer. Numerical errors have a great impact in designing a robust collision detection algorithm. Consider the following problem that we often encounter in a point–triangle case. It is possible that the point lies on the negative side from an exact computation but the computed value indicates that it lies on the positive side. This happens when the point lies very near to the triangle. The wrong decision of the side where a point locates with respect to the triangle may lead to intersection of two triangles. We must have to avoid this problem by ensuring that the computed distance between the point and the triangle must be larger than the maximum accumulated numerical error.

This drives us to adopt the (front-) thresholding scheme when we determine whether there is collision. The idea is that the distance between the features should be larger than a certain threshold. Let this threshold be ϵ_H. (ϵ_H should be larger than the machine epsilon ϵ_M.) If this threshold is sufficiently large, we can make sure that the sign of the signed distance between two features will be the same for the exact sign and the computed sign. Therefore, we can maintain their relative orientation throughout the animation. However, this scheme leads to a subtle problem.

Although the thresholding is useful, it does not help us fully solve the problem. Consider that there are two features colliding with each other. The distance between them is d. Assume that $\tilde{d}$ is very near to ϵ_H and $\tilde{d}$ is just smaller than $\tilde{\epsilon}_H$ by a machine epsilon. In the next frame, owing to a very small perturbation to these two features, their distance become $\tilde{d} + \tilde{\epsilon}_0 > \tilde{\epsilon}_H$, where ϵ_0 is larger than a machine epsilon. If we advance to the next frame, another small perturbation may make these two features collide with each other near the beginning of the frame. As a result, the phenomenon of ghost particle pulling is produced. This pattern may replicate throughout the simulation for other parts of the deformable surfaces. The bouncy phenomenon makes the motion unnatural. This problem must be resolved.

Although we could apply interval arithmetic [124] to compute the distance interval in order to avoid the problem, it is an expensive operation. An alternative approach is to adopt a second-level thresholding. We use another threshold ϵ_s to determine whether the colliding features move apart or not. The threshold ϵ_s should be larger than ϵ_H. We need to determine the minimum value for ϵ_s. Consider that the maximum accumulated error introduced in the distance is d_{err}. Then, the threshold should be chosen as $\epsilon_H + d_{err} + \epsilon_M$.

The value of d_{err} depends on the configuration of the objects. In order to realize how d_{err} changes in different configurations of the objects, we consider the computed distance between a point and a triangle. We restrict that the length of the edges of the triangle is at almost 10 units. The point is set to be very near to the triangle. We performed empirical experiments and obtained the distances from the computation of the single and double precision. The distance error is up to 10^{-4} and 10^{-11}, respectively.

In the empirical experiments, we generated randomly triangles which satisfied the restriction imposed on the length of edges. The point is computed by setting it as a point of the triangle which is displaced with a small distance in the normal direction of the triangle. After that, we computed the distance $\tilde{d}$ between the point and the triangle. Then, we randomly rotated the point and the triangle about the origin and computed their distance $\tilde{d}'$ again. We recorded the largest absolute distance error $|\tilde{d} - \tilde{d}'|$. Similarly, experiments were carried out for the edge–edge case for computing the largest distance error in the edge-edge case.

The second-thresholding scheme fully solves the bouncy problem due to the small perturbation of the features. However, ghost particle pulling still prevails if collisions happen early in the interval. We need to avoid collisions occurring near the beginning of the frame. There is a way to ameliorate the problem of ghost particle pulling by using a much larger threshold for the scheme of the second-thresholding. Another solution is that if there are early collisions, the time step should be reduced adaptively.

Appendix G

Self-Collision Detection for a Closed Orientable 2-Manifold Using $(\pi, \beta, \mathbf{I})$-Surface Decomposition Scheme

Theorem G.1 : The first contact point of a closed orientable two-manifold (triangular) mesh S is detected among the $(\pi, \beta, \mathbf{I})$-surfaces of S.

Proof: In a closed orientable 2-manifold triangular mesh, all its triangles are interior triangles with respect to the mesh. If two triangles T_1, T_2 collide and they are assigned to the same $(\pi, \beta, \mathbf{I})$-surface S^π, there exists at least one triangle T not belonging to S^π. The triangle T is either an adjacent triangle of T_1 or T_2 but not both. Without loss of generality, assume T is adjacent to T_1. Then T must collide with T_2 at the same feature as T_1 and T_2 collide. If there exists such T, then we are done.

Assume that there is no such triangle T. Then all the adjacent triangles of T_1 and T_2 belong to the same $(\pi, \beta, \mathbf{I})$-surface. Notice that T_1, T_2, Adj(T_1) and Adj(T_2)[1] satisfy the $(\pi, \beta, \mathbf{I})$-surface condition. If T_1 and T_2 collide, then there must exist edges crossing each other in the image plane. The crossing occurs before T_1 and T_2 collide. If these edges collide in the object space, then they must occur before T_1 and T_2 collide.

---

[1] Adj($\cdot$) is the adjacent triangles of ($\cdot$).

If the edges do not belong to T_1 and T_2, the edges must not collide with each other in the object space. But then T_1 and T_2 must collide with each other in a way that T_1 is moving in the back (front) side of T_2 or vice versa. But then T_1 must collide the triangles behind (in front of) T_2 before T_1 collides with T_2. This is a contradiction.

Therefore, the colliding edges must belong to T_1 and T_2. In this way, at least one of the triangles connecting the edges will flip its orientation. We choose this triangle as T and T does not belong to S^π.

If T is adjacent to both T_1 and T_2, then T will degenerate into a line or a point. This violates our assumption that the triangles do not degenerate into a line or a point.

$\square$

Bibliography

[1] ATI OpenGL Extension Support. World Wide Web, `http://www.ati.com/developer/atiopengl.pdf`, page 463. Last visit on 6th December 2004.

[2] IEEE Standard 754 Floating Point Numbers. World Wide Web, `http://stevehollasch.com/cgindex/coding/ieeefloat.html`. Last visit on 6th December 2004.

[3] SIGGRAPH COURSE 1998: Subdivision for Modeling and Animation. World Wide Web, `http://www.multires.caltech.edu/teaching/courses/subdivision/`. Last visit on 6th December 2004.

[4] Using P-Buffers for Off-Screen Rendering in OpenGL. World Wide Web, `http://developer.nvidia.com/attach/6533`. Last visit on 6th December 2004.

[5] T. Agui, Y. Nagao, and M. Nakajma. An Expression Method of Cylindrical Cloth Objects-An Expression of Folds of a Sleeve using Computer Graphics. *Trans. Soc. of Electronics, Information and Communications (In Japanese)*, J23-D-II(7):1095–1097, 1990.

[6] M. Aono. A Wrinkle Propagation Model for Cloth. *CG International'90: Computer Graphics Around the World*, pages 95–115, 1990.

[7] N.S. Asaithambi. *Numerical analysis : theory and practice*. Saunders College Publishing, 1995.

[8] G. Baciu and W.S.K. Wong. Rendering in Object Interference Detection on

Conventional Graphics Workstations. In *Proc. of Pacific Graphics*, pages 51–58. IEEE, Oct. 1997.

[9] G. Baciu and W.S.K. Wong. The Impulse Graph: A New Dynamic Structure for Global Collisions. *Computer Graphics Forum*, 19(3):229–238, 2000.

[10] G. Baciu and W.S.K. Wong. Hardware-Assisted Self-Collision for Deformable Surfaces. In *Proc. of the ACM Symposium on Virtual Reality Software and Technology*, pages 129–136, Nov 2002.

[11] G. Baciu and W.S.K. Wong. Image-Based Techniques in a Hybrid Collision Detector. *IEEE Transactions on Visualization and Computer Graphics*, 9(2):254–271, 2003.

[12] G. Baciu and W.S.K. Wong. Image-Based Collision Detection for Deformable Cloth Models. *IEEE Transactions on Visualization and Computer Graphics*, 10(6):649–663, 2004.

[13] G. Baciu, W.S.K. Wong, and H. Sun. RECODE: An Image-Based Collision Detection Algorithm. In *Proc. of Pacific Graphics*, pages 125–133. IEEE, Oct. 1998.

[14] G. Baciu, W.S.K. Wong, and H. Sun. RECODE: An Image-Based Collision Detection Algorithm. *Journal of Visualization and Computer Animation*, 10(4):181–192, 1999.

[15] K. Bala, B. Walter, and D.P. Greenberg. Combining Edges and Points for Interactive High-quality Rendering. In *Proc. of SIGGRAPH*, pages 631–640, 2003.

[16] G. Banel. Cloth Simulation: From the Movie Final Fantasy, The Spirits Within to the Game. In *Proc. of the Game Developers Conference (GDC2002)*, March 2002.

[17] D.E. Baraff. Analytical Methods for Dynamic Simulation of Non–penetrating Rigid Bodies. *Computer Graphics*, 23(3):223–232, 1989.

[18] D.E. Baraff. Curved Surfaces and Coherence for Non–penetrating Rigid Body Bodies. *Computer Graphics*, 24(4):19–28, July 1990.

[19] D.E. Baraff. Dynamic Simulation of Non–penetrating Flexible Bodies. *Computer Graphics (SIGGRAPH)*, 26(2):303–308, July 1992.

[20] D.E. Baraff and A. Witkin. Large Steps in Cloth Simulation. *Proc. of SIGGRAPH*, pages 43–54, 1998.

[21] D.E. Baraff, A. Witkin, and M. Kass. Untangling Cloth. *ACM Transactions on Graphics*, 22(3):862–870, 2003.

[22] G. Barequet, B. Chazelle, L.J. Guibas, J.S.B. Mitchell, and A. Tal. BOXTREE: A Hierarchical Representation for Surfaces in 3D. *Computer Graphics Forum*, 15(3):387–396, 1996.

[23] A.H. Barr. Global and Local Deformation of Solid Primitives. *Computer Graphics*, 18(3):21–30, 1984.

[24] R. Barzel and A.H. Barr. A Modeling System Based on Dynamic Constraints. *Computer Graphics*, 22(4):179–188, August 1988.

[25] C. Bennis, J.M. Vézien, G. Iglésias, and A. Gagalowicz. Piecewise surface flattening for non-distorted texture mapping. In *Proc. SIGGRAPH*, pages 237–246, 1991.

[26] J. Berkley, S. Weghorst, H. Gladstone, G. Raugi, D. Berg, and M. Ganter. Fast Finite Element Modeling for Surgical Simulation. In *Proc. of Medicine Meets Virtual Reality*, pages 55–61, 1999.

[27] P. Berman, B. Dasgupta, S. Muthukrishnan, and S. Ramaswami. Improved Approximation Algorithms for Rectangle Tiling and Packing. In *Symposium on Discrete Algorithms*, pages 427–436, 2001.

[28] M. Bern and P. Plassmann. *Handbook of Comp. Geometry*, chapter Mesh Generation. J. Sack and J. Urrutia, Eds. Elsevier Science, 1999.

[29] E. Bethel and S. Uselton. *Shape Distortion in Computer–Assisted Keyframe Animation*, pages 215–224. Springer-Verlag, 1989.

[30] M. Botsch and L.P. Kobbelt. A Robust Procedure to Eliminate Degenerate Faces from Triangle Meshes. In *Proc. of the Vision Modeling and Visualization Conference*, pages 283–290, 2001.

[31] D. E. Breen, D. H. House, and P. H. Getto. A Physically-Based Particle Model of Woven Cloth. *The Visual Computer*, 8(5–6):264–277, June 1992.

[32] D.E. Breen, D.H. House, and M.J. Wozny. A Particle-Based Model for simulating the Draping Behaviour of Woven Cloth. *Textile Research Journal*, 64(11):63–685, 1994.

[33] R. Bridson, R. Fedkiw, and J. Anderson. Robust Treatment of Collisions, Contact and Friction for Cloth Animation. *ACM Transactions on Graphics*, 21(3):594–603, 2002.

[34] J. Brown, S. Sorkin, C. Bruyns, and J.C. Latombe. Real-Time Simulation of Deformable Objects: Tools and Application. In *Computer Animation*, 2001.

[35] A. Cagnoni, A. Dobrzeniecki, R. Poli, and J. Yanch. Genetic Algorithm-Based Interactive Segmentation of 3D Medical Images. *Image and Vision Computing*, 17(12):881–895, 1999.

[36] C. Larboulette M.P. Cani. Real-Time Dynamic Wrinkles. In *Computer Graphics International*, pages 522–525, 2004.

[37] M. Carignan, Y. Yang, N. Magnenat-Thalmann, and D. Thalmann. Dressing Animated Synthetic Actors with Complex Deformable Clothes. 26(2):99–104, July 1992.

[38] S.F. Chen, J.L. Hu, and J.G. Teng. A Finite-Volume Method for Contact Drape Simulation of Woven Fabrics and Garments. *Finite Elements in Analysis and Design*, 37:513–531, 2001.

[39] K.J. Choi and H.S. Ko. Stable but Responsive Cloth. *ACM Transactions on Graphics*, 21(3):604–611, 2001.

[40] K. Chung and W. Wang. Quick Collision Detection of Polytopes in Virtual Environments. In *Proc. of the ACM Symposium on Virtual Reality Software and Technology*, pages 125–132. ACM, July 1996.

[41] L. Coconu and H.C. Hege. Hardware-accelerated Point-based Rendering of Complex Scenes. In *Proc. of 13th Eurographics Workshop on Rendering Techniques*, pages 43–52, 2002.

[42] J. Cohen, M.C. Lin, D. Manocha, and M. Ponamgi. I–COLLIDE: An Interactive and Exact Collision Detection System for Large–Scale Environments. In *Proc. of ACM Interactive 3D Graphics Conference*, pages 189–196. ACM, 1995.

[43] S. Coquillart. Extended Free-Form Deformation: A Sculpturing Tool for 3D Geometric Modeling. *Computer Graphics*, 24(4):187–196, 1986.

[44] F. Cordier, P. Volino, and N. Magnenat-Thalmann. Integrating Deformations between Bodies and Clothes. *Journal of Visualization and Computer Animation*, 12(1):45–53, Feb. 2001.

[45] K. Daubert, H.P.A. Lensch, W. Heidrich, and H.P. Seidel. Efficient Cloth Modeling and Rendering. In *Proc. of 12th Eurographics Workshop on Rendering Techniques*, pages 63–70, 2001.

[46] C. Davatzikos and R.N. Bryan. Using A Deformable Surface Model To Obtain A Shape Representation Of The Cortex. In *SCV95*, 1995.

[47] M. de Berg, M. van Kreveld, M. Overmars, and O. Schwarzkopf. *Computational Geometry: Algorithms and Applications*. Springer, 1997.

[48] M. Desbrun, P. Schröder, and Alan Barr. Interactive Animation of Structured Deformable Objects. In *Graphics Interface*, pages 1–8, June 1999.

[49] S.G. Dhande, P.V.M. Rao, S. Tavakkoli, and C.L. Moore. Geometric Modeling of Draped Fabric Surfaces. In *Graphics, Design and Visualisation (Proc. IFIP Int'l Conf. on Computer Graphics)*, pages 173–180, 1993.

[50] B. Eberhardt, A. Weber, and W. Strasser. A Fast, Flexible, Particle-System Model for Cloth Draping. *IEEE Computer Graphics and Applications*, 16(5):52–59, September 1996.

[51] J. Fan, Q. Wang, S.F. Chen, M. F. Yuen, and C. C. Chan. A Spring-Mass Model-Based Approach for Warping Cloth Patterns on 3D Objects. *The Journal of Visualization and Computer Animation*, 9(4):215–227, 1998.

[52] S. Fisher and M.C. Lin. Deformed Distance Fields for Simulation of Non-Penetrating Flexible Bodies. In D. Thalmann J.F. Canny, N. Magnenat-Thalmann, editor, *Computer Animation and Simulation: Proc. of Eurographics Workshop on Computer Animation and Simulation*, pages 99–112, 2001.

[53] J.D. Foley, A. van Dam, S.K. Feiner, J.F. Hughes, and R.L. Philips. *Introduction to Computer Graphics*. Addison-Wesley, 1996.

[54] A. Fuhrmann, Clemens Groβ, V. Luckas, and A. Weber. Interactive-free Dressing of Virtual Humans. *Computers & Graphics*, pages 71–82, 2003.

[55] A. Garcia-Alonso, N. Serrano, and J. Flaquer. Solving the Collision Detection Problem. *IEEE Computer Graphics and Applications*, 13(3):36–43, 1994.

[56] S. Gibson and B. Mirtich. A Survey of Deformable Modeling in Computer Graphics. Technical Report TR-97-19, Mitsubishi Electric Research Lab., Cambridge, November 1997.

[57] E.G. Gilbert, D.W. Johnson, and S.S. Keerthi. A Fast Procedure for Computing the Distance between Objects in Three–dimensional Space. *Journal of Robotics and Automation*, 4(2):193–203, 1988.

[58] S. Gottschalk. Separating axis theorem. Technical Report TR96-024, Department of Computer Science, UNC Chapel Hill, 1996.

[59] S. Gottschalk, M.C. Lin, and D. Manocha. OBBTree: A Hierarchical Structure for Rapid Interference Detection. In *Proc. of SIGGRAPH*, pages 171–180. ACM, Aug 1996.

[60] A. Gray. *Modern Differential Geometry of Curves and Surfaces*. CRC Press, Inc., 1993.

[61] U. Güdükbay, Bülent Özgüç, and Y. Tokad. A Spring Force Formulation for Elastically Deformable Models. *Computers & Graphics*, 21(3):335–346, 1997.

[62] J.K. Hahn. Realistic Animation of Rigid Bodies. *Computer Graphics*, 22(4):299–308, 1988.

[63] T. Hallgren and C.W. Halpegamage. An Algorithm for Interference Detection in Cloth Animation. In *ICVC99 - International Conference on Visual Computing*, pages 129–133. Fontasey Typesetters Pvt. Ltd., 1999.

[64] M. Held, J.T. Klosowski, and J.S.B. Mitchell. Evaluation of Collision Detection Methods for Virtual Reality fly–throughs. In *Canadian Conference on Computational Geometry*, pages 205–210, 1995.

[65] B.K. Hinds and J. McCartney. Interactive Garment Design. *The Visual Computer*, 6(2):53–61, March 1990.

[66] K.E. Hoff III, A. Zaferakis, M.C. Lin, and D. Manocha. Fast and Simple 2D Geometric Proximity Queries using Graphics Hardware. In *Proc. of the 2001 Symposium on Interactive 3D Graphics*, pages 145–148, 2001.

[67] D.H. House, R.W. DeVaul, and D.E. Breen. Towards Simulating Cloth Dynamics Using Interacting Particles. *International Journal of Clothing Science and Technology*, 8(3):75–94, 1996.

301

[68] J. Hu and Y.F. Chan. Effect of Fabric Mechanical Properties on Drape. *Textile Research Journal*, 68(1):57–64, 1998.

[69] P.M. Hubbard. Collision Detection for Interactive Graphics Applications. *IEEE Transactions on Visualization and Computer Graphics*, 1(3):218–228, 1995.

[70] P.M. Hubbard. Approximating Polyhedra with Spheres for Time-Critical Collision Detection. *ACM Transactions on Graphics*, 15(3):179–210, 1996.

[71] F. Jaillet, B. Shariat, and D. Vandorpe. Deformable Object Reconstruction with Particle Systems. *Computers & Graphics*, 22(2–3):189–194, March 1998.

[72] S. Jimenez and A. Luciani. Animation of Interacting Objects with Collisions and Prolonged Contacts. In B. Falciedieno and T.L. Kunii, editors, *Modeling in computer graphics–methods and applications. Proc. of the IFIP WG 5.10 Working Conference*, pages 129–141. Springer-Verlag, 1993.

[73] C. Kane, E. Repetto, M. Ortiz, and J. Marsden. Finite Element Analysis of Nonsmooth Contact. *Comput. Methods Appl. Mech. Eng.*, pages 1–26, 1999.

[74] Y.M. Kang, J.H. Choi, H.G. Cho, and C.J. Park. Fast and Stable Animation of Cloth with and Approximated Implicit Method. In *Proc. of the Conference on Computer Graphics International (CGI-00))*, pages 247–256. IEEE, 2000.

[75] M. Kass. *An Introduction to Physically-based Modeling: An Introduction to Continuum Dynamics for Computer Graphics.* 1995.

[76] S. Khanna, S. Muthukrishnan, and M. Paterson. On Approximating Rectangle Tiling and Packing. In *Proc. of the 9th Annual ACM-SIAM Symposium on Discretre Algorithms SODA'98*, pages 384–393, New York, 1998. ACM Press.

[77] Y.J. Kim, M.A. Otaduy, M.C. Lin, and D. Manocha. Fast Penetration Depth Computation for Physically-Based Animation. *Proc. of SIGGRAPH*, pages 23–31, 2002.

302

[78] J. Klein and G. Zachmann. Point Cloud Collision Detection. *Computer Graphics Forum*, 23(3):567–576, 2004.

[79] J.T. Klosowski, M. Held, S.B.J. Mitchell, H. Sowizral, and K. Zikan. Efficient Collision Detection Using Bounding Volume Hierarchies of k-DOPs. *IEEE Transactions on Visualization and Computer Graphics*, 4(1):21–36, Jan. 1998.

[80] D.E. Knuth. *Sorting and Searching: The Art of Computer Programming*. volume 3. Second Edition. Addison-Wesley, 1997.

[81] L.P. Kobbelt and M. Botsch. An Interactive Approach to Point Cloud Triangulation. *Computer Graphics Forum*, 19(3):479–487, 2000.

[82] T.L. Kunii and H. Gotoda. Modeling and Animation of Garment Wrinkle Formation Processes. In N. Magnenat-Thalmann and D. Thalmann, editors, *Computer Animation (Second workshop on Computer Animation)*, pages 131–147. Springer-Verlag, April 1990.

[83] T.L. Kunii and H. Gotoda. Singularity Theoretical Modeling and Animation of Garment Wrinkle Formation Processes. *The Visual Computer*, 6(6):326–336, December 1990.

[84] B. Lafleur, N. Magnenat-Thalmann, and D. Thalmann. Cloth animation with self-collision detection. In *IFIP conference on Modeling in Computer Graphics proceedings*, pages 179–197. Springer-Verlag, 1991.

[85] C. Lennerz, E. Schömer, and T. Warken. A Framework for Collision Detection and Response. In *11-th European Simulation Symposium, ESS'99*, pages 309–314, 1999.

[86] S. Leopoldseder and H. Pottmann. Approximation of Developable Surfaces with Cone Spline Surfaces. *Computer Aided Design*, 30(7):571–582, 1998.

[87] M.C. Lin. *Efficient Collision Detection for Animation and Robotics*. PhD thesis, University of California, Berkeley, 1993.

[88] M.C. Lin and J.F. Canny. Efficient Collision Detection for Animation. In *Third Eurographics Workshop on Animation and Simulation*, Cambridge, 1992.

[89] M.C. Lin and S. Gottschalk. Collision Detection Between Geometric Models: A Survey. In *Proc. of IMA Conf. on Mathematics of Surfaces*, pages 37–56, 1999.

[90] M.C. Lin and D. Manocha. Fast Interference Detection between Geometric Models. *The Visual Computer*, 11(10):542–591, 1995.

[91] Li Ling. Animation of Stochastic Motion of 3-D Cloth Objects. *Computers and Graphics*, 21(6):769–775, November 1997.

[92] J.D. Liu, M.T. Ko, and R.C. Chang. Collision Avoidance in Cloth Animation. *The Visual Computer*, 12(5):234–243, 1996.

[93] J.D. Liu, M.T. Ko, and R.C. Chang. A Simple Self-Collision Avoidance for Cloth Animation. *Computers and Graphics*, 22(1):117–128, 1998.

[94] M. Matsumoto and T. Nishimura. Mersenne Twister: A 623-dimensionally equidistributed uniform pseudorandom number generator. *ACM Trans. on Modeling and Computer Simulation*, 8(1):3–30, 1998.

[95] T. McInerney and D. Terzopoulos. Deformable Models in Medical Image Analysis. *Medical Image Analysis*, 1(2):91–108, 1996.

[96] Leonard Meirovitch. *Elements of Vibration Analysis*. McGraw-Hill, 1986.

[97] S. Melax. BSP Collision Detection As Used In MDK2 and NeverWinter Nights. In *Proc. of the Game Developers Conference (GDC2001)*, March 2001.

[98] D.N. Metaxas. *Physics-Based Deformable Models: Applications to Computer Vision, Graphics and Medical Imaging*. Kluwer Academic Publishers, 1997.

[99] B. Mirtich. *Impulse-Based Dynamic Simulation of Rigid Body Systems*. PhD thesis, University of California, Berkeley, 1996.

[100] B. Mirtich. V-Clip: Fast and Robust Polyhedral Collision Detection. *ACM Trans. on Computer Graphics*, 17(3):177–208, Jul. 1998.

[101] T. Möller. A Fast Triangle-Triangle Intersection Test. *Journal of Graphics Tools*, 2(2):25–30, 1997. ISSN 1086-7651.

[102] M. Moore and J.P. Wilhelms. Collision Detection and Response for Computer Animation. In *Computer Graphics (SIGGRAPH'88)*, volume 22, pages 289–298. ACM, 1988.

[103] K. Myszkowski, O.G. Okunev, and T.L. Kunii. Fast Collision Detection between Computer Solids using Rasterizing Graphics Hardware. *The Visual Computer*, 11:497–511, 1995.

[104] L.P. Nedel and D. Thalmann. Modeling and Deformation of the Human Body using an Anatomically-Based Approach. In *Proc. of Computer Animation'98*, pages 34–40, 1998.

[105] H. Ng. *Techniques for Modeling and Visualization of Cloth*. PhD thesis, University of Sussex, UK, 1996.

[106] H.N. Ng and R.L. Grimsdale. *GEOFF - A Geometrical Editor for Fold Formation*, pages 124–131. Springer-Verlag, 1995.

[107] H. Okabe, H. Imaoka, T. Tomiha, and H. Niwaya. Three Dimensional Apparel CAD System. *Computer Graphics*, 26(2):105–110, 1992.

[108] L. Piegl and W. Tiller. *The NURBS Book*. 2nd Edition. Springer, 1995.

[109] J.C. Platt and A.H. Barr. Constraint Methods for Flexible Models. *Computer Graphics*, 22(4):21–30, August 1988.

[110] M. Ponamgi, D. Manocha, and M.C. Lin. Incremental Algorithms for Collision Detection between General Solid Models. In *Proc. of SIGGRAPH*, pages 293–304. ACM, 1995.

[111] M.K. Ponamgi, D. Manocha, and M.C. Lin. Incremental Algorithms for Collision Detection Between Polygonal Models. *IEEE Transactions on Visualization and Computer Graphics*, 3(1):51–64, 1997.

[112] W.H. Press, S.A. Teukolsky, W.T. Vetterling, and B.P. Flannery. *Numerical Recipes in C: The Art of Scientific Computing. Second Edition.* Cambridge University Press, Cambridge, 1992.

[113] X. Provot. Deformation Constraints in a Mass-Spring Model to Describe Rigid Cloth Behaviour. In *Graphics Interface*, pages 147–154, 1995.

[114] X. Provot. Collision and Self-Collision Handling in Cloth Model Dedicated to Design Harments. In *Comp. Animation and Simulation*, pages 177–189, 1997.

[115] S. Redon, A. Kheddar, and S. Coquillart. Fast Continuous Collision Detection between Rigid Bodies. *Computer Graphics Forum*, 21(3), 2002.

[116] W. T. Reeves. Particle systems- a technique for modeling a class of fuzzy objects. *ACM Transactions on Graphics*, 2(2):91–108, 1983.

[117] T.W. Sederberg and S.R. Parry. Free-Form Deformation of Solid Geometric Models. *Computer Graphics*, 20(4):151–160, 1986.

[118] M.I. Shamos and F.P. Preparata. *Computational Geometry: An Introduction.* Springer-Verlag, N.Y., 1985.

[119] W.J. Shanahan, D.W. Lloyd, and J.W.S. Hearle. Characterizing the Elastic Behavior of Textile Fabrics in Complex Deformations. In *Textile Research Journal*, volume 48, page 495, August 1978.

[120] J. Shewchuk. An Introduction to the Conjugate Gradient Method without the Agonizing Pain. Technical Report CMU-CS-TR-94-1125, Carnegie Mellon University, 1994.

[121] M. Shinya and M.C. Forgue. Interference Detection through Rasterization. *Journal of Visualization and Computer Animation*, 2:131–134, 1991.

[122] K. Sims. Particle Animation and Rendering Using Data Parallel Computation. *Computer Graphics*, 24(4):405–413, 1990.

[123] A. Smith, Y. Kitamu, H. Takemura, and F. Kishino. A Simple and Efficient Method for Accurate Collision Detection among Deformable Polyhedral Objects in Arbitrary Motion. In *Virtual Reality Annual International Symposium*, pages 136–145. IEEE, 1995.

[124] J. Snyder. Interval Analysis for Computer Graphics. *Computer Graphics*, 26(2):121–130, July 1992.

[125] M. Sun and E. Fiume. A technique for constructing developable surfaces. In *Cannadian Human-Computer Communications Society*, pages 176–185, 1996.

[126] S. Suri, P.M. Hubbard, and J.F. Hughes. Collision Detection in Aspect and Scale Bounded Polyhedra. In *Proc. of Ninth ACM-SIAM Symp. Discrete Algorithms*, pages 127–136. ACM, Jan 1998.

[127] R. Szeliski and D. Tonnesen. Surface Modeling with Oriented Particle Systems. *Computer Graphics*, 26(2):185–194, 1992.

[128] F. Taillefer. Mixed Modeling. In *Compugraphics*, pages 467–478, 1991.

[129] J.G. Teng, S.F. Chen, and J.L. Hu. A Finite-Volume Method for Deformation Analysis of Woven Fabrics. *Int.J. Numerical Methods in Engineering*, 46:2061–2098, 1999.

[130] D. Terzopoulos and K. Fleischer. Modeling Inelastic Deformation: Viscoelasticity, Plasticity, Fracture. *Computer Graphics*, 22(4):269–278, 1988.

[131] D. Terzopoulos, J. Platt, A. Barr, and K. Fleischer. Elastically Deformable Models. *Computer Graphics*, 21(4):205–214, July 1987.

[132] D. Terzopoulos and A. Witkin. Physically Based Models with Rigid and Deformable Components. *IEEE Computer Graphics and Applications*, 8(6):41–51, 1988.

[133] M. Teschner, S. Kimmerle, G. Zachmann, B. Heidelberger, L. Raghupathi, A. Fuhrmann, M.P. Cani, F. Faure, N. Magnetat-Thalmann, and W. Strasser. State of the art report. In *Eurographics*, 2004.

[134] N. Tsopelas. Animating the Crumpling Behavior of Garments. In *Proc. 2nd Eurographics Workshop on Animation and Simulation*, pages 11–24, 1991.

[135] X. Tu and D. Terzopoulos. Artificial Fishes: Physics, Locomotion, Perception, Behavior. *Computer Graphics*, 28(Annual Conference Series):43–50, 1994.

[136] E. Turquin, M.P. Cani, and J. Hughes. Sketching Garments for Virtual Characters. In John F. Hughes and Joaquim A. Jorge, editors, *Eurographics Workshop on Sketch-Based Interfaces and Modeling*. Eurographics, August 2004.

[137] G. van den Bergen. Efficient Collision Detection of Complex Deformable Models using AABB Trees. *Journal of Graphics Tools*, 2(4):1–14, 1999.

[138] T. Vassilev, B. Spanlang, and Y. Chrysanthou. Fast Cloth Animation on Walking Avatars. *Computer Graphics Forum*, 20(3):260–267, Sep. 2001.

[139] P. Volino, M. Courchesne, and N. Magnenat-Thalmann. Versatile and Efficient Techniques for Simulating Cloth and Other Deformable Objects. In *Proc. of SIGGRAPH*, pages 137–144, 1995.

[140] P. Volino and N. Magnenat-Thalmann. Efficient Self-Collision Detection on Smoothly Discretised Surface Animation using Geometrical Shape Regularity. *Computer Graphics Forum, Eurographics proceedings*, 13(3):155–166, Sep. 1994.

[141] P. Volino and N. Magnenat-Thalmann. Collision and Self-Collision Detection: Efficient and Robust Solutions for Highly Deformable Surfaces. In *Computer Animation and Simulation*, pages 55–65, 1995.

[142] P. Volino and N. Magnenat-Thalmann. Accurate Collision Response on Polygonal Meshes. In *Proc. of the Computer Animation Conference*, pages 179–188, 2000.

[143] P. Volino and N. Magnenat-Thalmann. Implementing Fast Cloth Simulation with Collision Response. In *Computer Graphics International*, pages 257–268, 2000.

[144] P. Volino, N. Magnenat-Thalmann, J.H. Shen, and D. Thalmann. An Evolving System for Simulating Clothes on Virtual Actors. *IEEE Computer Graphics and Applications*, 16(5):42–51, September 1996.

[145] P. Volino and N. Magnenat Thalmann. *Virtual Clothing, Theory and Practice*. Springer-Verlag, 2000.

[146] B. von Herzen. *Applications of Surface Networks to Sampling Problems in Computer Graphics*. PhD thesis, California Institute of Technology, Computer Science Dept., Caltech-CS-TR-88-15, 1989.

[147] B. von Herzen, A.H. Barr, and H.R. Zats. Geometric Collision for Time–dependent Parametric Surfaces. *Computer Graphics (SIGGRAPH'90)*, 24(4):39–48, 1990.

[148] J. Weil. The Synthesis of Cloth Objects. In *Computer Graphics*, pages 49–54, August 1986.

[149] S.K. Wong. Real-Time Hardware-Assisted Collision Detection, MPhil Thesis, The Hong Kong University of Science and Technology, 1999.

[150] W.S.K. Wong and G. Baciu. Dynamic Interaction between Deformable Surfaces and Nonsmooth Objects. *Submitted to IEEE Transactions on Visualization and Computer Graphics, accepted*, 2004.

[151] W.S.K. Wong and G. Baciu. Hardware-Based Collision and Self-Collision for

Rigid and Deformable Surfaces. *Submitted to MIT Presence Special Issue, accepted*, 2004.

[152] W.S.K. Wong, G. Baciu, and J.L Hu. Multi-Layered Deformable Surfaces for Virtual Clothing. In *Proc. of ACM Symposium on Virtual Reality Software and Technology*, pages 24–31, 2004.

[153] Y.Q. Xu, Y.Y. Chen, S. Lin, H. Zhong, E. Wu, B. Guo, and H.Y. Shum. Photorealistic Rendering of Knitwear Using Lumislice. In *Proc. of SIGGRAPH*, pages 391–398, 2001.

[154] D. Terzopoulos Y. Lee and K. Waters. Realistic Face Modeling for Animation. In *Proc. of SIGGRAPH*, pages 55–62, 1995.

[155] Y. Yang and N. Magnenat-Thalmann. An Improved Algorithm for Collision Detection in Cloth Animation with Human Body. In *First Pacific Conference on Computer Graphics and Applications*, pages 237–251, 1993.

[156] D. Zhang and M.M.F. Yuen. Collision Detection for Clothed Human Animation. In *Proc. of Pacific Graphics*, 2000.

[157] D. Zhang and M.M.F. Yuen. Cloth simulation using multilevel meshes. *Computers & Graphics*, 25(3):383–390, 2001.

[158] D. Zhang and M.M.F. Yuen. A coherence-based collision detection method for dressed human simulation. *Computer Graphics Forum*, 21(1):33–42, 2002.

[159] O.C. Zienkiewicz and R.L. Taylor. *The Finite Element Method*. McGRAW-HILL Book Company, 1991.

[160] M.J. Zyda, D.R. Pratt, D. Osborne, and J.G. Monahan. NPSNET: Real–Time Collision Detection and Response. *The Journal of Visualization and Computer Animation*, 4(1):13–24, 1993.

Wissenschaftlicher Buchverlag bietet

kostenfreie

Publikation

von

wissenschaftlichen Arbeiten

Diplomarbeiten, Magisterarbeiten, Master und Bachelor Theses
sowie Dissertationen, Habilitationen und wissenschaftliche Monographien

Sie verfügen über eine wissenschaftliche Abschlußarbeit zu aktuellen oder zeitlosen
Fragestellungen, die hohen inhaltlichen und formalen Ansprüchen genügt,
und haben **Interesse an einer honorarvergüteten Publikation**?

Dann senden Sie bitte erste Informationen über Ihre Arbeit per Email
an info@vdm-verlag.de. Unser Außenlektorat meldet sich umgehend bei Ihnen.

VDM Verlag Dr. Müller Aktiengesellschaft & Co. KG
Dudweiler Landstraße 125a
D - 66123 Saarbrücken

www.vdm-verlag.de